# BLESSED ONE

# BLESSED ONE

## Protestant Perspectives on Mary

BEVERLY ROBERTS GAVENTA

CYNTHIA L. RIGBY

*Editors*

Westminster John Knox Press
LOUISVILLE • LONDON

Scripture quotations from the New Revised Standard Version of the Bible are copyright © 1989 by the Division of Christian Education of the National Council of the Churches of Christ in the U.S.A. and are used by permission.

"Ignored Virgin or Unaware Woman: A Mexican-American Protestant Reflection on the Virgin of Guadalupe" by Nora O. Lozano-Díaz from *A Reader in Latina Feminist Theology: Religion and Justice*, edited by Maria Pilar Aquino, Daisy L. Machado, and Jeanette Rodriguez. Copyright © 2002. Courtesy of the University of Texas Press.

"Mary: A Reformed Theological Perspective" by Daniel L. Migliore is used by permission of *Theology Today*.

*Book design by Sharon Adams*
*Cover design by Pam Poll*
*Cover illustration: "Annunciation" by William Congdon, courtesy of Portsmouth Abbey School*

*First edition*
Published by Westminster John Knox Press
Louisville, Kentucky

This book is printed on acid-free paper that meets the American National Standards Institute Z39.48 standard. ⊚

PRINTED IN THE UNITED STATES OF AMERICA

03 04 05 06 07 08 09 10 11 — 10 9 8 7 6 5 4 3 2

**Library of Congress Cataloging-in-Publication Data**

Blessed one : Protestant perspectives on Mary / Beverly Roberts Gaventa, Cynthia L. Rigby, editors.
    p. cm.
  Includes bibliographical references and index.
  ISBN 0-664-22438-5 (alk. paper)
    1. Mary, Blessed Virgin, Saint—Theology. 2. Protestant churches—Doctrines.
  I. Gaventa, Beverly Roberts. II. Rigby, Cynthia L.

BT613 .B57 2002
232.91'088'2044—dc21                                                          2002066175

# Contents

## Part 1 *Encountering* Mary

## Part 2 *Living* Mary

Contents

# Contributors

Nancy J. Duff is Associate Professor of Theological Ethics at Princeton Theological Seminary.

Beverly Roberts Gaventa is Helen H. P. Manson Professor of New Testament Literature and Exegesis at Princeton Theological Seminary.

Joel B. Green is Professor of New Testament Interpretation at Asbury Theological Seminary.

E. Elizabeth Johnson is J. Davison Philips Professor of New Testament Language, Literature, and Exegesis at Columbia Theological Seminary

Cheryl A. Kirk-Duggan is the Executive Director of the Center for Women and Religion at the Graduate Theological Union.

Nora O. Lozano-Díaz is Assistant Professor of Theological Studies at the Hispanic Baptist Theological School.

Lois Malcolm is Associate Professor of Systematic Theology at Luther Seminary.

Bonnie J. Miller-McLemore is Professor of Pastoral Theology and Counseling at Vanderbilt Divinity School.

Daniel L. Migliore is Charles Hodge Professor of Systematic Theology at Princeton Theological Seminary.

Kathleen Norris is the author of many highly regarded volumes, including *The Cloister Walk* and *Meditations on Mary*.

Cynthia L. Rigby is Associate Professor of Theology at Austin Presbyterian Theological Seminary.

Katharine Doob Sakenfeld is W. A. Eisenberger Professor of Old Testament Literature and Exegesis at Princeton Theological Seminary.

# Foreword

A friend who had spent a sabbatical working with refugees in Southeast Asia once sent me a homemade Christmas card that put the more colorful cards to shame; it consisted of a black-and-white snapshot of a Cambodian mother holding her infant in her arms. What struck me most was the youth of the mother and the fact that this unposed photograph was instantly recognizable as a madonna and child. The mother beholding the child, in love and wonder. I don't think it matters what breed of Christian my friend is—he is, in fact, a Roman Catholic bishop—but what is significant is that he "got" Mary. In silence, the photograph spoke powerfully about Mary as a presence in our world, a constant reminder that in the incarnation the omnipotent God chose to take on human vulnerability. And a vulnerability of the most extreme sort, a child born not to wealth and power but to an impoverished peasant woman and her uneasy husband in the rural backwater of a small, troubled, colonized country.

I think that many Protestants, if they think about Mary at all, get hung up on what they are supposed to believe about her. And she doesn't make it easy. It's as if her calm visage belies our seeking after labels. Is Mary a cultural artifact or a religious symbol? A literary device or a theological tool? A valuable resource for biblical exegetes or the matrix of an extrabiblical piety that we, as Protestants, must avoid at all costs? The point about Mary is that she is all these things, and more, always more. She is poor yet gloriously rich. She is blessed among women yet condemned to witness her son's execution. She is human yet God-bearer, and the Word that she willingly bears is destined to pierce her soul. Had we a more elastic imagination, we might be less troubled by Mary's air of serene contradiction. But ours is a skeptical and divisive age. We are more comfortable with appraisal than with praise, more adept at cogent analysis than meaningful synthesis.

Mary is useful to us as a corrective to our ordinary state of mind, the epitome of "both/and" passion over "either/or" reasoning. She has a disarming way of challenging the polarities that so often bring human endeavors to impasse: the subjective and objective, the expansive and the parochial, the affective and the intellectual. Mary's designation as both virgin and mother, for example, no longer seems to be an impossible "model" for women that justifies their continued oppression within church and society. Instead, Mary constitutes a challenge as to what is possible for me, as a married, childless, Christian woman: to what extent can I remain "virgin," one-in-myself, able to come to things with newness of heart, and in what sense must I become "mother," losing myself in the nurture and service of others and embracing life's circumstances with the ripeness of maturity? This Mary is a gender-bender; she asks the same question of any Christian man.

If Mary points us beyond our traditional divisions, ideologues of all persuasions—conservative and liberal, feminist and anti-feminist—have long attempted to use Mary to argue their causes, with varying degrees of success. But Mary ultimately resists all causes. Like our God, she is who she is. And Mary is, in the nationally televised words of the Rev. Jimmy Swaggart (who prefaced his remark by saying, memorably, "The Catholics got *one* thing right") "the mother of God." From the Council of Ephesus to the less-respectable reaches of contemporary American evangelism, Mary holds her own.

As *theotokos*, Mary is also the mother of Wisdom. Unlike Zechariah, who responds to his annunciation concerning the birth of John the Baptist by inquiring of the angel, "How will I know that this is so?" Mary asks, simply, "How can this be?" It's an existential question, not an intellectual one. God responds to Zechariah by striking him dumb—for the entire gestation of his child, a nice touch—while Mary finds her voice, making the ancient song of Hannah her own. For me, the essential question is not what author placed Hannah's words in Mary's mouth, and with what theological intent. What is far more important is how I respond to this threading of salvation history from 1 Samuel to the Gospel of Luke. How do I answer when the mystery of God's love breaks through my denseness and doubt? Do I reach for a reference book, or the remote control? Am I so intent on my own plans that I ignore the call, or do I dare to carry the biblical tradition into my own life's journey? When I am called to answer "Yes" to God, not knowing much about where this commitment will lead me, Mary gives me hope that it is enough to trust in God's grace and the promise of salvation.

When I first began visiting Benedictine monasteries some twenty years ago, I was so ignorant of Scripture, despite an upbringing in Methodist and Congregational churches, that I did not know where the prayer the monks and nuns prayed each night came from. Gradually, I learned that it was a passage from the first chapter of Luke, and that for centuries before the Reformation it had been employed as the church's traditional vespers canticle. It was called the "Magnificat" because it begins with that word, in Latin translation; in English, it reads, "My soul magnifies the Lord."

I did not know that I was one of many Protestants, both laity and clergy, who had begun filling monastery guest rooms and choir stalls, and discovering there much common ground. What could be more refreshing to a Protestant than a daily immersion in Scripture, not only in communal prayer based on the Psalms but with a rhythm of hearing and responding to entire books of the Bible read aloud? I sensed that I was drawing from the tap roots of Christianity, from traditions and practices of prayer that had existed before the church split into the Roman Catholic and Orthodox churches, and long before the Reformation. I could claim as my prayerbook the entire Psalter (and not just psalms deemed suitable for Sunday morning); I could open my eyes and ears to the literary and theological treasurehouse of the early church; and I could reclaim Mary as a significant figure in my Christian faith.

No doubt it was my repeated exposure to the Magnificat in monastery choirs that led me to make it the focus of encountering Mary in the Scriptures. Each time I pray, "My soul magnifies the Lord, and my spirit rejoices in God my savior," I am compelled to ask, with Mary, "How can it be" that salvation has ways of working around all of the obstacles of sin, ignorance, and defiance that I place in its path? "How can it be" that God troubles with so wretched, self-centered, inconstant, and spiritually impoverished person as myself? Who, after all, am I?

The correct answer, to paraphrase a line from the Episcopal hymnal, is that I am called to be a person whose soul, like Mary, can be God's earthly sanctuary. Like Mary, I am invited each day to bring Christ into the world in my prayers, thoughts, and actions. And each evening, as I pray the Magnificat, I am asked to consider how I have done in this regard. Have I been so rich, stuffed full of myself, my plans, and my possessions, that I have in effect denied Christ a rightful place on earth? Or am I poor and despairing, but in my failures, weakness, and emptiness more ready and willing to be filled with God's purpose?

This book would have been helpful to me as I forged a meandering path through monastery retreats back to membership in a Protestant church. Rediscovering Mary was no small part of that journey, but I felt very much alone with my new understanding of her, and of her place in my life of faith. The church in which I was raised had a curious attitude towards Mary, an odd mixture of hubris and bashfulness. We dragged Mary out at Christmas, along with the angels, and placed her at center stage. Then we packed her safely in the crèche box for the rest of the year. We effectively denied Mary her place in Christian tradition and were disdainful of the reverence displayed for her, so public and emotional, by many millions of Catholics around the world. The more pilgrimages Catholics made to Lourdes, or Knock, or Czestochowa, the more silent we became. Even when the feminist movement opened the way for increased study of women in Scripture, few Protestants wrote about Mary, few preachers discussed her in their sermons.

Mary was mysterious, and therefore for Catholics; our religion was more proper, more masculine. Anything we couldn't explain—or explain away—was either ignored or given short shrift. I recognize the church of my childhood in this description by Nancy Mairs: a church with "all the mystery scrubbed out of it by a vigorous and slightly vinegary reason." But mystery endures, and I end this foreword as I began, by contemplating a madonna and child. The young woman's face is calm, yet creased with worry, expressing both love and pity. She knows hard times, all the pain and suffering this world can bring, and she knows that this child will someday die. But salvation always has a price. For now it is enough to hold the child, holding life and death all at once in her arms. It is enough to hold on, and to gaze at the child with a look of love and joy that is eternally comforting, both human and divine.

# Introduction

Beverly Roberts Gaventa and Cynthia L. Rigby

"Surely, from now on all generations will call me blessed."
—*Mary (Luke 1:48)*

The time has come for Protestants to join in the blessing of Mary. The Lukan story in which Mary visits Elizabeth draws attention repeatedly to the blessedness of Mary. Filled with the Holy Spirit, Elizabeth twice proclaims that Mary is blessed (1:42, 45). In the soaring opening of the Magnificat, Mary herself declares that "from now on all generations will call me blessed" (1:48). This rich blessing of Mary has scarcely extended to Protestant faith and life, however. Although we Protestants identify Scripture as authoritative, the Lukan blessing of Mary has rarely inspired Protestants to act accordingly.

Perhaps that is too harsh an indictment. Perhaps we have blessed Mary, at least during the weeks of December. But then we have sent her on her way, not expecting her to stay and occupy a place among us. This is true theologically, as evidenced in our nearly complete silence about Mary in both biblical studies and systematic theology. It is true liturgically, where Mary is confined to Advent hymns and texts and to our profession of the Apostles' Creed. And it is certainly true devotionally, since Protestant resistance to seeking intercession from the saints seems to render any reflection on Mary suspect. So fearful have we been of what seems to us excessive attention to Mary in Roman Catholic and Orthodox traditions that Mary is virtually absent among us.

Developments in recent decades have prompted a number of Protestants to think again about Mary. It is as if her very absence has itself become a presence. As questions of feminism and theology come together, it seems imperative to ask about Mary's place in Christian thought. Renewed interest in spiritual life among Protestants finds us listening to the music of earlier

Christian generations, where much attention is lavished on Mary. Theological reflection on childbirth and parenting require a coming to terms with the mother of Jesus. The absence of Mary not only cuts Protestants off from Catholic and Orthodox Christians; it cuts us off from the fullness of our own tradition. We have neither blessed Mary nor allowed her to bless us.

Toward an invitation to Mary to be present once again in Protestant faith and life, we invited a group of Protestant scholars to think about Mary—exactly *as* Protestants. They are individuals with particular scholarly expertise who represent varied theological and cultural traditions. Some contributors have chosen to begin with biblical texts, others with images of Mary drawn from tradition or contemporary life. The resulting essays vary significantly, as would be expected. But they converge and diverge in ways that we hope will constitute an invitation to others to join the discussion. That conversation itself makes for a small step toward fulfilling Mary's words.

Three sets of questions frame the collection. The first question is simply, Who is Mary? It is addressed in Part 1, "*Encountering* Mary." Not surprisingly, Protestants turn to Scripture first when considering this question. A second question concerns the ways in which Mary's story, encountered first in Scripture, intersects with contemporary life. Referred to here as "*Living* Mary" (Part 2), this area of exploration concerns what we learn from Mary about ourselves and, in turn, how our own lives influence the ways in which we interpret Mary. A third framing question is what Mary teaches us about God (thus Part 3, "*Bearing* Mary"). Although the book presents these as three distinct categories and three distinct sets of essays, the essays and the questions overlap and intersect repeatedly.

## ENCOUNTERING MARY

The Gospel writers tell us that Mary is the one "of whom Jesus was born" (Matt. 1:16) and that she is the "favored one" (Luke 1:28). But she is also a surprise. At least if our expectations consist entirely of a smiling Mary kneeling before a kindly Gabriel, then the opening lines of the New Testament will come as something of a shock. Matthew's Gospel opens with the genealogy of Jesus, in which four women appear as Mary's predecessors. These predecessors bear the names, not of Sarah and Rebekah, but of Tamar, Rahab, Ruth, and "the wife of Uriah." Even before Jesus' birth, as Katharine Doob Sakenfeld demonstrates in her essay, Mary already stands with those who do not comply with human expectations. She is a surprise by virtue of the company she keeps.

Mary also resists expectations by escaping the manger scene in Bethlehem and becoming a witness to the scandal of the cross. In Luke's Gospel, Mary is an interpreter of events as the Magnificat proudly declares God's intervention for Israel's salvation. She "ponders" Simeon's anticipation of the rejection and death of Jesus, and she worries over the troublesome behavior of her adolescent son in the Jerusalem temple. Even before the death of her son, she is integrally connected with his humiliation and suffering, Beverly Gaventa argues.

As encountered in the Gospels, Mary is also a challenge to narrow construals of what it means to be a family or to value the family. The comparatively harsh treatment of Mary and the remainder of Jesus' family in the Gospel of Mark underscores the gospel's disruption and redefinition of family in light of Jesus' death and resurrection, as E. Elizabeth Johnson demonstrates. A similar dynamic takes place in the Lukan story. Joel Green shows that, by identifying herself with God's family rather than with patriarchal family structures, Mary constitutes a challenge to the status quo. The Lukan Mary assists readers in understanding a story world that "intersects the canons and conventions of our own worlds at sometimes odd angles," Green further explains (see page 10). This combination of the expected and the extraordinary comes into view time and again in these essays, and it prompts reflection on the ways of God as well as on our own ways.

## *LIVING* MARY

Mary surprises us not only because she is different from what we might expect but because she teaches us unexpected things about ourselves. One of the first things we notice about biblical portrayals of Mary is that this woman, called to bear God, is not otherwise extraordinary. Protestants believe that Mary is not superior to us but is, as Nancy Duff explains, imperfect and sinful. To elevate Mary to a status beyond ordinary personhood is to abdicate the very hope of the incarnation—that God has met us in the mundane and beautiful context of creaturely existence. Respecting the ordinariness of Mary (as surprising as it is), Duff notes, is to accept our own vocation as the ordinary and imperfect, called and loved, people of God.

Mary reminds us of our creaturely status not in order to put us down but to lift us up in response to the call of God. Cheryl Kirk-Duggan works with the idea that Mary is proud of who she is and what she has accomplished. In contrast to the submissive and self-sacrificing portraits of Mary that convey that we, too, should shun pride, Kirk-Duggan argues that Mary surprises us by teaching us to care for ourselves as well as others. Bonnie Miller-McLemore is similarly concerned that notions of a self-sacrificing Mary prevent us from acknowledging the depth of her struggle and therefore from identifying with her. Mary's pondering—the anguish Mary experiences especially as a mother—cannot be leveraged for the happiness or safety of her child. It is instead characteristic of how she lives in relationship to Jesus. Similarly, our living as believers, with Mary, demands something that might be more demanding, even, than self-sacrifice. It requires a surprising degree of self-reflection, uncertainty, and struggle: the constant pondering of a mother in relationship to her child.

It is with our imperfections, our pride, and our anguish that we are called to discern and to bear witness to God's liberative work in the world. Nora Lozano-Díaz argues that this may involve struggling with the value of religious and cultural symbols that do not immediately resonate with our experience. Latina Protestants are among those who need to do this, she explains, if they are ever to gain a clear understanding of what Mary teaches us about living as Christian believers.

## *BEARING* MARY

Protestant thinkers consistently note that the most surprising thing about Mary is what she reveals about God. Contrary to what we would expect, Mary as God-bearer (*theotokos*) reminds us that God does not stand at a distance from us but has entered into existence with us in the person of Jesus Christ.

Protestants insist that Jesus Christ alone occupies center stage, but Mary as a person of faith directs us to participate in the ministry of her son. Daniel Migliore encourages us to stand with Mary as those who respond to God's election, proclaim God's surprising grace, are subject to God's transforming Word, and prayerfully await the coming of the Spirit. Again, Mary is not a superhuman being who models an ideal that real-life disciples cannot emulate. Migliore argues that Mary is our sister in Christ, a fellow believer with whom we struggle to understand and to serve God.

Mary's faithfulness directs us to the surprising reality of God's goodness, despite appearances to the contrary. As Lois Malcolm explains, it is not Mary's circumstances that reveal the character of God but Mary's experience of God's "bare" goodness that relativizes our experiences. The rich might be filled with good things and the hungry sent, empty, away—but this is not the reality of God's coming reign. God's kingdom is, in fact, marked by a reversal of what we so often see in this world. Mary knows that. As one who grieved much as well as knew great joy, Mary did not cease to uphold what was right and true. She continued to trust in who God is regardless of her circumstances. She believed she would be used by God, regardless of her circumstances, because she trusted the God who told her so.

The idea that we participate in the coming of God's new creation might be the most surprising of all. It is also one that will be met with suspicion by

Protestants, for whom there can be no compromise on the Reformation insight that there is *nothing* we can contribute to our salvation. In what sense does Mary, and in what sense do we—ordinary, sinful, often-mistaken creatures—participate in what God is doing in the world? As Cynthia Rigby explores, the coming of God in Mary as *theotokos* reveals not only that God enters into existence with us but that we are drawn, in and through Jesus Christ, into fellowship with God. Remarkably, God has made possible our participation in the coming kingdom by entering into our world and beseeching our care, our service, our friendship, and our love. The Word is made flesh, the Word that is God. It is *this* Word that is carried, nurtured, and fretted over by Mary. Such a thing is not only surprising; it is impossible to fathom. Mary reminds us, however, that all things are possible with God—even that we who have nothing to contribute will in some sense be bearers of God.

## BLESSING MARY BLESSING US

It is our hope that this volume will help Protestant believers think in new ways about Mary, blessing her and being blessed by her. We hope this because, finally, it is the Protestant conviction that Mary is who we are. She is a person of faith who does not always understand but who seeks to put her trust in God. She is one who is blessed not because she sins less, or has keener insight into the things of God. She is instead blessed (as we are) because she is called by God to participate in the work of God. To bless her in this work, even as Luke and Elizabeth do, is both to wish her an abundant life and to express the desire that God's purposes come to fruition. To call Mary blessed is to recognize the blessedness of ordinary people who are called to participate in that which is extraordinary. It is to encounter Mary and yearn to live with her as one who bears God.

Our hesitancy, as Protestants, to call Mary "blessed" stems from our suspicion that to do so would mean we are elevating her to a position higher than ourselves, perhaps even on a par with Christ. While this suspicion has kept us from consideration of Mary for far too long, it is founded in an insight that must continue to be upheld: Mary is like us, and only thereby can she make manifest that we, too, can participate in the things of God. To recognize Mary's blessedness, then, should not mean we elevate her to superhuman status. From a Protestant perspective, it is not even, first, to acknowledge who she is. Instead, to say Mary is the "Blessed One" is to join with the Spirit of the Magnificat, to prophesy about who *God* is and what God has done. Mary is the Blessed One because of what God has done in her and through her. Not to bless Mary is to turn away from the work of God.

In addition, is there not also a sense in which we are blessed *by* Mary? This idea might make Protestants even more nervous, for we emphasize that blessing comes from God, not by priests, saints, or other human mediators. If blessing Mary means acknowledging God's particular presence and activities in salvation history, perhaps being blessed *by* Mary is allowing these particular occasions of God's activity (i.e., those related to Mary) to have their impact on us. This volume is full of explorations about how Mary has blessed us and how she may bless us still: What does she tell us about motherhood? About suffering? About creativity? About "family values"? As we look to the particular experiences and insights of our brothers and sisters in order to live life more fully, so we are charged to look to the particular calling and contribution of Mary. What does she offer to our self-understanding and to our understanding of God?

Perhaps the stark absence of Mary in contemporary Protestantism is about to come to an end. Surely, when Mary is present with us, we will not turn to her as our mediator or redeemer, but we will relate to her as a member of the Great Cloud of Witnesses, as an ordinary sister in Christ who, extraordinarily, was called to be the Mother of God. Joining with her in the ministry of Christ, how can we not be blessed by her presence, knowing that we, too—as ordinary human beings—are called to participate in the extraordinary reversals of God's new creation?

The editors wish to offer special thanks to our authors for their contributions to this volume. We are also grateful for the vision and guidance of Stephanie Egnotovich of Westminster John Knox Press. Finally, the completion of the project was made possible by the talents and efforts of two colleagues at Austin Presbyterian Theological Seminary: Dhawn B. Martin, M. Div. candidate, who assisted with research, editing, and formatting; and Alison Riemersma, faculty secretary, who facilitated communications and coordinated logistical details. We are deeply appreciative of their efforts.

# PART I

## *Encountering* Mary

# 1

# Blessed Is She Who Believed

*Mary, Curious Exemplar in Luke's Narrative*

JOEL B. GREEN

Among the New Testament writings, none contributes more to our portrait of Mary, mother of Jesus, than the two-volume narrative attributed to Luke the evangelist: the Gospel of Luke and the Acts of the Apostles.[1] In large part, this is due to the significant role Luke gives to his account of the birth and childhood of Jesus. Of course, the Gospel of Matthew devotes its opening two chapters to Jesus' birth and infancy as well; for Matthew, however, Mary is a secondary figure, known typically in relation to Joseph. By contrast, in the first chapters of Luke, Mary is a prominent actor in her own right; she makes decisions, acts, speaks, and is spoken to. Indeed, in Luke 2:5 Joseph is introduced in relation to Mary (and not vice versa); in 2:16 she is named before Joseph; in 2:33–34 Simeon, having blessed "them" both, addresses himself to Mary (and not to Joseph); and in 2:48 Mary speaks for herself and her husband. Throughout his narrative, Luke mentions Mary by name thirteen times[2] and refers to her directly, though without mentioning her name, an additional three times.[3] Although our interests may lead us to wish Luke had given us more, it is nonetheless clear from what he has provided that Mary serves an important role in his narrative.

Students of Luke–Acts, and of Mary, have largely agreed in general terms on the role Mary serves in the Lukan narrative. As important as her status as the mother of Jesus might be, her identity is developed along other lines; she is a "model for all Christians,"[4] "the exemplary disciple, a Christian prototype,"[5] "the first believer,"[6] "the perfect Christian."[7] If this portrayal of Mary is generally agreed on, it is not especially helpful, since it remains to be ascertained whether Luke in fact attributes some sort of unique status to Mary, and because references to Mary as a model believer remain rather abstract. How does she serve this role?

9

As I will demonstrate, a more apt category for Mary's role in Luke–Acts is that of "accessible exemplar." I borrow this category from the work of Garrett Green, particularly from his insights into how literature of all kinds, but, for religious communities, especially the Scriptures, shape the way persons imagine the world.[8] Accordingly, an "accessible exemplar" would provide us with ways of seeing beyond the world, whose rhythms and patterns we take for granted, to fresh ways of making sense of our lives, including especially our relatedness to God and our relationships with one another. Reading Luke–Acts as Scripture, we open ourselves, as communities of believers, to having our identity and deepest beliefs formed and reformed by this narrative. We also find ourselves stirred to transform the world around us so that it might conform to this vision, this Word. Attending to the portrait of Mary within the Lukan narrative provides us ready access to what may seem to be the curious horizons of a world whose values and commitments are measured by the good news of the kingdom of God. Studying Luke's portrait of Mary helps us to recognize a life-world that intersects the canons and conventions of our own worlds at sometimes odd angles.

My approach in this essay is oriented toward recent work in narrative theory that reads narrative texts as cultural products.[9] This approach is concerned at a basic level with how Luke's narrative draws on and broadcasts widespread assumptions from within the world of Luke, as well as how Luke's narrative works to counter the taken-for-granted values and assumptions that pervade its world. As narrative, Luke–Acts invites its readers into its discourse as participants, ready to be prodded and encouraged, challenged and formed; hence, our reading of Luke–Acts is not a matter of mere antiquarian interest. The question is not primarily, How can I make sense of this ancient message? Rather, it is, How does this narrative tell the story of our worlds, our lives, those of us who enter into it so as to indwell it? Given this approach, I argue that Mary's appearance in the Lukan narrative assaults the theological imaginations of its readers, subverting conventional wisdom about the determination of people's statuses and roles in favor of communities among whom the image of the merciful God may be embodied. In short, Luke's portrait of Mary invites a conversion of the imagination,[10] together with reformed allegiances and dispositions, in which the character of the people of God is reevaluated in light of the newly found understanding of God's purpose in the good news.

I take as my point of departure the brief dialogue between Jesus and an unnamed woman from the crowd regarding Mary's status as "the blessed one," found in Luke 11:27–28. This text brings forward earlier references to Mary in the Gospel and anticipates the final testimonial to Mary that occurs in Acts 1:14, where she is explicitly numbered within the community of Jesus' faithful disciples. Focusing on Mary as accessible exemplar allows me to demonstrate that, for Luke, Mary is not only a model for women disciples; nor is she unique in exhibiting the strange ways of God. Finally, to highlight Mary's vocation as one who points Luke's readers to a new way of seeing the world, I urge that Luke invites us to join Mary in that work to which he repeatedly draws attention—namely, the sort of pondering that allows for previously unimaginable interpretations of the events and world around us (Luke 2:19, 51).

## BLESSED IS SHE, BLESSED ARE THEY

> While he was saying this, a woman in the crowd raised her voice and said to him, "Blessed is the womb that bore you and the breasts that nursed you!" But he said, "Blessed rather are those who hear the word of God and obey it!" (Luke 11:27–28 NRSV)

The interchange between Jesus and the unnamed woman from the crowd interrupts Jesus' defense of himself and his ministry. The larger narrative unit (11:14–36) begins with a brief account of one occasion in which Jesus engaged in exorcism—for him a characteristic activity in the Gospel of Luke (see Luke 13:10–17; Acts 10:38). Jesus casts out a demon, and this act leads to three kinds of response, each of which then receives fuller development: amazement (11:14c → 11:27–28); the charge that Jesus is in league with Beelzebul, Lord of the Flies, ruler of demons (11:15 → 11:17–26); and the demand for a sign from heaven (11:16 → 11:29–36). Although these responses appear in summary form as though they were elicited directly by Jesus' ministry of exorcism, it makes sense to see them as links in a chain of cause and effect. Jesus casts out a demon, an act that raises the question, By whose authority does he cast out demons? His reply pits the sovereignty of God against the rule of Satan, positions Jesus' ministry on the frontlines of the clash against these two kingdoms, and insists on a view of Jesus as the agent of God's salvation. This reply constitutes a claim to considerable status before God that leads this unnamed woman from the crowd to her exuberant pronouncement of blessing. Jesus again responds, again through redirection and refocus. Finally, he observes the wrongheaded thinking that results in misrepresentations of the character of his ministry. People do not grasp who he is and the significance of what he is about; they therefore demand signs as proof because they are possessed by inner dispositions turned away from God's saving design. Thus, in the face of these three forms of response to his ministry, Jesus calls for a conversion of one's moral, emotional, and cognitive orientations, a transformation of one's imagination. He argues for an alternative identification of the source of his power and invites an alternative, fourth response, one that recognizes in his work the powerful and gracious presence of the dominion of God that leads to faithfulness before God.

The woman's declaration—"Blessed is the womb that bore you and the breasts that nursed you!"—brings to the surface conventional values regarding the status and role of women in an expression that likely had already achieved proverbial status.[11] Her announcement is enmeshed with two intertwined perspectives regarding women: (1) that they find their place in traditional society in terms of relatedness to a man, typically their father, husband, or, if widowed, son; (2) that they find value in childbearing and may be regarded as blessed through being the mother of a son who is granted great honor. This kind of cultural value, whereby honor is obtained through bearing children, is on display in the Scriptures of Israel—such as in the account of the rivalry between Leah and Rachel—wherein steps on the ladder of status and fortune are counted in numbers of pregnancies (Gen. 29:31–30:24). After all, had God's blessing of humanity not come with the command, "Be fruitful and multiply . . ." (Gen. 1:28)?[12] The ideal of fecundity and the value for women of bearing children was also largely taken for granted in Rome, not least so as to maintain the family name and to propagate the potency of the empire.[13] Read against such a backdrop, this woman's pronouncement of blessedness seems only fitting and, one might think, marks her as a woman of keen insight into Jesus' character. By referring to his mother, Mary, in this way, has she not characterized him with high honorifics indeed?

What, then, are we to make of Jesus' reply: "Blessed rather are those who hear the word of God and obey it"? Although it is possible, grammatically, to read his words as a contradiction of the woman's pronouncement, the fact that Elizabeth had spoken similar words, and done so under the inspiration of the Holy Spirit (1:41–42), makes this option doubtful.[14] Neither is it appropriate to imagine that Luke thus narrates Jesus' simple agreement with this woman's assessment.[15] Simply because a statement was made earlier in the narrative by a woman under the guidance of the Spirit does not mean that such a statement is incapable of further nuance. In fact, we must allow for the progression of thought within the narrative concerning what constitutes a state of divine blessedness shared among the people of God.[16] Rather, the sense that best fits this narrative context is that the words of this woman are not altogether wrong but are in need of substantive modification.[17]

Jesus' response to the woman, then, should be interpreted as a corrective. In speaking thus, he amends both her pronouncement and the pervasive cultural values to which she gives voice. That is, he is engaged in cultural critique at this juncture in the narrative, calling into question one of the primary means by which women would have found honor in the world about which Luke writes and within which Luke's narrative would be read. Here, then, it is imperative that we note the basis on which Mary would be a candidate for blessedness. Luke has portrayed Mary as one who hears and reflects on the divine word and one who embraces it positively; indeed, she is even one who proclaims the word in the fashion of a prophet (1:26–38, 46–55; 2:19, 51). Although Jesus' words generalize concerning how anyone might achieve a state of blessedness ("[B]lessed are those who . . ."), Elizabeth had already declared Mary as blessed on account of her faith (1:45). Taking seriously the criterion Jesus introduces in this narrative account is important because the alternative might restrict Mary's hope (and, with her, that of other women) for divine fortune to her role as mother—that is, to the fruitfulness of her belly and breasts.[18] Jesus' beatitude allows no room for conventional boundaries to divine fortune, for his message works to construct a new world that undermines the dispositions and practices of the present, in the same way that his mission signals the downfall of the realm of Satan (11:17–26).

We have already dropped hints about the connection of this brief interchange with the encounter between Mary and Elizabeth narrated by Luke in his opening chapter (1:39–45). In fact, the categories for making sense of blessedness that appear in Jesus' parley with the unnamed woman in 11:27–28 seem already to have been presented by Elizabeth. She provides Mary with a dual greeting:

> "Blessed are you among women, and blessed is the fruit of your womb. . . . And blessed is she who believed that there would be a fulfillment of what was spoken to her by the Lord." (1:42, 45 NRSV)

At first sight these two pronouncements may appear to be at odds with one another, a reading for which some might find support in 11:27–28. The former blessing focuses on Mary's motherhood, after all, while the second declares her fortunate on account of her faith. Locating this exchange more firmly in the Lukan birth account suggests a different focus, one that emphasizes God's gracious initiative leading to Mary's response. In what way does Mary merit divine fortune? Luke makes clear that it is not because of Mary's motherhood. Her state of pregnancy is the consequence of her blessedness, not its cause. Her role in the actualization of God's saving plan is thus highlighted, but, again, this is the result of divine blessing, not its impetus. In other words, Mary is not due honor on account of the fruitfulness of her belly, and there is no real tension between Elizabeth's words of greeting and the criterion of blessing later offered by Jesus in 11:27–28. Instead, Luke underscores the graciousness of God's initiative and the importance of openhanded response to God's word.

The question remains, Who is Mary? What has she done to merit this signal honor? To this question, Luke's answer is as profound as it is subtle. With other characters in Luke's birth account—including Zechariah, Elizabeth, Joseph, Simeon, and Anna—stature is marked in terms of pedigree and by references to unassailable character (1:5–7, 27; 2:4, 25–27, 36–37), both typical measures of social standing in most any world. Elizabeth and Zechariah, for example, are children of Aaron. Zechariah thus lays ancestral claim to the advanced honor accorded those of the priesthood: he has unrivaled access to holy places and holy paraphernalia, the power to pronounce blessings on God's behalf and to determine who and what is pure, and an indispensable role in temple worship and sacrifice (Exod. 28–29; Lev. 8–10) for which he was set apart from God. What is more, Zechariah and Elizabeth's portrayal invites our association of this couple with Abraham and Sarah: blameless before the Lord, advanced in years, and childless.[19] Joseph, who has almost no role to play in the Gospel of Luke, is twice mentioned as a member of David's household. Simeon and Anna are each, in different ways, painted as prophetic figures of exemplary piety.

Such marks of honor as these are conspicuous by their absence in the case of Luke's introduction of Mary, however. She is presented as a young girl, perhaps twelve or thirteen years old, not yet or only recently having achieved puberty, who resides in an insignificant town far removed from the Jewish and Roman centers of power and purity. Her family of origin is never mentioned. She is betrothed to Joseph but has not yet joined his household and, thus, has no claims to his status. In fact, she is not introduced in any way that would commend her to us as one particularly noteworthy or deserving of honor. Her insignificance seems to be her primary significance for the Lukan narrative. Yet she is the one who is granted the highest status allocated anyone within this narrative, an honorable greeting by the archangel of the Lord and an invitation to participate in the actualization of God's saving purpose. Here already is the inversion of the social realities of the world Mary occupies. Opening this Gospel with a mural so stark in contrast to issues of honor and position, Luke has begun the process of undercutting the conventions of competitive maneuvering for positions of status that mark the world of his narrative. Mary, who seems to measure low on any status scale (with reference to ancestral heritage, gender, age, or location), turns out to be the one favored by God, the one who finds her status and identity ultimately in her embrace of God's blessing to her.[20] Luke's narrative is profoundly theocentric at precisely this juncture, for he thus makes transparent his emphasis on the gracious initiative of God in setting in motion the fulfillment of the ancient plan of God. God chooses Mary, as it were, for no good reason— at least, for no reason that would be convincing to persons whose values are at home in the world of honor and shame of the ancient Mediterranean.

At the same time, it is worth reflecting on the sort of person who finds her status and identity ultimately in her embrace of God's blessing to her. Doing so will remind us of the way Mary performs in the Lukan narrative as curious exemplar. Mary's memorable reply to Gabriel's words of annunciation, taken on their own, suggest the extraordinary quality of the new reality on display in Luke's account. Gabriel announces the birth to Mary of a son of greatly exalted status: "holy," "Son of the Most High," "Son of God" (1:32–35). Mary replies, "Here I am, the servant [or slave] of the Lord; let it be to me according to your word" (1:38 NRSV). Mary thus shows herself to be one who hears and embraces God's word, one who submits herself to the divine purpose, and, crucial for our purposes here, one who claims a place in God's own household. Luke has mentioned no family of origin for Mary, but Mary makes up for this lacuna in the narrative by naming the head of her family as God. In a world where identity was found in relatedness to others, Mary thus delineates her own self-identity with reference to God's family. This is strange because it diverges from conventional wisdom and practice, but also because it is presented to us as the deliberate act of a woman—indeed, a young girl—whose behavior thus departs from acceptable norms. In the words of Thomas D'Sa, Mary thus presents herself as a contrarian who acts against the grain of her male-dominated culture and who thus models living life according to patterns and rhythms that originate in the saving work of God.[21] Within her social world, Mary has a script to follow. This script would involve her relative seclusion, not a journey of some seventy miles (no chaperone or traveling companions are mentioned by Luke!)[22], and her submission to her father or husband, not her purposeful resolve. Turning from such conventions, she steps to the curious rhythms of the new era being ushered in by God and adopts behaviors appropriate to this fresh (but ancient) work of God. In doing so, she portends the appearance of others in the Third Gospel whose behavior departs from the norm but is nonetheless regarded as exemplary: a centurion who invites Jesus' beneficence (7:1–10), a woman who expresses authentic hospitality to Jesus (7:36–50), and a woman who relentlessly pursues justice (18:1–8), to name three.

The exemplary quality of Mary can be pursued even further by taking a path Luke has only opened but not yet developed: the redefinition of family transparent in Mary's claim to status as a servant in God's household. Her response to Gabriel relativizes, even places in jeopardy, her pending marriage to Joseph and her place in his household—both because she has agreed to a pregnancy apart from the honor and security of marriage and because she has declared her primary and ultimate allegiance to God rather than to a life of subservience to her husband-to-be. For her, partnership in the aims of God transcends the claims of family, and her words anticipate Jesus' own message in 8:19–21, and especially verse 21: "My mother and my brothers are those who hear the word of God and do it." In this text, Mary and Jesus' physical brothers are not characterized as model disciples and, therefore, not counted among Jesus' family[23]

because, in his urgent call for the renewal of God's people, Jesus insists that all
other responsibilities and relationships be subordinated to faithfulness to
God's word. This redefinition reaches even to notions of family, where kinship
is defined not with reference to blood ties but on the basis of hearing and doing
the word of God. A perspective known in the larger world of the ancient
Mediterranean, both within and outside of Jewish circles, this message continues to be developed elsewhere in the Gospel of Luke.[24] As for Mary (and
Jesus' brothers), at this juncture in the narrative the jury is still out on how she
will comport herself in relation to Jesus. Only later will Luke inform us that,
in the end, Mary is Jesus' kin when measured in relation to her responsive faith
(see Acts 1:12–14).[25]

## MARY, INTERPRETER OF GOD'S WORK

It is difficult to imagine a more powerful reflection on the significance of the
coming of Jesus than Mary's prophetic words in Luke 1:46–55, the Magnificat
or Mary's Song. Images of the divine warrior and gracious God coalesce in this
celebration of the advent of salvation in Jesus. Here, Mary identifies the shape
of Israel's restoration as it will be narrated in the words and deeds of Jesus in
subsequent chapters, and invites others, her audience in- and outside the narrative, to make their home in this redemptive vision. As insightful as Mary's
Song may be into the character of God's work, it is nonetheless true that Mary
herself does not appear to grasp fully the significance of her own provocative
and rousing words. That is, even after her revelatory encounter with Gabriel,
even after the confirmation of Gabriel's message through Elizabeth's words of
greeting, even after proclaiming the faithful work of the Savior-God, and even
after the wondrous events surrounding the birth of her son, she is left to puzzle over the meaning of it all.

Twice, in Luke 2:19, 51, we are told that Mary "preserved all of these matters in her heart" (au. trans.).[26] This phrase is reminiscent of texts from Israel's
Scriptures in which persons mull over the significance of revelatory moments,
such as Jacob's recall of Joseph's dream concerning the honor he would receive
(Gen. 37:11) or Daniel's reflection on the vision he has experienced (Dan.
7:28). These scriptural precursors serve to underscore the revelatory significance of the events surrounding Jesus' birth and childhood. They also highlight the reality that even these events do not contain within them their own
interpretation, so that Mary must engage herself in hermeneutical reflection
to grasp their meaning. Indeed, given what we have found to be the generally
alien nature of the words and practices that monopolize the unfolding of God's
presence and purpose, the need for the penetrating work of interpretation is

all the more evident. Such interpretive activity is represented by Luke not as a matter of cognitive discovery or logical deduction but as one centered in "the heart"—in ancient psychology, the center of affect and volition.[27] The narrator thus points to the sort of integration of revelatory experience and rumination that might generate the insight and commitment requisite for a life of faithful discipleship. If Mary, who has been portrayed in such positive terms, nevertheless holds hasty conclusions in abeyance in favor of careful consideration, then we may see that Luke invites us, his audience, to do the same. "Preserving" must lead to "obedience," and it does in the case of Mary. Faithful hearing, the sort that leads to faithful doing, however, involves the struggle of interpretation.

Mary shows the way. She knows already that the ways of God being brought about in the birth of Jesus have deep roots in the promises to Israel of old, and to Abraham in particular. As Mary's Song shows, she knows that the significance of Jesus' mission lies above all in its relation to the ancient narrative of God's engagement with God's people as related in Israel's Scriptures. For Luke, the story of Jesus picks up where the scriptural story leaves off. Bringing the birth narrative to a close with Mary continuing "to ponder all these things in her heart," rather than with final answers or well-crafted propositions, invites readers to respond in the same way. They are asked to eschew hasty conclusions about what must or will be and, instead, maintain an openness to the course Luke's own narrative will take as it develops this vision of restoration. The true significance of "all these things" will become clear only as the story is told.

## CONCLUSION

We have seen how Luke's narration in chapters 1–2 departs from conventional norms and his own literary proclivities in order to emphasize Mary's lack of merit, according to ordinary measures of human worth. God's gracious initiative stands at center stage, and typical categories for determining status and ordinary boundaries meant to hem divine fortune are thus erased. Luke's narrative strategy has deployed Mary so as to pull back the curtain on a curious world, curious in that it works with norms that are strange and surprising. I have also observed that Mary herself is characterized by behaviors that seem more at home in this curious world of God's reign than in the world inhabited by others, both in- and outside Luke's narrative. Mary seems readily to embrace the patterns and rhythms of God's kingdom, irrespective of their alien quality. This does not mean that discipleship comes easily for Mary, or naturally. She exhibits the need to ponder events infused with the presence of God.

However, Mary's contemplation on how these matters might be understood against the backdrop of God's ancient purpose and engagement with Israel invites Luke's audience to join her. Luke's portrayal of Mary thus provides us with access to a way of perceiving the world and life in it that runs counter to the world of normal perception. It also provides an exemplar of one whose life is in sync with God's saving plan: Mary herself.

## NOTES

1. The Gospel of Luke (sometimes known as the Third Gospel because of its position in the sequence of New Testament books) and the Acts of the Apostles do not name their common author, though tradition has identified Luke, sometime coworker with Paul, in this role (the evidence is briefly surveyed in Joel B. Green, "Luke," in *Eerdmans Dictionary of the Bible*, ed. David Noel Freedman et al. [Grand Rapids, Mich.: Wm. B. Eerdmans Pub. Co., 2000], 827–28). In this essay, "Luke" refers to the narrator of Luke–Acts, without bias as to actual authorship. Among recent presentations of the Lukan portrait of Mary, see especially Joseph A. Fitzmyer, "Mary in Lucan Salvation History," in *Luke the Theologian: Aspects of His Teaching* (New York/Mahwah: Paulist Press, 1989), 57–85; Beverly Roberts Gaventa, *Mary: Glimpses of the Mother of Jesus* (Columbia, S. C.: University of South Carolina Press, 1995; Minneapolis: Fortress Press, 1999).
2. Luke 1:27, 30, 34, 38, 39, 41, 46, 56; 2:5, 16, 19, 34; Acts 1:14.
3. Luke 2:41–52; 8:19–21; 11:27–28.
4. John McHugh, *The Mother of Jesus in the New Testament* (Garden City, N.Y.: Doubleday, 1975), 347.
5. Turid Karlsen Seim, *The Double Message: Patterns of Gender in Luke and Acts* (Nashville: Abingdon Press, 1994), 115.
6. Fitzmyer, "Mary," 69.
7. Anthony J. Tambasco, *What Are They Saying about Mary?* (New York/Mahwah: Paulist Press, 1984), 26; see p. 28: "first example of the Christian who keeps God's word."
8. Garrett Green, *Imagining God: Theology and the Religious Imagination* (Grand Rapids, Mich.: Wm. B. Eerdmans Pub. Co., 1989).
9. See Joel B. Green, *The Gospel of Luke*, New International Commentary on the New Testament (Grand Rapids, Mich.: Wm. B. Eerdmans Pub. Co., 1997).
10. "Imagination" is " . . . the power of taking something as something by means of meaningful forms, which are rooted in our history and have the power to disclose truths about life in the world. Creative imagination arises out of the openness of these forms both to new experiences and to new and illuminating combinations of forms" (David J. Bryant, *Faith and the Play of Imagination: On the Role of Imagination in Religion*, Studies in American Biblical Hermeneutics 5 [Macon, Ga.: Mercer University Press, 1989], 5).
11. For example, Petronius had written, "How blessed is the mother who gave birth to such a one as you" (*Satyricon* 94.1; mid–first century c.e.). See also Ovid *Metamorphoses* 4.320–24; Gen. 30:13; 49:25; *2 Apoc. Bar.* 54:10.
12. The import of this directive for Second Temple Judaism is suggested in Tal Ilan, *Jewish Women in Greco-Roman Palestine* (Peabody, Mass.: Hendrickson, 1995),

105–07; Léonie J. Archer, *Her Price Is Beyond Rubies: The Jewish Woman in Graeco-Roman Palestine*, Journal for the Study of the Old Testament Supplement Series 60 (Sheffield: Sheffield Academic Press, 1990), 123–26.

13. Cf. Beryl Rawson, "The Roman Family," in *The Family in Ancient Rome: New Perspectives*, ed. Beryl Rawson (Ithaca, N.Y.: Cornell University Press, 1986), 1–57.

14. James Malcolm Arlandson (*Women, Class, and Society in Early Christianity: Models from Luke-Acts* [Peabody, Mass.: Hendrickson, 1997]) regards the unnamed woman as an outsider, contradicted by Jesus (123–24).

15. Contra Darrell L. Bock, *Luke*, 2 vols., Baker Exegetical Commentary on the New Testament 3 (Grand Rapids, Mich.: Baker Books, 1994/96), 2:1094; M. Philip Scott, "A Note on the Meaning and Translation of Luke 11:28," *Irish Theological Quarterly* 41 (1974): 235–50.

16. So Robert L. Brawley, *Centering on God: Method and Message in Luke-Acts*, Literary Currents in Biblical Interpretation (Louisville, Ky.: Westminster/John Knox Press, 1990), 52–53.

17. Cf. *Mary in the New Testament: A Collaborative Assessment by Protestant and Roman Catholic Scholars*, ed. Raymond E. Brown et al. (Philadelphia: Fortress Press; New York/Mahwah/Toronto: Paulist Press, 1978), 171–72; Fitzmyer, "Mary," 77. The Greek word *menoun* is capable of various renderings (see the survey in C. F. D. Moule, *An Idiom Book of New Testament Greek*, 2d ed. [Cambridge: Cambridge University Press, 1959], 162–64), so narrative context must be determinative.

18. This is noted by Luise Schottroff, *Let the Oppressed Go Free: Feminist Perspectives on the New Testament*, Gender and the Biblical Tradition (Louisville, Ky.: Westminster/John Knox Press, 1993), 116: "[Jesus'] . . . answer in 11:28 criticizes the beatitude of Mary, which has reduced her to belly and breasts."

19. See, e.g., Gen. 11:30; 15:16; 16:1; 17:1, 17; 18:11–12.

20. This is discussed more fully in Joel B. Green, "The Social Status of Mary in Luke 1, 5–2, 52: A Plea for Methodological Integration," *Biblica* 73 (1992): 457–71.

21. Thomas D'Sa, "Mary the Contrary: A Reflection on the Annunciation and Visitation as Models of Commitment and Evangelization," *Vidyajyoti* 58 (1994): 623–35.

22. Cf. Archer, "Her Price Is beyond Rubies," 101–22, 239–50.

23. Cf. Robert C. Tannehill, *The Narrative Unity of Luke–Acts: A Literary Approach*, vol. 1: *The Gospel according to Luke*, Foundations and Facets (Philadelphia: Fortress Press, 1986), 212–13. Contra Joseph A. Fitzmyer, *The Gospel according to Luke*, 2 vols., Anchor Bible 28–28A (Garden City, N.Y.: Doubleday 1981/85), 1:222–25.

24. Cf. 9:57–62; 12:51–53; 14:25–26; 18:23–30. With regard to how this message would have been heard in the world of the New Testament, cf. Stephen C. Barton, "The Relativisation of Family Ties in the Jewish and Graeco-Roman Traditions," in *Constructing Early Christian Families: Family as Social Reality and Metaphor*, ed. Halvor Moxnes (London/New York: Routledge, 1997), 81–100.

25. Gaventa (*Mary*, 69–72) notes how Acts 1:14 resolves a narrative tension regarding Mary's identity as a disciple. Her exemplary response to Gabriel leads eventually to Mary's pondering (2:19, 51), with no immediate provision on Luke's part regarding the outcome(s) of her reflection. Presented in 8:19–21 on the boundary between disciples and the crowds, as neither in nor out, the status of Mary's discipleship remains open. This tension is resolved, finally, when we find Mary's name among the disciples in Acts 1:12–14.

26. The phrasing is almost identical in the Greek of 2:19 and 2:51. Cf. Dan. 4:28 LXX.
27. This point is suggested in François Bovon, *Das Evangelium nach Lukas*, vol. 1, Evangelisch-Katholischer Kommentar zum Neuen Testament (Zürich: Benziger; Neukirchen-Vluyn: Neukirchener, 1989), 131.

# 2

# Tamar, Rahab, Ruth, and the Wife of Uriah

*The Company Mary Keeps in Matthew's Gospel*

KATHARINE DOOB SAKENFELD

The Gospel of Matthew places Mary in an astonishing company of women. The opening verses present Jesus' lineage schematically, recognizing three classic time periods of the Old Testament story: the time of the ancestors beginning with Abraham; the time of the Jerusalem monarchy beginning with King David; and the time following the deportation to Babylon, when there was no longer a ruling king. A striking feature of the Matthean genealogy is the mention of four women within the long list of men's names: Tamar, Rahab, Ruth, and "the wife of Uriah" (Bathsheba). Why are these four women mentioned? And what might their presence have to do with Mary?

When the Old Testament presents a single line of descent, it normally does not include women's names.[1] Matthew's genealogy for Jesus does not conform to this typical pattern. The stories of these four women are varied, yet they share some irregularity compared to ordinary Old Testament patterns of marriage and family. These four names may thus be intended to prepare the reader for the irregularity of Mary's conception and Jesus' birth. Matthew's genealogy ends with "Joseph the husband of Mary, of whom Jesus was born . . ." (1:16).[2] Clearly the genealogy is for Joseph, son of David (v. 20); yet equally clearly, Mary's child is "from the Holy Spirit" before she and Joseph live together (v. 18). This essay will review briefly the stories of these four Old Testament women, with a focus on how their stories show God's purpose at work even in situations that challenge ordinary human expectations and values.

## TAMAR (GENESIS 38)

Of the four women mentioned in Matthew, Tamar is probably the least known (Matt. 1:3), as the themes of her story are hardly the stuff of church school lessons. The story must be understood within the framework of the ancient Israelite concept of "levirate marriage" (see Deut. 25:5–10). When an Israelite married man died before his wife had borne a son, the brother of the dead man was expected to take the widow as his own wife. According to Deuteronomy, the first son she bore would then be considered a descendant of the dead man so that his genealogical line would not end.

Tamar was chosen by Judah as wife for his oldest son, Er. For a reason never supplied by the account in Genesis 38, God took the life of Er before a son was born. So Judah instructed his second son, Onan, to take Tamar as wife according to the levirate rule. Onan, knowing that a child conceived would not be his, "spilled his semen on the ground." For this disobedience, God took his life also. Now Judah, not knowing or inquiring why his sons had died, worried that Tamar was at fault for their deaths. So he sent her home to her own family, alleging that he would eventually give Tamar to the third son when that son was older. But time passed, the third son grew up, and Judah took no action. Tamar therefore took the matter of offspring into her own hands. She disguised herself as a prostitute and waited along the roadside where Judah was expected to be traveling. Sure enough, Judah came along and approached her, unaware of her identity. Tamar asked for his signet, cord, and staff (identifiable personal property) as surety that he would send the promised payment. Payment never arrived, so she kept the property. Several months later news came to Judah that Tamar was pregnant from acting as a prostitute. The story does not tell who conveyed the news, but given the overall plot it seems reasonable to suppose that Tamar herself may have arranged for the message to be sent. In a show of righteous indignation, Judah insists that Tamar be put to death. As she is being brought out, she sends the signet, cord, and staff to Judah to show him who was responsible for her pregnancy. As he recognizes his own property, he says, "She is more in the right than I, since I did not give her my [third] son Shelah" (v. 26). The result of the pregnancy is twins, Zerah and Perez; and the line of Perez leads from Judah on to David.[3]

Why did Tamar seek to become pregnant by Judah rather than by the third son Shelah? The narrator of the story does not address the question, not even indirectly. Mention is made of the death of Judah's wife before the encounter at the roadside, but this does not erase the seeming scandal of what transpires. Certainly Tamar's behavior is not within the parameters of expected Israelite practice. Prostitution is never condoned, and though we may say that the story deals only with the appearance of prostitution, engaging in anonymous sex for pay is not in any usual circumstances considered an appropriate solution to a problem. Rabbinic tradition from a time later than the NT period seeks to exonerate both Judah and Tamar by laying the whole encounter at the hand of God, who set desire in Judah's heart so that he would turn aside to Tamar and thus set in motion the Davidic ancestry.[4] In the Genesis narrative, however, the focus of Judah's self-criticism is on his failure to give his third son to Tamar, not on his visit to a woman whom he imagined to be a prostitute. A broad thematic connection to Mary's story is not difficult to discern. In both cases, the pregnancies came about outside the structure of marriage. Through deft allusion to Judah's declaration of Tamar's righteousness, Mary is implicitly vindicated as well.

Commentators both ancient and modern have suggested a second thematic connection to the Gospel of Matthew, which is generally held to look toward a mission to all nations in the era of the post-resurrection followers of Jesus (Matt. 28:16–20). The narrator of Genesis identifies Judah's first wife, Shua, as a Canaanite (38:2), and it is popularly thought that Tamar also was a non-Israelite, as are Rahab and Ruth and possibly Bathsheba. Neither Genesis 38 nor any other Old Testament reference supports this claim concerning Tamar's non-Israelite origin, and it is not possible to know whether the author of Matthew viewed her as Israelite or foreigner. In any case, it is not necessary to identify a single thread (such as being non-Israelite) to connect all of the four women.

## RAHAB (JOSHUA 2, 6)

The traditional song "Joshua Fit the Battle of Jericho" centers on the best-known part of the Jericho story, the walls that "came tumblin' down." Less familiar, though still probably more familiar than the story of Tamar, is the story of Rahab (Matt. 1:5), an inhabitant of the town of Jericho. Since there is no explicit sexual activity in the story recorded in Joshua, Rahab can more safely be conveyed in children's Bible story books. From the Israelite camp on the east side of the Jordan River, Joshua sends two men to spy out conditions in Jericho. Immediately on arriving at the city, they enter the house of Rahab, who is identified as a prostitute. Drama builds quickly. The king of Jericho somehow gets word of the presence of spies at Rahab's house and sends officials to demand that she turn them over to the authorities. Rahab meanwhile has hidden the spies under flax stalks on her flat rooftop, and she tells the officials that the spies have already left the town. As the king's searchers go chasing across the countryside, Rahab returns to the roof to have a conversation with the spies. She confesses the power of the LORD, who "is indeed God in heaven above and on earth below" (2:11), and asks that the Israelites spare her

life and that of her extended family in return for the protection she has given
the spies. The spies agree, but they stipulate that she must continue to keep
their secret, and Rahab, whose house is in the city wall, aids their escape. As
they depart, the spies arrange that she display a crimson cord in her window
at the time of the attack, and they advise her that all her family must stay
together in the house in order to avoid death.

The spies return to Joshua, but their report as recorded says nothing of
Rahab, indeed nothing that could not already have been known except that "all
the inhabitants of the land melt in fear before us" (2:24). The Israelites cross
the Jordan, and the ritualized siege of Jericho begins. The text focuses on cir-
cular marching (probably silent for the first six days) and eventually trumpet-
blowing and shouting, not the usual stuff of siege attack warfare. As the walls
fall flat, the Israelites rush forward to attack the people of the city. Only now
is Rahab mentioned again, as Joshua instructs the two spies to keep their
promise by bringing out "from the prostitute's house" (6:22) Rahab and all her
family. The family is placed outside the Israelite camp as Jericho is destroyed,
and the narrator reports that "her family has lived in Israel ever since" (6:25).
With this final comment, Rahab and her family disappear completely from the
pages of the Old Testament. Beyond her inclusion in Matthew's genealogy, she
is mentioned twice in the New Testament, once in the so-called "roll call" of
heroes of Old Testament faith (Heb. 11:31) and once alongside Abraham, as a
"prostitute also justified by her works when she welcomed the messengers and
sent them out by another way" (Jas. 2:25).

Matthew's genealogy attributes to Rahab a family: Salmon as her husband
and Boaz as her son. However, there is no other known testimony to this tradition. Johnson notes that in the oldest extant Jewish literature Rahab appears
only in Josephus (who presents her as an innkeeper, not a prostitute); she is
not referenced in the Apocrypha, the Pseudepigrapha, or Philo.[5] In the later
rabbinic tradition she appears as a convert, but when her family relations are
mentioned, she is the wife of Joshua, not Salmon. In her marriage to Joshua,
according to the Rabbis, Rahab gave birth only to daughters, who are said to
be ancestors of the prophetess Huldah (2 Kgs. 22:14–20 ), the prophet Jeremiah, and other faithful persons mentioned in the book of Jeremiah.[6] Thus
nowhere in known Jewish sources is Rahab featured in the genealogy of David.

We do not know whether the author of Matthew drew on some tradition
unknown to modern scholars in portraying Rahab as a female ancestor of
David and therefore of the Messiah. However it happened that her name was
included in the genealogy, her presence prepares us for the possibility that God
uses unlikely people to work for our good. As a prostitute, Rahab was among
the most marginalized members of her Canaanite community. The story gives
readers no clue about what became of her vocation and her family once they

began living in the midst of the Israelite community. Even those who confessed the God of Israel were not easily integrated if they were perceived as ethnic outsiders. Yet according to Matthew, God included her among the ancestors of the Messiah. For many of us today, the life of some ancestor generations ago may be a matter of historical curiosity, but we do not think of it counting much for the present, especially if we do not know many details. But for ancient readers, genealogy was critically important. If such an unlikely woman was among the Messiah's female ancestors, how much less odd that God would choose to have the Messiah born of Mary, a village girl of no account from a human point of view.

The presence of Rahab points also to the importance of persons from beyond the Jewish community who recognized the power of the God of Israel. Readers of Joshua 2 often ask whether Rahab praises the God of Israel just because she believes the Israelites will take over the land and she sees her chance to save her life and that of her family. From this perspective, her words do not really count as a confession of faith but are uttered only to satisfy the spies. The spies and Rahab are thought to make a deal, each for their own lives, so that in the two-way transaction God hardly enters the picture. Whether a prostitute who is guilty of lying to the authorities (even to save the spies) can be taken seriously as a follower of the true God is often a question on the lips of these readers. To be sure, it is possible to read the text in this way. If we step back from the sense that this story is part of our Christian sacred book, then such a reading seems a quite plausible interpretation. Surely the Canaanite residents of Jericho would be likely to view the traitor Rahab in such a way. The question of Rahab's motivation is not addressed by the narrator, and, of course, the New Testament references represent much later reflection on the story. Thus Rahab's motives, viewed in the immediate context of the story, may well have been completely self-serving, or at least ambiguous (as is often said of "foxhole" religion). But the story needs also to be read canonically. When we consider the larger Old Testament context, Rahab's speech is easily recognizable as a classic Israelite "affirmation of faith," reciting the events of Israel's deliverance, especially at the Red Sea, as a basis for believing in the saving power of the LORD (cf. Deut. 6:21–23; 26:5–9).[7]

## RUTH (THE BOOK OF RUTH)

In Ruth (Matt. 1:5) we encounter another foreign woman who confesses faith in the God of Israel. Although some modern scholars have raised questions about Ruth's sincerity,[8] Jewish tradition views her as a model proselyte,[9] and most readers assume that she accepts the faith of her Israelite mother-in-law.

The biblical narrative is longer and more complex than those involving the other three women. Still, the plot can be briefly outlined.

Elimelech, a citizen of Bethlehem, takes his wife Naomi and his two sons to the neighboring territory of Moab because of a famine. The two sons marry Moabite women, Ruth and Orpah. The women remain childless and after some time the father and two sons all die. The widowed Naomi, full of sadness and indeed bitterness, decides to return to Bethlehem and seeks to dissuade her two widowed daughters-in-law from accompanying her. Complying with Naomi's wish, Orpah returns home, but Ruth insists on coming to Bethlehem. In the context of this decision Ruth utters to her mother-in-law, young woman to old, words that today are mostly used in marriage ceremonies:

> "Where you go, I will go;
>     where you lodge, I will lodge;
> your people shall be my people,
>     and your God my God.
> Where you die, I will die—
>     there will I be buried."
>                 (Ruth 1:16–17a)

On their arrival in Bethlehem, Ruth seeks food for the two of them by going out to glean in the barley fields. She comes unknowingly to the field of Boaz, a prominent man of the village who turns out to be a relative of Naomi. Boaz is kind to her, but the time of the barley and wheat harvests passes, and no more is heard of this connection.

When the time of threshing arrives, Naomi suggests that Ruth prepare herself attractively and approach Boaz during the night as he sleeps by the village threshing floor. Ruth agrees to this risky and potentially humiliating course of action. The narrator fills the scene with vocabulary that has ordinary meaning but can also have overtones of sexual relations; what happens physically between Ruth and Boaz is thus shrouded in mystery. What is clear is that Ruth suggests to Boaz that he should marry her. Boaz, for his part, recognizes that there is pertinent Israelite customary law to be considered, for there is another man who has prior rights and/or an obligation with regard to marrying Ruth. The next morning, Boaz calls a meeting of the village elders and offers the other man the chance to marry Ruth. Once the man declines, Boaz announces his intention to marry her, and the villagers (probably the men) join in wishing him God's blessing in the form of children by his new wife, so that the house of Boaz "may be like the house of Perez, whom Tamar bore to Judah" (4:12). The two are married; Ruth conceives; and when the baby boy Obed is born, he is described both as a caretaker for Naomi in her old age and as an ancestor of King David. The book concludes with a genealogy that moves from Perez (see Tamar above) through Salmon (see Rahab above) to Boaz and his son Obed, on down to David (cf. 1 Chr. 2:5–15).

Such a summary can scarcely do justice to the carefully crafted literary design of the book of Ruth, with its wonderful surplus of subtle nuances and wordplays, as well as its many plot intricacies, all of which are obscured by abbreviation. The story deserves repeated reading in full, with plenty of time for readers to observe and savor its artistry.

Many scholars believe that this story was told and preserved not simply to give information about the ancestry of the famous King David but to challenge the Israelite community to be more open to foreigners who accepted the God of Israel and followed Israelite customs. Although the evidence is not completely uniform, much of the Old Testament tradition portrays Moabites as among Israel's classic enemies; they were one of only two foreign peoples explicitly forbidden to participate in any temple worship (Deut. 23:3; cf. Neh. 13:1). According to tradition, apostasy had resulted when Israelite men became sexually involved with Moabite women (Num. 25:1–2). Antipathy toward outsiders and the idea that foreign women would lead Israelite men away from loyalty to the LORD is associated with stories from many periods of biblical history. Abraham, for example, wants his son Isaac to marry one of his own people (Gen. 24); King Solomon's foreign wives are supposed to have turned his heart away from God (1 Kgs. 11). In the years after the exiles returned from Babylon, Ezra and Nehemiah required all the leaders of the community to divorce their foreign wives (Ezra 9–10; Neh. 10:28–30; 13:3, 23–30). Against this widespread and longstanding fear of the foreign woman, the story of Ruth stands as a notable contrary signal. Her faithfulness to her mother-in-law is praised by Boaz, the male leader of the village.[10] Boaz invokes God's blessing upon Ruth and takes her in marriage with the approbation of the entire community.

Yet the path to that eventual marriage is not at all conventional. In this regard Ruth's story is like those of the other women of Matthew's genealogy, a story demonstrating that honor rather than suspicion may belong to a woman who finds herself in unusual circumstances. As with Mary, what appears to the ordinary eye to be inappropriate behavior turns out to be highly regarded. In Ruth's case, Boaz has already expressed a positive attitude and concern for her at the time of their initial meeting (2:11–12). Still, this does not prepare the reader for what transpires later on. For a woman to go out alone in the dark of night, to go secretively to where a man lies sleeping, to lie down next to such a man and "uncover his feet" (3:7, a reference to his lower body, possibly even to his genitals)—for such a woman to wait to see what the man's reaction would be upon discovering her presence—none of this from beginning to end fits the image of proper behavior for any woman in biblical culture. In an era and culture like ours in contemporary North America, where sexual activity outside of marriage has become almost commonplace, the shock value of such a description of Ruth's actions is perhaps hard to imagine, just as it is hard for us to realize how shocking Mary's mysterious pregnancy would have been, not just to Joseph, but to all of her family and neighbors. To appreciate Ruth's courage and perhaps the desperation she and Naomi felt as they realized that they could not survive (i.e., they would not have bread enough to eat) without a male protector, we must abandon the all-knowing viewpoint of the reader who already knows how the story will end. We must enter rather into Ruth's mind and heart as she moves out into the night, approaches Boaz and lies down, and awaits his response. When he awakes, she does not follow Naomi's advice to do whatever Boaz suggests, but rather she takes the initiative. Answering his question, "Who are you?", she does not stop with her name but rushes head-long into what is ornamented cultural language for a proposal of marriage (3:9). With Boaz's favorable response to this astonishing sequence of events, the stage is set for Ruth to become the great-grandmother of King David and eventu-ally to be remembered by Matthew as an ancestor of the Messiah. But nothing has happened in an ordinary way—from the beginning of the story when Ruth first married outside her own Moabite culture, to the ending, when she who was previously childless is promptly given conception by the LORD and when the men who had prayed for Boaz's wife to bear a child are joined by the women of the village, who rejoice that new life has indeed been brought forth.

## BATHSHEBA (2 SAMUEL 11–12)

Matthew's genealogy does not use Bathsheba's name but instead identifies her as "the wife of Uriah" (Matt. 1:6). It is as if the writer wants to remind the read-ers starkly of the unusual circumstances of the relationship out of which Solomon was born. Like her predecessors in the genealogical list, and like Mary, Bathsheba's experience in relation to marriage and the child of the lin-eage is not that of a typical young woman. Unlike Tamar and Ruth, however, it is not Bathsheba's own initiative that brings her into the story. Rather, it is the desire and plotting of King David that lead to her presence in this list of women. Although she is familiar to us by her name Bathsheba, the narrative of 2 Samuel 11–12 uses her name only twice, once at the very beginning when David inquires as to the identity of the woman he has seen bathing (11:3), and once at the very end when he consoles her after the death of their first son and has sexual relations with her that lead to the conception and eventual birth of Solomon (12:24). Otherwise in these chapters she is identified either as "the woman" (11:5) or as "the wife of Uriah (the Hittite)" (11:26; 12:10, 15).[11] Thus her identity as the wife of another is kept in view. Uriah as a Hittite was a foreign mercenary leader in David's army. Although the text is not explicit about Bathsheba's background, it is assumed by tradition and many modern commentators that she too was a non-Israelite. Thus Matthew's focus on foreign women who formed part of the Messiah's genealogy continues here.

It is striking how little space is given in this story to the relationship between David and the wife of Uriah—only nine verses out of fifty-two. The story opens with just five verses given to David's noticing Bathsheba, summoning her to him for sexual relations and then sending her home, followed by her report that she has become pregnant. The next nineteen verses detail David's scheming first to get Uriah to sleep with Bathsheba, and when that plan fails, to have Uriah killed. A two-verse interlude then reports how Uriah's wife becomes David's wife and bears a son. Then a twenty-three-verse section details the visit to David by the prophet Nathan to announce God's condemnation of David's action, which is followed by David's response during the illness and death of the child. Two more brief verses then report the conception, birth, and naming of Solomon.

Western art and drama has made much of the relationship between David and the wife of Uriah, often romanticizing the contacts, extending the time frame, and/or portraying Bathsheba as the initiator of the events.[12] The biblical narrative is so succinct as to be ambiguous, but our knowledge of the cultural setting suggests a different perspective. There is no indication in the text that Bathsheba intended to be seen by anyone. Regardless of her intention, David could have averted his eyes or not asked who she was. David does the summoning. It is unlikely that the wife of a foreign mercenary in the royal army would feel that she had much choice about accepting the summons. The prophet Nathan makes quite clear that David is completely culpable in the taking of Uriah's wife and, of course, in arranging for Uriah's death. The narrative mentions briefly Bathsheba's mourning following her husband's death and David's consoling her for the death of her child; otherwise, the story gives us no insight into Bathsheba's world. Indeed, even these two events are included primarily as time markers for the activities of David. All in all, the narrator presents a story about David.

Yet Matthew's genealogy remembers "the wife of Uriah." Allusion to a woman's story that is out of the ordinary once again prepares the way for understanding Mary's situation and Joseph's obedient response to the angel who reveals to him the source of her pregnancy.

## CONCLUSION

The stories of the four women included in Matthew's genealogy do not offer any tidy pattern by which to explain their selection. Two of the women (Rahab,

Ruth), and possibly a third (Bathsheba), are foreigners, but the fourth (Tamar) is not known as a foreigner in biblical tradition. Three of them have children by relationships that are extraordinary in one way or another, but in the case of the fourth (Rahab) we have no information about her marriage. Some premodern Christian interpreters sought to find commonality in the sinfulness of the women, but as we have seen, such a possibility has little basis once the androcentric perceptions of readers have been challenged. What the women do have in common is that none of their stories "fits the way things are 'supposed' to be."[13] Thus these four women anticipate Mary's pregnancy, and indeed the life of her son Jesus, a pregnancy and a life that did not "fit" with human expectations, even though they were the work of God.

## NOTES

1. Marshall D. Johnson, *The Purpose of the Biblical Genealogies*, 2d ed. (Cambridge: Cambridge University Press, 1988), 153 n. 2.
2. All biblical quotations are taken from the NRSV.
3. It should be noted that despite the law in Deuteronomy and despite the references to raising up offspring for the dead husband, Er (Gen. 38:8,9), the actual genealogy is recorded with the biological father Judah as the father of Perez with the indication that "Judah had five sons in all" (1 Chr. 2:4).
4. *Genesis Rabbah* 85, as cited in Johnson, *Biblical Genealogies*, 160. Johnson comments that "a tendency to exonerate Tamar appears early" (159) and seems surprised when ancient Jewish commentators explain away her behavior or present her as virtuous. On the one hand, one may ask whether Tamar's exoneration should be surprising, given Judah's declaration that she is righteous. On the other hand, Judah makes a comparative rather than an absolute statement ("[S]he is more righteous than I"), which opens the door to lay blame where it is often laid, at the feet of a woman engaged in illicit sex, regardless of her circumstances or the purpose of her action.
5. Ibid., 162.
6. Ibid., 164.
7. Many other texts, such as Psalm 78; 114; Jer. 2:4–7; Isa. 43:14–21, represent this classic tradition in a variety of settings.
8. Dana Nolan Fewell and David Gunn, *Compromising Redemption: Relating Characters in the Book of Ruth*, Literary Currents in Biblical Interpretation (Louisville, Ky.: Westminster/John Knox Press, 1990), 32, 104.
9. D. R. G. Beattie, *Jewish Exegesis of the Book of Ruth*, Journal for the Study of the Old Testament Supplement Series 2 (Sheffield: JSOT Press, 1977), 173–75.
10. In the biblical story, Boaz is presented as an ideal Israelite village leader. Matthew's genealogy, wherein Boaz is the son of Salmon and Rahab, would make Boaz already half-Canaanite, a man of mixed ethnicity. One might suppose that such a background could explain his openness to Ruth as a foreigner. As stated above, however, there is no evidence anywhere outside of Matthew that the tradition regarded Rahab as Boaz's mother.

11. In 1 Kgs. 1, the story of the final dispute among David's sons over succession to his throne, Solomon's mother is regularly called Bathsheba.
12. See J. Cheryl Exum, *Plotted, Shot, and Painted: Cultural Representations of Biblical Women*, Journal for the Study of the Old Testament Supplement Series 215 (Sheffield: Sheffield Academic Press, 1996).
13. Beverly Roberts Gaventa, *Mary: Glimpses of the Mother of Jesus*, Studies on Personalities of the New Testament (Columbia, S.C.: University of South Carolina Press, 1995; Minneapolis: Fortress Press, 1999), 38.

# 3

# "Who Is My Mother?"

## Family Values in the Gospel of Mark

### E. Elizabeth Johnson

Jesus' mother plays a minor role in Mark's Gospel: she speaks a single line in one scene and remains silent in a second. Neither appearance is particularly flattering. Early in Jesus' career, his mother and brothers worry that he is "beside himself" and seek him out only to be rebuffed in favor of his inner circle of followers (Mark 3:20–35). Later, people in his hometown ask contemptuously who he thinks he is to pass himself off as a sage or wonder-worker when they all know his mother Mary; his brothers James, Joses, Judas, and Simon; and his (unnamed) sisters. Jesus likens the community's disrespect to his family's dishonoring of him and laments that such is the fate of prophets (6:1–6a). At the end of the book, a Mary identified as the mother of James the younger, Joses, and Salome observes Jesus' death and burial and prepares to anoint his body (15:40, 47; 16:1). Mark does not say this woman is Jesus' mother, although the coincidence of the names is at the very least provocative. These two—or perhaps three—glimpses of Jesus' mother in Mark[1] do not amount to a full characterization of her nor have they contributed much to religious devotion to her. In all of early Christian literature, Mark's Gospel offers the least sympathetic portrayal of Mary, so it is scarcely surprising that it seldom figures prominently in studies of her.[2]

Christian piety has honored Mary as one who recognizes her son as God's Messiah and nurtures faith in him. Mark's Mary does neither. Her marginal role in the Second Gospel has been taken to signify different things, both about her and about the early church. Some readers think Mark's unattractive picture reflects historical reminiscence that Jesus' mother was not among his followers as later Christians contended. On the other hand, some say the negative portrait of Mary is designed precisely to oppose nascent veneration of her.[3] Some interpreters simply pass over Mark as adding little to the much fuller and more interesting descriptions of her in Matthew, Luke, John, and later texts. Alternatively, many devotional studies harmonize a picture of Jesus' mother from the many positive ones in Christian tradition and use the composite to soften the rough edges of Mark's story and reduce its offensive features.

Instead of a historical or theological investigation, this essay explores the character of Mary in Mark's Gospel. It seeks to understand the way one early Christian tells stories about Mary and what those stories might reveal about the author's faith and life.[4] The narrative of Mark marginalizes the figure of Jesus' mother in the same way that it relativizes and redefines all domestic relations within the Christian community. For Mark, the invasion of God's redemptive realm in the death and resurrection of Jesus Christ upsets the prevailing cultural values of the patriarchal household and family honor. This invasive character of God's good news in Jesus Christ destabilizes and reorders the bonds of kinship even as it establishes new familial bonds within the church. The person of Mary in Mark's Gospel thus illustrates—or better, perhaps, embodies—both the domestic disorientation that the Christian message effects and the reorientation of kinship among believers that it establishes. Jesus' mother demonstrates the apocalyptic family values that characterize some of the earliest Christian communities.[5]

First, a preliminary word about the term *apocalyptic*, a topic to which we shall return. Judaism and Christianity of the first century abound with books that call themselves "apocalypses," revelations from heavenly beings to human beings reported in visionary, cryptic language full of bizarre, symbolic imagery. The best-known apocalypses are in the Bible—Daniel 7–12 and Revelation— although there are many more as well. These books shape the way Christians like Mark understand God, the world, and their own places in it, and we call their worldview "apocalyptic" when it shares literary and conceptual traits with those books.[6] Mark is an apocalyptic storyteller because what he says about Jesus—and Mary—is cast in revelatory terms and reflects his conviction that Jesus has inaugurated the new age of God's salvation.

## THE REJECTED MOTHER

The first scene in which Jesus' mother appears (Mark 3:20–35) casts her and her other children alongside Jesus' enemies. They are as hostile to him as are the scribes from Jerusalem:

> After his family[7] heard, they went out to seize him because they kept saying,
> "He is beside himself."

> And the scribes who came down from Jerusalem kept saying,
> "He has Beelzebul," and,
> "He casts out demons by the power of the chief demon." (3:21–22)[8]

This is a shocking scenario, and commentators ancient and modern have devoted great quantities of imagination and ink to the family's defense. Matthew and Luke remove Mark 3:21 altogether from their versions of the story, and various translations of it provide someone other than Jesus' relatives to restrain him or question his emotional stability (emphasis added):[9]

> And when his *friends* heard *of it*, they went out to lay hold on him: for *they* said, "He is beside himself." (KJV)
> And when His *own people* heard *of this*, they went out to take custody of Him; for *they* were saying, "He has lost His senses." (NAS)
> And when his *family* heard it, they went out to seize him, for *people* were saying, "He is beside himself." (NRSV)

Still others translate so that people do not think Jesus is out of control but that the crowd is, because it is either so enthusiastic or so hostile.[10] Surely, it has seemed to many readers, Mark 3:21 cannot mean what it seems to say, that Jesus' family—particularly his mother—considers his ministry demonic or delusional.

The full story in Mark, however, is far less generous than these attempts to massage one sentence of it would suggest. The family comes out to "seize" Jesus, after all, which is what other hostile forces attempt (12:12) and finally accomplish when they arrest him (14:1, 44, 46, 49; cf. 6:17; 12:12; 14:51).[11] Not only does Mark place Jesus' kinfolk on stage right beside the scribes, he gives them similar lines to speak—"[H]e is beside himself" (3:21); "[H]e has Beelzebul," "[H]e casts out demons by the power of the chief demon" (3:22)—and later summarizes all three lines with the words "[H]e has an unclean spirit" (3:30). In antiquity to say someone is deranged is not so much to make a medical or psychological diagnosis as it is to identify the presence of evil powers. In John 10:20, for example, "[H]e has a demon" and "[H]e is mad" are synonymous parallels.[12] The structure of the passage further demonstrates that it is Jesus' family rather than anonymous outsiders who attack him the way the scribes do. Mark relates the incident with the scribes between two appearances of Jesus' kinfolk, with the result that the incidents prove mutually interpretive. The passage abounds with references to "calling" and to "houses" (a virtual synonym for "families"[13]), and the repeated accusations against Jesus ("they kept saying"[14]) frame his parables about himself and Satan, which stand at the center of the story.[15]

Jesus calls the Twelve and goes home.[16]
The family keeps saying he is disturbed (3:21).
The scribes keep saying he is Satanic (3:22).
Jesus calls a group and responds in parables (3:23–27).
    If a kingdom is divided it cannot stand.
    If a house is divided it cannot stand.
    If Satan is divided he cannot stand.
    Only one stronger can rob a strong man's house.
Jesus condemns those who keep saying he is possessed (3:30).
Jesus' mother and brothers call him; he embraces those who do God's will
    (3:31–35).

From Mark's perspective, the statements of the relatives and the scribes are equally wrong. From the moment Jesus appears in Mark's Gospel, he engages in hand-to-hand combat with Satan and his minions. God's Spirit rips apart the sky at Jesus' baptism to anoint him (1:10–11) and then drives him into the wilderness to do battle with the devil (1:12–13). There is far more "temptation" in Matthew's and Luke's versions of this story[17] and more "testing" in Mark's[18] because what Satan "tests" in Mark is Jesus' mettle as an opponent. After Jesus rebuffs the devil's challenge in the desert, he embarks on a ministry of exorcism and healing, attacking and defeating demonic forces (1:21–28, 34, 39; 3:22; 5:1–20; 7:25–30; 9:14–29).[19] Although Jesus is called "Teacher," it is not his words that evoke people's wonder and praise but his exorcisms: "What is this? A new authoritative teaching! He subjugates even the unclean spirits and they obey him!" (1:27).

The narrative that precedes chapter 3 thus makes abundantly clear that Jesus is Satan's enemy, not his ally, so when his relatives allege that he is "beside himself" (3:21) and the scribes charge that "he has Beelzebul" (3:22), the accusations appear both absurd and malicious. Jesus condemns these assessments of his power as blasphemy against the Holy Spirit (3:28–29) because in fact he is the stronger one promised by the Baptist (1:7), the one who is tying Satan up and plundering his house (3:23–27). It is blasphemous to attribute to Satan Jesus' work of exorcism because it is really God's work.

Jesus repudiates his family of origin and instead embraces as kin those who know the true source of his power and obey God by becoming his followers (3:31–35). Whether his mother and brothers hear him judge them blasphemous is unclear, since Mark says they are outside the house where Jesus is speaking (3:31). The staging of this scene, with their standing outside and his sitting inside, highlights the distance between them.[20] A fivefold repetition of the words "mother and brothers" in so brief a paragraph poignantly drives home the contrast between who is and who is not "really" Jesus' family.[21] So also, Jesus' mother and brothers come looking for him and "call him" (3:31).

Perhaps this verb "call" no more than reflects the mob scene Mark describes in 3:20: so many people have gathered at the house that Jesus' mother and brothers must call out in order to be heard over the crowd. It is curious, however, that Mark does not say the relatives "cry out" or "shout," but that they "call" Jesus. Elsewhere Mark uses this verb and its cognates when Jesus summons people into relationship with himself. At 1:20 he calls James and John to leave their father Zebedee and follow him; at 2:17 he says his mission is to call sinners rather than the righteous; at 3:13 he calls together the Twelve. That Jesus' mother and brothers should "call" him from the house where he is with his disciples suggests that their call to him conflicts with his call to them. One responds either to the call of family or to the call of Jesus, Mark implies, and Jesus himself provides the model response at 3:35. He claims as kin those who do God's will and rejects those who confuse God's power with that of Satan.

When Matthew and Luke tell this story, they recast it considerably. Although Mark makes it look as though the scribes' charge arises unprovoked,[22] Matthew and Luke say Jesus' exorcism of a mute person prompts the scribes to conclude that he is an agent of the devil (Matt. 12:22–32; Luke 11:14–23). Furthermore, Matthew separates Jesus' controversy with the scribes (Matt. 12:22–32) from his redefinition of his family (12:46–50) by inserting three stories between these two events. Matthew reports on two separate occasions that the scribes accuse Jesus of Satanic alliance—"[H]e casts out demons by the power of the chief demon" (9:34; 12:24)—but not once that Jesus' family thinks he is mad. Luke distances the Beelzebul controversy (Luke 11:14–23) from the story of Jesus' relatives (8:19–21) by reversing the order of those events, and, like Matthew, deletes the family's charge that he is mad. Matthew and Luke thus narrate the story of Jesus' true kinfolk to show that he enlarges his family to include those who do God's will. Mark's version, by contrast, excludes Jesus' family of origin because they oppose him as his enemies do, and it replaces them with the fictive kinship of the household of faith.[23]

The role Jesus' mother plays in this unhappy episode is indistinguishable from that of her other children. She misunderstands the source of Jesus' power and attempts to stop his ministry. As a consequence, Jesus dismisses her as his mother and replaces her with people who know and support him. It is difficult to recognize this woman as the mother who elsewhere learns from an angel of her child's identity (Luke 1:26–38) or expresses faith in his miraculous power (John 2:1–12).

## THE REJECTED SON

The second episode in Mark that mentions Jesus' mother provides a bit more information about her, for here we learn her name is Mary (6:1–6a). This picture of her is scarcely more positive than the first one, however, and she speaks not a word. When Jesus comes home to Nazareth after establishing his reputation in the surrounding area, his preaching and healing evoke from the villagers both astonished approval—"From where does this one get these things? What wisdom has been given to this one! What sorts of powers are happening through his hands!"—and scornful skepticism—"Isn't this the woodworker, the son of Mary and the brother of James and Joses and Jude and Simon? And aren't his sisters here with us?" (6:2–3). Joel Marcus notes the remarkable similarities between the first half of this scene and the one in 1:21–28—both are set in a synagogue where Jesus teaches and people are thrilled by what he says and does—but here in chapter 6 the story "makes an unexpected swerve" as the Nazarenes are offended by his ostensibly praiseworthy behavior.[24]

Jesus' neighbors are both impressed by his deeds and appalled that it is he who does them. He accomplishes remarkable feats that manifest wisdom and power, but he is the wrong sort of person to be doing those things. The people offer three objections. First, Jesus is a *techtōn*, a word that is frequently translated "carpenter" but that describes woodworking crafts more than building construction.[25] Jesus works with his hands, which means in Greco-Roman culture that he comes from the lower economic and social echelons.[26] Second, Jesus' power cannot be honorable if he himself is illegitimate. It is ironic that Mark calls Jesus' hometown his "fatherland" (*patrida*, 6:1) because the sneering crowd calls him "Mary's son" (6:3). One is conventionally identified by the name of one's father, so the remark alludes to questions about Jesus' paternity.[27] The slur becomes bitterly ironic in the context of Mark's Gospel, because Mary is no longer Jesus' mother. She and his brothers and sisters were replaced at 3:31–35 by those who do God's will. Third, Jesus' neighbors accuse him—correctly, we must acknowledge—of abandoning his family. "Aren't his sisters here with us?" they ask contemptuously, rather than being with their brother who ought to care for them and for his mother.[28]

Jesus' neighbors scoff at him because he has no legitimate claims to fame. Despite his miraculous deeds and impressive teaching, Jesus bears no honor and a great deal of shame in a culture that cares desperately about those values. One's honor in antiquity derives chiefly from family identity[29] and Jesus' family gives him precious little of it. To make matters worse, he has rejected and dishonored what family he once had. By any moral standard of the day, Jesus is rightly scorned, which makes his use of a popular saying to interpret his rejection astonishing: "A prophet is not dishonored except in his hometown and among his kinfolk and in his household" (6:4). Conventional wisdom recognizes that an out-of-towner is likely to receive more respect than a local, but Mark says far more when he adds "kinfolk" and "household" to the proverb about those who dishonor prophets.[30] What the culture deems shameful Mark's Jesus embraces as probative of his prophetic identity. Jesus' rejection of his mother and brothers in 3:31–35 results in their reciprocal rejection of him in 6:1–6a, and their village takes the side not of the upstart Jesus but of the family he has left behind.

## DOMESTIC DISORIENTATION AND APOCALYPTIC FAMILY VALUES

Mary is not the only abandoned parent in the Gospel of Mark, nor is hers the only broken family. Mark's story teems with domestic disorientation. At the very beginning, James and John leave their father Zebedee to follow Jesus (1:16–20), and Jesus later promises reward to all who forsake "house or brothers or sisters or mother or father or children or fields" to do likewise (10:29). Among the persecutions in store for his disciples are disrupted households and domestic strife: "Siblings will hand each other over to death, and parents will hand over their children; children will rise up against parents and have them put to death; and you will be hated by everyone because you carry my name" (13:12–13). The notion that family members, in particular siblings, should deal treacherously with each other is a watchword in antiquity for the very depths of domestic dishonor,[31] yet Mark predicts those dynamics will arise in the Christian family itself.

It seems to some interpreters that Mark calls for universal renunciation of conventional kinship. Howard Clark Kee, for instance, says of this Gospel, "All genetic, familial and sex distinctions are eradicated in this new concept of the true family."[32] Mark's story does not consistently bear out such a claim, though. Jesus calls James and John to leave their father (1:19–20), but the men maintain their fraternal bond after they become disciples (3:17; 5:37; 9:2; 14:33).[33] Similarly, the brothers Simon and Andrew leave their family business to follow Jesus (1:16–18) but do not abandon their family entirely, since Jesus heals Simon's mother-in-law in what is still apparently their home (1:29–31). Even as Jesus calls disciples to leave their parents and sends his own mother away, he twice invokes the biblical commandment to honor parents (7:9–13; 10:19; cf. Exod. 20:12). Although Mark tells stories of parents who beg Jesus to heal their children (5:21–43; 7:24–30; 9:14–29), says those who welcome children welcome Jesus (9:37), and calls children models of discipleship (10:13–16), he also praises those who abandon their children for the sake of the gospel mission (10:29). On the one hand, Mark's Jesus grounds marriage in the very fabric of God's creation and prohibits divorce and remarriage (10:1–12); on the other hand, he endorses celibacy and describes the redeemed life as asexual (12:25). Clearly there is no consistent replacement in Mark of the traditional family with a new Christian household, no matter how harsh Jesus' words to his mother and brothers.

Other interpreters instead view Mark's attitude toward family and kinship as a reflection of some form of social compensation, with the early church creating a family for believers who lose their families of origin when they convert to Christianity. Joel Marcus reads the predictions in chapter 13 that family members of Jesus' followers will turn against them in the last days as indicating "experiences of familial alienation and persecution common among early Christians," even "the alienation of some Markan Christians from their own family members."[34] Greco-Roman antiquity knows numerous people whose altered religious convictions cost them their family relationships, and other first-century religious and philosophical groups similarly use family metaphors to constitute themselves as alternative households.[35] The characters in Mark, however, do not make such clear transitions from conventional families to the household of faith. When the Gerasene rescued from the demonic Legion begs to "be with" Jesus (in language suspiciously reminiscent of Jesus' call of the Twelve, 3:14; 5:18),[36] Jesus refuses his request and returns the man to his "home and family"[37] to bear witness to Jesus' power and the mercy of God (5:19). Jesus calls the bleeding woman he heals "Daughter" and, rather than inviting her to follow him, sends her home in peace (5:34); and when he raises Jairus's daughter from the dead, he hands her back to her parents (5:43). Mark's story is consistently inconsistent about the respective values of traditional and alternative households. Jesus' new family of those who obey God neither simply displaces nor merely compensates for the loss of his followers' families of origin. The call of Jesus to join his household instead disorients and reorients extant household relationships because it is an apocalyptic power.

Some interpreters speak of the apocalyptic character of Mark (and of other early Christian literature) primarily in terms of eschatology, as if all that were "revealed" in it concerns time, particularly the end of time. This is easy to understand: Jesus promises the disciples, "There are those standing here who will not taste death until they have seen that the kingdom of God has come with power" (9:1), and they ask him, "Tell us, when will these things be, and what is the sign that all these things are about to happen?" (13:4). On the other hand, however, the very first revelation in Mark[38] is not about the turning of the cosmic calendar, but of the Spirit of God who breaks out of heaven (1:11; 15:38) and is, in the words of Donald H. Juel, "on the loose" in the ministry of Jesus. "Mark's narrative is about the intrusion of God into a world that has become alien territory—an intrusion that means both life and death."[39] Obviously God's invasion of the world has temporal consequences; Mark summarizes Jesus' preaching about the nearness of God's redemptive dominion by saying, "[T]he time has been fulfilled" (1:15). The present consequences of that nearness, though, occupy Mark far more than predictions of what is yet to come.

The disruptive presence of God in Jesus' ministry means that no prevailing definitions of human life and community are safe from change. Jesus makes God's salvation emphatically present in people's lives as he transgresses important boundaries between religious and impious, Jew and non-Jew, male and female, clean and unclean, rich and poor, sick and healthy, even between the human and the nonhuman realms. Those boundaries are essential markers of reality in antiquity, not merely social conventions that identify people, and when Jesus crosses them things are never again the same.[40] The revelation of God's salvation replaces the "either-or" of the old world and its pairs of opposites with the "both-and" character of the new world. Jesus' parables about mending clothes and making wine warn that new and old cannot coexist, or the new will destroy the old (2:21–22). The images of ripped clothing and fermenting wine that bursts its container signal "the violent, apocalyptic change that Jesus' advent involves."[41] All the tidy distinctions between and among people that serve to structure conventional life are left behind in the wake of Jesus' call to follow him. Among the most treasured of those distinctions in Greco-Roman antiquity are the ones that fashion family identity, and the multiple visions of household order in Mark manifest an apocalyptic reordering of values that places loyalty to God's Crucified Messiah at the defining center of all other human relationships. Traditional family structures are neither established as Christian nor are they abandoned as obsolete; they are instead (re)shaped by the death of Jesus who honors what society shames and dismisses what the world around him most honors.

## THE RESURRECTED MOTHER[42]

Although Jesus predicts three times in Mark that he will be crucified and raised from the dead (8:31; 9:31; 10:34), his arrest, trial, and execution leave his disciples demoralized and scattered. A trio of women, however, stays to watch after the Twelve flee (15:40–41). Two of the women watch Joseph of Arimathea bury Jesus' body (15:47), and all three return the next day to anoint it (16:1). While Mark does not call these women "disciples," he does report that they see to Jesus' burial, a function the disciples of the Baptist perform for him (6:29).[43] The women watch "from afar," just as Peter follows Jesus to his trial "from afar" (14:54; 15:40), which suggests that they too are at best hesitant disciples. They stay with Jesus even though they demonstrate no greater faith than do the Twelve, since their loyalty is to a dead body rather than to a living lord. They nevertheless function in Mark's story as witnesses of Jesus' death and resurrection, no minor role in a book that calls itself "the beginning of the gospel" (1:1). Although they "say nothing to anyone" within the narrative itself (16:8), the Christian reader of Mark knows full well that the women's testimony will eventually result in the creation of the church.

Mark describes the second of these women in three different but evidently related ways: she is "Mary the mother of James the younger and Joses" (15:40), "Mary the mother of Joses" (15:47), and "Mary the mother of James" (16:1). All three recall Mark 6:3, where Jesus is "the son of Mary and the brother of James and Joses and Jude and Simon." Is this Mary also the mother of Jesus? Other early Christians think she observes her son's execution (John 19:25–27); if Mark does too, why does he not say so? If this woman is Jesus' mother, why is her son James called "the younger" at 15:40 and not at 6:3? Why these odd variations among the descriptions of her? Interpreters have struggled for centuries to make sense of the puzzle. Perhaps Mark is merely clumsy in knitting together what he has heard about who does what on Good Friday and Easter; other Gospels call this woman "the other Mary" (Matt. 28:1), "Mary of James," (Luke 24:10), or "the wife of Clopas" (John 19:25).[44] For some commentators, she is simply a woman who just happens to be named Mary, just happens to have sons with names the same as Jesus' brothers, and just happens to be among those who care for Jesus at the end of his life.[45]

There is a less strained and more natural reading of Mark's story, however, that recognizes the three descriptions deliberately call attention to Mary and her sons James and Joses.[46] The reader or listener who has attended to Mark's narrative from its beginning cannot help remembering that these characters have appeared in it before. Although the names Mary, James, and Joses are among the most common in first-century Judaism,[47] the coincidence is too great that they should all three occur in two different households in the same small circle of people without any mention of the similarities. More important, Christian tradition knows these people as well as it knows the Easter message the women in Mark 16:8 are afraid to tell. Paul says, "James, the brother of the Lord," is a well-known leader in the church (Gal. 1:19; 2:9, 12; 1 Cor. 15:7), and Acts tells of his rise to prominence (12:17; 15:13) after the martyrdom of James the son of Zebedee (12:2).[48] Josephus, a first-century Jewish historian, reports the arrest and execution of "the brother of Jesus who is called James" (*Antiquities* 20.200). Although no comparable tradition exists about a brother named Joses, Paul knows of more than one Christian missionary related to Jesus because he mentions the (plural) "brothers of the Lord" who travel with Christian wives (1 Cor. 9:5). Finally, Christian tradition is sure that Mary becomes a Christian, despite the picture of her as an outsider in Mark 3:31–35.[49]

Mark repeatedly calls attention to information like this that exists beyond the pages of his book. He refers to people he expects his reader to know, like Bartimaeus (10:46) or Simon, Alexander, and Rufus (15:21). He assumes so much about Christian faith in the telling of his story that it is difficult to imagine how an unbeliever might understand it. Jesus assures the sons of Zebedee, for example, that they will be "baptized" and they will "drink the cup" of Christian discipleship (10:35–40), and he addresses God with the Aramaic word for "father" that some Christians use when they are adopted by God at baptism (*Abba*, 14:36; cf. Rom. 8:15; Gal. 4:6).[50] Several important narrative threads in Mark remain loose at the end of the book.[51] Is Jesus really raised? Do the women ever speak? Are Jesus and Peter reconciled? Does Mary return to Jesus' family as a disciple? Although Mark does not answer these questions, the open-ended character of the story invites readers who in fact know those answers to reflect on them.

When Mary, James, and Joses return to Jesus' family circle at the end of Mark, they come as disciples whose kinship to him and to each other has been disrupted and reconstructed because of his death and resurrection. The brothers Jude and Simon named in Mark 6:3 receive no similar mention here, perhaps because Mark is unaware of their joining Jesus' movement. Much later in the first century a tradition will arise that Jesus' brother Jude also becomes a Christian, but there is no evidence of the tradition prior to that time.[52] The figure of Mary in Mark thus exemplifies the disorientation and reorientation of family life that the Christian message provokes among its hearers.[53]

## NOTES

1. My phrase deliberately echoes that of Beverly Roberts Gaventa, *Mary: Glimpses of the Mother of Jesus* (Columbia, S.C.: University of South Carolina Press, 1995; Minneapolis: Fortress Press, 1999). Both her approach to the task and her decision not to include the Second Gospel in that study have encouraged me to think about Mary in the Gospel of Mark.
2. An important exception is the discussion of Mark in Raymond E. Brown, et al. eds., *Mary in the New Testament* (Philadelphia: Fortress Press, 1978), 51–72. More recently, interest in family relations in early Christianity has renewed attention to Mark's picture of Mary. See particularly Katrina McCaughan Gampf Klawe Poetker, "'You Are My Mother, My Brothers, and My Sisters': A Literary Anthropological Investigation of Family in the Gospel of Mark" (Ph.D. Dissertation, Emory University, 2001) and the literature cited there.
3. A helpful survey of the many pitfalls in the quest of the historical Mary appears in Brown et al., *Mary in the New Testament*, 7–31.
4. We call the author "Mark" for tradition's sake even though the book itself makes no such claim. For a helpful discussion of the literary and historical problems, see Raymond E. Brown, *An Introduction to the New Testament*, Anchor Bible Reference Library (New York: Doubleday, 1997), 158–167.

5. I propose a similar argument about Paul's letters in "Apocalyptic Family Values," *Interpretation* 56 (2002): 34–44.
6. A good introduction to revelatory literature is John J. Collins, *The Apocalyptic Imagination* (New York: Crossroad Books, 1984).
7. Joel Marcus makes the case that "those around him" in 3:21 means "his relatives" by pointing to similar usage of the phrase in the LXX and other Hellenistic literature (*Mark 1–8*, Anchor Bible 27 [New York: Doubleday, 2000], 270). The immediate literary context provides even stronger evidence that Mark has family in mind when he speaks of the people near to Jesus: the preceding paragraph enumerates the Twelve and describes their closeness to Jesus (3:13–19); in the following paragraph Jesus replaces his mother, brothers, and sisters with those who do God's will (3:31–35); and the scene itself takes place "at home" (3:20).
8. All translations of the New Testament are mine unless otherwise indicated.
9. The original is sufficiently ambiguous to bear all (or most) of the translation possibilities.
10. "When they heard it, his followers went out to calm it down, for they said it was out of control with enthusiasm" (H. Wansbrough, "Mark iii.21—Was Jesus Out of His Mind?" *New Testament Studies* 18 [1971–72]: 233–235, quoted in Brown et al., *Mary in the New Testament*, 57, n. 98).
11. Ched Meyers calls it "political detainment" (*Binding the Strong Man: A Political Reading of Mark's Story of Jesus* [Maryknoll, N.Y.: Orbis Books, 1988], 167).
12. Marcus, *Mark 1–8*, 271.
13. Ibid., 273.
14. The imperfect tense in 3:21, 22, 30 carries a customary or habitual meaning, "they kept saying," rather than a simple past, "they were saying."
15. James R. Edwards argues that the second of two stories so woven together, in this case the Beelzebul dispute and Jesus' response in parables, "provides the key to the theological purpose of the sandwich" ("Markan Sandwiches: The Significance of Interpolations in Markan Narratives," *Novum Testamentum* 31 [1989]: 193–216, 196).
16. This "home" seems to be Jesus' base of operations in Capernaum (cf. 1:21; 2:1), as distinct from his "hometown" of Nazareth (6:1; cf. 1:24).
17. Matt. 4:1–11; Luke 4:1–13.
18. The same word can be translated "test" and "tempt."
19. Donald H. Juel, *A Master of Surprise: Mark Interpreted* (Minneapolis: Fortress Press, 1994), 65–75; idem, *The Gospel of Mark*, Interpreting Biblical Texts (Nashville: Abingdon Press, 1999), 70–72, 107–118.
20. Correctly Stephen P. Ahearne-Kroll, "'Who Are My Mother and My Brothers?' Family Relations and Family Language in the Gospel of Mark," *The Journal of Religion* 81 (2001): 1–25, 14.
21. Stephen C. Barton, *Discipleship and Family Ties in Mark and Matthew*, Society for New Testament Studies Monograph Series 80 (Cambridge: Cambridge University Press, 1994), 73. The phrase "his mother and his brothers" recurs as well in later gospel literature: the *Gospel of Thomas* 99, the *Gospel of the Nazarenes* 2, and the *Epistle to the Apostles* 5.
22. A summary statement about Jesus' healings and exorcisms at 3:9–12 is followed by his going up a mountain with the Twelve (v. 13) and then going home (v. 19). His relatives arrive in response to the regathering of the crowd ("when they heard," v. 21), not to his exorcisms or his calling the Twelve. The scribes come

down from Jerusalem (v. 22), where Jesus has not yet gone, so they respond to his reputation, not to anything they have seen for themselves.

23. Sociologists and anthropologists use the phrase "fictive kinship" to describe family relations that are modeled after but not created by legal (marriage, adoption, etc.) and biological (birth) bonds. A convenient and accessible introduction to the subject is K. C. Hanson, "BTB Readers Guide: Kinship," *Biblical Theology Bulletin* 24 (1994): 183–194.

24. Marcus, *Mark 1–8*, 378.

25. John P. Meier describes the social status of the *techtōn* as "somewhere at the lower end of the vague middle, perhaps equivalent—if we may use a hazy analogy—to a blue collar worker in lower-middle-class America" (*A Marginal Jew: Rethinking the Historical Jesus. Volume One: The Roots of the Problem and the Person*, Anchor Bible Reference Library [New York: Doubleday], 282).

26. See the discussion in Abraham J. Malherbe, *The Letters to the Thessalonians*, Anchor Bible 32B (New York: Doubleday, 2000), 166–167.

27. See the discussions in Brown et al., *Mary in the New Testament*, 63–64 and Marcus, *Mark 1–8*, 375.

28. Myers, *Binding the Strong Man*, 212.

29. The discussion about families in the first-century Mediterranean world, particularly those of Jews and Christians, is lively. A particularly engaging and accessible introduction is Paul Veyne, ed., *A History of Private Life From Pagan Rome to Byzantium* (Cambridge, Mass.: Belknap, 1987). See also Carolyn Osiek and David Balch, *Families in the New Testament World* (Louisville, Ky.: Westminster John Knox Press, 1997); Halvor Moxnes, ed., *Constructing Early Christian Families* (New York: Routledge, 1997); Shaye J. D. Cohen, ed., *The Jewish Family in Antiquity*, Brown Judaic Studies 289 (Atlanta: Scholars Press, 1993).

30. Both Matthew and Luke remove the reference to relatives and Luke deletes also the mention of households in this saying (Matt. 13:57; Luke 4:24). John 4:44, which probably reports the saying without knowing Mark's version of it, mentions only prophets' hometowns. See the perceptive discussion in Marcus, *Mark 1–8*, 376–378.

31. Joseph H. Hellerman (*The Ancient Church as Family* [Minneapolis: Fortress Press, 2001], 43–51) discusses sibling solidarity as a primary value of Mediterranean kinship.

32. *Community of the New Age: Studies in Mark's Gospel* (London: SCM, 1977), 107.

33. James and John are identified repeatedly by their relationship to their father Zebedee (1:19–20; 3:17; 10:35) even though at 3:17 Jesus bestows on them a symbolic name, "Boanerges," which Mark says means "Sons of Thunder." The name sounds like a reference to the battle between the forces of God and the forces of Satan into which Jesus recruits these disciples. In the same context Jesus dubs Simon "Peter" or "Rock," another sobriquet with apocalyptic resonance.

34. Marcus, *Mark 1–8*, 280.

35. See Abraham J. Malherbe, "God's New Family in Thessalonica," in *The Social World of the First Christians: Essays in Honor of Wayne A. Meeks*, ed. L. Michael White and O. Larry Yarbrough (Minneapolis: Fortress Press, 1995), 116–125; idem, *The Letters to the Thessalonians* (Anchor Bible 32B; New York: Doubleday, 2000).

36. Marcus, *Mark 1–8*, 353.

37. The phrase "your own people" seems to mean "relatives" since it is parallel to "your home."

38. Although Mark does not mention "revelations," he employs countless images and words drawn from the tradition of Jewish apocalyptic literature. See Adela Yarbro Collins, *The Beginning of the Gospel: Probings of Mark in Context* (Minneapolis: Fortress Press, 1992).

39. Juel, *A Master of Surprise*, 35–36.

40. J. Louis Martyn calls these pairs of opposites "antinomies" in his discussion of the character of Paul's apocalyptic theology ("Apocalyptic Antinomies," in *Theological Issues in the Letters of Paul* [Nashville: Abingdon Press, 1997], 111–123; and *Galatians* [Anchor Bible 33A; New York: Doubleday, 1997], 97–105).

41. Marcus, *Mark 1–8*, 238.

42. I owe this image to James S. Hanson, who says of Mark, "[T]he inevitability of the disciples' own 'resurrection' in the face of their utter failure (and here I would include the women at the tomb) represents the Gospel's rhetorical goal" (*The Endangered Promises: Conflict in Mark*, Society of Biblical Literature Dissertation Series 171 [Atlanta: Society of Biblical Literature, 2000], 245).

43. C. Clifton Black, "Christ Crucified in Paul and in Mark: Reflections on an Intracanonical Conversation," 184–206 in *Theology and Ethics in Paul and His Interpreters: Essays in Honor of Victor Paul Furnish*, ed. Eugene H. Lovering, Jr. and Jerry L. Sumney (Nashville: Abingdon Press, 1996], 198).

44. R. C. H. Lenski opines that she is "the wife of Cleopas and a sister of the mother of Jesus," even though he does not explain why two sisters might both be named Mary (*The Interpretation of St. Mark's Gospel* [Minneapolis: Augsburg Books, 1946], 728).

45. Raymond E. Brown surveys the literature exhaustively in *The Death of the Messiah: From Gethsemane to the Grave: A Commentary on the Passion Narratives in the Four Gospels*, vol. 2; Anchor Bible Reference Library (New York: Doubleday, 1994), 1016, 1152–1153, 1277. Most commentators simply pass over the matter in silence. Others see the similarities between the names in 6:3 and 15:40, but offer no explanation: Mark "makes no attempt to reconcile" the lists of names (Donald H. Juel, *Mark*, Augsburg Commentaries on the New Testament [Minneapolis: Augsburg Press, 1990], 231); the second Mary's identity is "impossible to determine" (C. Clifton Black, note to Mark 15:40, *HarperCollins Study Bible*, ed. Wayne A. Meeks, et al. [San Francisco: HarperCollins, 1993], 1950). Most who note the oddity labor mightily to find an alternative identity for the woman, averring that Mark could not (or should not) have referred to Jesus' mother this way: "The way the mother of these brothers is named, not to mention that she is named after Mary Magdalene among the women at the crucifixion of Jesus, makes it virtually impossible that she is the same Mary as the mother of Jesus" (Donald A. Hagner, "James," *Anchor Bible Dictionary* [1992], 3.618). There are nevertheless several interpreters who suspect she is indeed Jesus' mother, although they draw widely differing conclusions about what her appearance at the end of Mark signifies: M. Barnouin, "'Marie, Mère de Jacques et de José' (Marc 15.40)," *New Testament Studies* 42 (1996): 472–474; John Fenton, *Finding the Way Through Mark* (London: Mowbray, 1995), 113; Robert H. Gundry, *Mark: A Commentary on His Apology for the Cross* (Grand Rapids, Mich.: Wm. B. Eerdmans Pub. Co., 1993), 977; Hisako Kinukawa, *Women and Jesus in Mark: A Japanese Feminist Perspective* (Maryknoll, N.Y.: Orbis Books, 1994), 91–96; C. D. Marshall, *Faith as a Theme in Mark's Narrative*, Society for New Testament Studies Monograph Series 64 (Cambridge: Cambridge University Press, 1989), 178; Myers, *Binding the Strong Man*, 396;

Poetker, "You Are My Mother"; Herman C. Waetjen, *A Reordering of Power: A Socio-Political Reading of Mark's Gospel* (Minneapolis: Fortress Press, 1989), 238.

46. John Fenton, "The Mother of Jesus in Mark's Gospel and its Revisions," *Theology* 86 (1983): 435.

47. Richard Bauckham, *Jude and the Relatives of Jesus in the Early Church* (Edinburgh: T & T Clark, 1990), 8.

48. The son of Zebedee is known in later tradition as "James the greater" (Brown et al., *Mary in the New Testament*, 53).

49. Gaventa, *Mary*, and the other treatments of Christian literature in the present volume.

50. Although he does not address use of *Abba* in Mark and Paul, Joel Marcus makes a persuasive case for understanding the two as theologically related in "Mark—Interpreter of Paul," *New Testament Studies* 46 (2000): 473–487. See also Black, "Christ Crucified in Mark and Paul."

51. Although numerous early Christians, and not a few modern ones, have attempted to tidy up the end of Mark, 16:8 is indeed its purposeful conclusion. See Juel, *A Master of Surprise*, 107–121.

52. The New Testament letter of Jude is sometimes attributed to Jesus' brother even now (e.g., Bauckham, *Jude*, 134–178), although the evidence is particularly difficult to assess.

53. Karl P. Donfried and Paul J. Achtemeier describe the true relatives of Jesus in 3:31–35 as his "eschatological family" (Brown et al., *Mary in the New Testament*, 58).

# 4

# "Standing Near the Cross"

## *Mary and the Crucifixion of Jesus*

### BEVERLY ROBERTS GAVENTA

For most Protestants, Mary is little more than a character in the Christmas story. She creeps into our consciousness along with the Advent wreath, making a brief appearance perhaps in sermon and song, and then she disappears along with the crèche, no later than Epiphany. Given customary Protestant anxiety about overemphasizing Mary's role and the fact that the Gospels of Matthew and Luke include her almost exclusively in the infancy narratives, the confinement of Mary to Advent and Christmas is predictable. Another vantage point is possible, however. In this essay, I consider Mary from a different angle of vision, one offered by the Gospel of John, in which Mary takes her place not at the manger but at the cross. Beginning with the Gospel of John and its location of Mary at the "hour" of Jesus' crucifixion may reorient understanding of Mary away from the often sentimental treatment of the infancy narratives to the impending story of suffering and rejection that culminates at the cross.

Considering Matthew and Luke in light of John's Gospel reveals that, although John's is the only Gospel explicitly to place Mary at the cross, the others foreshadow the cross with their treatment of Mary even at Jesus' birth. From the point of view of the maternal thinking advocated by Bonnie Miller-McLemore, this should not come as a surprise, since any threat to a child also constitutes a threat to the mother who gave birth to that child.[1] The fact that it may take readers by surprise only reflects the predisposition to reduce Mary's role. Theologically this connection between Mary and the cross reinforces the scandal of the gospel, that is, the scandal of God's Son enduring humiliation, rejection, and death at human hands. Not only did Jesus' birth necessitate explanation, but his death did as well.

## MARY AND JESUS' "HOUR" IN THE GOSPEL OF JOHN

As with much else in the Gospel of John, the treatment of Mary is unique.[2] The Fourth Gospel never identifies her by name, referring instead to "the mother of Jesus" and "his mother." And even when Jesus addresses her directly, he does so with the puzzling address "Woman" instead of "Mother." She appears in the story twice, once at the beginning of the Gospel and once again near its conclusion. Although the first scene involving Jesus' mother, a wedding feast at Cana, provides the occasion for Jesus' first miracle, it also introduces the ominous theme of Jesus' death. In the second scene, the mother stands near the cross. The other Gospels contain no parallel to either story.

The story of the wedding at Cana is familiar (2:1–11). The "mother of Jesus" attends a wedding, to which Jesus and his disciples are also invited. The wine supply gives out, prompting Jesus' mother to say to him, "They have no wine." He responds with an extremely enigmatic question and a statement, "My hour has not yet come." In spite of this response, his mother tells the servants to do whatever he commands. Jesus instructs that "six stone water jars," each of which would hold twenty or thirty gallons, be filled with water. He then orders that some of this "water" be taken to the steward, who declares it extraordinary that the bridegroom has withheld the good wine, when hosts normally serve the good wine first.

Given the unusual nature of this story, in which Jesus provides neither food for the hungry nor healing for the sick but vast quantities of wine for a wedding feast, it comes as no surprise to find that John 2 has produced a bewildering array of interpretations, especially regarding Mary's place in the story. That diversity of viewpoints reflects the diversity of the interpreters, but it also reflects something inherent in the story itself. The story abounds with symbolic features (a wedding, water, wine), but its importance extends far beyond any specific symbolic or allegorical application. The story points forward, anticipating the gifts of God that Jesus will introduce, the coming "hour" of Jesus' revelation, and the necessity of human beings to make a decision about Jesus.

The role played by Jesus' mother in the story of the wedding at Cana is a simple one, but it is also profound. At one level she is no more than a function of the plot in that she sets the stage for the miracle that follows. By telling Jesus that there is no wine and then telling the servants to do whatever Jesus instructs them, she in some sense initiates the event. From a literary point of view, her words to Jesus and to the servants provoke the transformation of water into wine. This is not to say, however, that she actually intends to prompt Jesus' miracle or even that she knows a miracle is possible. Had some other woman, otherwise unknown to us, taken this part in the story, interpreters would probably not see her as advocating a miracle or understanding Jesus' identity. If anything, interpreters would distance Jesus from her in order to avoid the notion that a woman influenced him.

In addition to setting the stage for the miracle, Mary also serves in this story to confirm the humanity of Jesus. The opening of John's Gospel, with its claim that Jesus is "word" and "light," "grace" and "truth," creates the impression that Jesus has only a kind of docetic existence (one that appears to be but is not really human). The end of chapter 1 and the beginning of chapter 2 correct that impression. Commentators sometimes assert that the Cana miracle separates Jesus from his mother, yet it is also true that the Cana miracle and the passage that precedes it *invest* Jesus with a human mother and father and brothers and home. Here the words of 1:14 find dramatic fulfillment: "And the Word became flesh and lived among us."

Jesus' mother has yet another role to play in the Cana story, however, and that is to anticipate the crucifixion. When Jesus initially refuses Mary's request, he says, "My hour has not yet come." This is the first reference to Jesus' "hour," by which the Gospel of John refers to the time of Jesus' death (see, for example, John 12:27; 13:1; 16:32; 17:1). Because she appears at only these two points in John's narrative, the wedding and the cross, the reference to the hour here surely points ahead to her second appearance in chapter 19.

Jesus' mother appears again at the crucifixion. The brief vignette reads,

> Meanwhile, standing near the cross of Jesus were his mother, and his mother's sister, Mary the wife of Clopas, and Mary Magdalene. When Jesus saw his mother and the disciple whom he loved standing beside her, he said to his mother, "Woman here is your son." Then he said to the disciple, "Here is your mother." And from that hour the disciple took her into his own home. (19:25b–27)

This is the second of three brief scenes at the cross. Prior to this moment, the soldiers gamble for possession of Jesus' clothing (19:23–25a), and immediately following this scene Jesus pleads for water, and then, as John reports, "he bowed his head and gave up his spirit" (19:28–30). By placing these three brief scenes together, the narrator depicts the separation of Jesus from his earthly existence. First, he is stripped of his clothing by persons who are indifferent or even hostile to him. Second, he takes leave of those who stand close to him, even his mother and the disciple whom he loves. Third, he takes a final drink of wine and gives up his own breath.

This scene portrays Mary, the mother of Jesus, in two distinct ways. She speaks not a single word, and the narrator devotes not a single word to her description. Her sole action is to stand near the cross, and Jesus addresses her only briefly. There is, in one sense, no "characterization" of Jesus' mother in this scene. Nevertheless, her presence at the cross recalls the story of the wedding at Cana, the only other scene in which she appears, where Jesus makes his initial announcement about his "hour." It also recalls the network of family that connects Jesus to earthly existence. When Jesus' mother and the Beloved Disciple are given to one another and depart the scene, Jesus' connections to earthly existence likewise depart from John's gospel. Her role in this incident, then, has to do with Jesus' separation from his own earthly life.

This interpretation of the reference to Jesus' mother at the cross differs from both of the customary readings of this passage. Protestant interpreters often understand this to be an emotional scene in which Jesus displays his devotion to his mother, but that is to read into the text issues that are strikingly absent from it. It is strange to suggest that Jesus demonstrates his filial piety when his first words call on her to see her "son," the Beloved Disciple. More important, the utter absence of emotion in the narrator's description of the incident argues against this interpretation. Nowhere in John does Jesus, who does weep for Lazarus and his sisters (11:35), and who later appears to a weeping Mary Magdalene (20:11), express emotional attachment to or concern for his own mother.

By contrast, Catholic interpreters often view Jesus' mother at the cross as symbolizing the church, but that approach also overinterprets the passage. The focus here is not on what happens to the Beloved Disciple and Jesus' mother but on the death of Jesus and, specifically, the separation of Jesus from those relationships that characterized his earthly existence. No longer the son of this woman, he may depart to be with his heavenly Father. In other words, the symbolism inheres in the scene as a whole rather than in some quasi-allegorical interpretation of the characters.

Mary's role in the Gospel of John consists exclusively of her relationship to Jesus. She remains unnamed because what makes her important is solely the fact that she is Jesus' mother. In this respect, she is like all the characters in John's story: they exist in the narrative to reveal something about Jesus rather than something about themselves. Yet perhaps something more can be said about Mary's very presence at the cross. If the mother of Jesus is not a sign of Jesus' devotion to family or a symbol for the church, she may nevertheless instruct readers about the place of believers at the cross. By contrast with Peter's denial of Jesus, his mother and her companions serve as the first witnesses to the fulfillment of Jesus' prophecy that he would be "lifted up" (John 3:14; 8:28; 12:32).

## MARY AND JESUS: ENDANGERED
## IN THE GOSPEL OF MATTHEW

Moving from the Gospel of John to that of Matthew means moving from the cross to Jesus' birth and infancy. Mary appears quite briefly later in the Gospel

(12:46–50; 13:53–58), but her primary location in Matthew is in chapters 1 and 2. Although Matthew does not place Mary at the cross, the undercurrent of danger that runs through this initial story anticipates the cross and suggests that Matthew's story also aligns Mary with the cross.

Deeply ingrained in the conventional wisdom about Matthew is the notion that the infancy narrative in his Gospel focuses on Joseph rather than on Mary. That view reflects the fact that Joseph is the one who receives the annunciation of Jesus' birth, and Joseph is the one whom angelic dreams direct first to flee Herod and then to return again to Galilee rather than Judea. Yet the focus on Joseph should not be exaggerated, since nowhere does he speak (except for the indirect report about the naming of Jesus in 1:25). The only time the narrator reports on Joseph's responses to events is when Joseph plans to divorce Mary, a plan that carries the potential for disaster (see below).

As for Mary, she also remains silent; she neither speaks nor is addressed by another character (here the contrast with Joseph's role is appropriate). No emotion, no judgment, no opinion is attributed to her. Yet by placing her where he does—in the company of certain women and alongside the infant Jesus in chapter 2—Matthew reveals something important about her.[3]

Mary's name first appears at the end of the long genealogy of Jesus in 1:1–17, the genealogy that begins with Abraham, traces the line through David, and then culminates with Jesus himself. As is well known, what makes this genealogy remarkable is that it contains the names of four women. The women named are themselves unusual, not exemplary and well-known figures such as Sarah and Rebecca. They are Tamar (who played the role of a prostitute to force Judah to provide her with the son she deserves under Israelite law); Rahab (a prostitute who assisted the spies in their conquest of Jericho); Ruth (the widow who remained loyal to her mother-in-law and eventually married the wealthy Boaz); and "the wife of Uriah," better known to readers as Bathsheba, who became David's wife only after he arranged the death of her husband to cover up their adulterous affair.[4]

The long history of exegesis has produced multiple explanations for the presence of these particular women in the genealogy. That debate need not be rehearsed here except to notice the tendency of interpreters to make all the women (including Mary) into a single woman with a single story. Yet their stories are not one story; they are not all sinners or all Gentiles, for example. Instead, what the stories have in common is that each of these women in some way threatens the status quo, and each is in turn threatened by that status quo. For example, the "wife of Uriah" threatens David with her report that she is pregnant, and he in turn threatens her by bringing about the death of her husband.

When Matthew introduces Mary's name at the end of the genealogy, readers anticipate that she has something in common with these other women. The story soon reveals Mary's own threat in a concise scene: Mary and Joseph are engaged to be married, but they have not yet married. Mary is pregnant. Matthew reveals to the reader that the conception is "from the Holy Spirit," but no such knowledge comforts Joseph. Matthew reports simply, "Her husband Joseph, being a righteous man and unwilling to expose her to public disgrace, planned to dismiss her quietly" (1:19).

As is well known, engagement in Palestine of the first century was not merely a private declaration that could be broken by either party and for any reason. Engagement gave to Joseph the legal rights of a husband, and it obligated Mary to him, regardless of the fact that he and Mary were not yet technically married. Her pregnancy, therefore, constitutes evidence of nothing less than adultery. Joseph could simply divorce her by handing her a "bill of divorce," or he could take legal procedures against her for adultery. If the provisions of Deuteronomic law were being observed at this time, Mary would have been liable to death for her supposed adultery.

Matthew describes Joseph as "a righteous man" who decided to "dismiss her quietly" so as not to disgrace Mary. In other words, he wants to avoid a scandal, and therefore he takes the mildest measures possible. With a single word, Matthew connects the report that Jesus decided to act *lathra*, which the NRSV translates here "quietly," with the action of King Herod in calling his advisors to him "secretly" (again *lathra*).[5] What Matthew leaves unexplained is how Joseph's action could remain quiet, or what Joseph thought would happen to Mary and her child. Pregnancy is difficult to hide, but a newborn for whom there is no father is impossible to conceal. In an age in which adultery and illegitimacy brought with them harsh treatment, even Joseph's righteous remedy would have had disastrous consequences for Mary and for her child. Joseph's private action would have public consequences.

Joseph does not take the action he plans, of course, because divine intervention in the form of an angelic visitation instructs him otherwise. Yet the decision of Joseph allows us to see how Mary has something in common with the four women of the genealogy. Like them, Mary also threatens the status quo insofar as her pregnancy threatens Joseph's honor. Joseph's initial perception is that his bride has both betrayed him and disgraced herself. As a result of his sense of being threatened by Mary, Joseph in turns contemplates an action that threatens Mary and her unborn child with ostracism and perhaps far worse.

"In the time of King Herod" signals the beginning of the second half of the Matthean infancy narrative, the half that focuses on Herod's threat to the child Jesus (2:1). Here it is not the good and righteous Joseph who schemes to put Mary away and leave her child without a name, but Herod who threatens to kill the child. Only a series of divine warnings, first to the wise men and then to Joseph, prevents Jesus from being slaughtered along with the other young children of Bethlehem. What is striking about Matthew's treatment of Mary in this chapter is that every reference to Mary here carries a reference to the baby and almost every reference to the baby carries a reference to Mary, as follows (italics added):

> The wise men see *"the child with Mary his mother"* (v. 11).
> An angel warns Joseph to flee to Egypt, taking with him *"the child and his mother"* (v. 13).
> Joseph then takes *"the child and his mother"* by night (v. 14).
> After Herod's death, the angel instructs Joseph to return, bringing *"the child and his mother"* (v. 20, 21).

The repetition of the phrase unmistakably connects the two figures, so that they become a single unit. If Herod succeeds in destroying this child, he will in some real sense also destroy the mother, just as Joseph's earlier plan to divorce Mary also jeopardized the life of her child. Whoever threatens the child, threatens his mother; whoever protects the child, protects his mother.

For Matthew, Mary the mother of Jesus remains a silent figure. Yet Matthew connects her closely with the theme of threats against Jesus. That theme begins when the adult Jesus encounters authorities who are threatened by him and who threaten him in return (see, for example, 12:14; 21:46; 26:3–5). It begins even before his birth, when the good Joseph assumes that he knows what he should do and has to be stopped. It continues when the raging Herod seeks Jesus' death. Mary shares Jesus's peril both from the well-intentioned and from the wicked. She stands close by the cross even before her son is born.

## THE SWORD THAT PIERCES MARY IN THE GOSPEL OF LUKE

By contrast with the slender appearances of Mary in John and Matthew, Luke's Gospel includes her in several scenes. It reports remarks made by Mary and to her and even reveals her responses to events. From the vantage point of contemporary readers, Luke still reveals far too little about Mary, but he nevertheless provides a fuller treatment than any of the other evangelists. In this more extended treatment, Mary plays three distinct but interrelated roles—those of disciple, prophet, and mother.[6] Despite the fact that the scenes involving Mary largely appear in the infancy narrative, these roles all connect Mary also with the cross.

As is well-established, Mary is a disciple; for Luke, indeed, she is the first disciple. In 1:38, Mary responds to Gabriel's annunciation with the words

"Here am I, the servant of the Lord; let it be with me according to your word."
With that statement she consents to God's will, specifically to God's plan to
bring about the salvation of all humankind through the intervention of Jesus
Christ. Mary identifies herself as a "servant" or "slave" (which better translates
the Greek word *doulos*). The designation "slave of the Lord" often generates
the response that Mary thereby becomes subservient, even a model for female
subservience. Yet such an interpretation is a strong misreading of the text,
which concerns not Mary's (much less womankind's) subservience to men but
her recognition of the prerogative of God to rule in her life. This is what it
takes to become a disciple, male *or* female: obedience to God's will.

By naming herself as God's slave, Mary identifies herself with all those who
rightly understand their relationship to God. In Peter's programmatic address
at Pentecost, he interprets the Spirit's outpouring as a fulfillment of the words
of the prophet Joel promising the gift of the Spirit to "my slaves, both men
and women" (Acts 2:18). Later, after the first incident in which apostles are
arrested for their proclamation of Jesus' name, the gathered community of
believers in Jerusalem prays to God, freely declaring themselves to be God's
slaves (4:29).[7] Much later in the narrative, a female slave who is possessed by
a demon ironically identifies Paul and Barnabas as "slaves of the Most High
God" (16:17). In Paul's farewell address to the Ephesian elders, he characterizes his ministry not by recalling great sermons and acts of miraculous power,
but by identifying himself as God's own slave (20:19; see also 20:22). As such,
Paul recognizes that he will not again see the Ephesian elders (20:25, 38), a
clear anticipation of his impending death. Mary is the first in the line of these
references to God's slaves. By consenting to God's will, she also anticipates
Jesus' own consent to the cross (22:39–46).

In the soaring language of the Magnificat, Mary takes on a second role, that
of a prophet (1:46–55). She praises God for God's action in her life and on
behalf of Israel. Luke does not explicitly refer to Mary's speech as prophetic;
neither does Luke say that she speaks through the Holy Spirit (as he does with
Zechariah in 1:67). Her conception takes place when the Holy Spirit overtakes
her (1:35), of course, which may explain why Luke does not feel it necessary
to specify that she speaks *via* the Spirit. More to the point, the Magnificat itself
reflects the prophetic themes of God's intercession on behalf of the weak and
powerless, God's scorn for the mighty, God's promises for God's people. This
reversal of things as they are, this assault on the status quo, anticipates another
reversal: that of the cross itself by God's action in the resurrection.

Mary is also a mother. This is both her most obvious and her most intricate
role (an assertion that may hold for all of us who become parents). In Luke's
narrative, Mary's maternity serves to introduce a certain tension into the story.
It enters with the familiar scene in which the shepherds comply with the angelic
instruction and go to see the infant Jesus. Luke observes that they "made known

what had been told them about this child" (2:17), but he also adds that "Mary treasured all these words and pondered them in her heart" (2:19). Virtually the same expression occurs at the end of Luke 2, where Mary and Joseph start their journey home from the Passover celebration in Jerusalem only to find that their twelve-year-old son is not with them. When Mary and Joseph do find Jesus, he is not only back in Jerusalem, but he is also amazing the teachers of Israel within the Temple itself. Mary bluntly confronts him with their anguish over his behavior, and he responds. Then Luke says, "But they [Joseph and Mary] did not understand what he said to them." All of them return to Nazareth.

The entire infancy narrative concludes with the words "His mother treasured all these things in her heart. And Jesus increased in wisdom and in years, and in divine and human favor" (2:52). That translation, however, suggests that Mary was simply storing up pleasant memories for the family album. Yet the Gospel writers do not usually indulge in sentimentality, and Mary's action is not so much to "treasure" as to ponder, to reflect, even to worry.[8]

This motif of maternal anxiety is reinforced by the second oracle of Simeon. Addressing Mary directly, Simeon declares, "This child is destined for the falling and rising of many in Israel, and to be a sign that will be opposed so that the inner thoughts of many will be revealed—and a sword will pierce your own soul too" (Luke 2:34–35). Commentators sometimes deny that this oracle refers to Mary's grief at Jesus' death, since Luke does not explicitly report that Mary is present at the cross. Yet it seems odd indeed to imagine that Mary must be present at the crucifixion to be grieved by it, and the oracle clearly connects Mary with the rejection that awaits her son.

Through the anticipation of Jesus' death, and especially through the motif of pondering, Luke introduces questions about Mary: What does she understand? What will she do? Will she persist in her discipleship? Will she, like others, turn away? These questions are not finally answered until the beginning of Luke's second volume, the Acts of the Apostles, when Mary joins the apostles in the Upper Room just before the day of Pentecost (Acts 1:14). In Luke's story, Mary is disciple, prophet, and mother. But it is as a worrying, troubled mother that she becomes a most interesting part of Luke's story. Mary's worry, her anguished looking for her Son, and especially the words Simeon directs her way, all anticipate the real loss of Jesus at the crucifixion. Even in Luke's Gospel, then, with the appearance of Gabriel and the shepherds' awe, the cross enters the story of Mary.

## MARY AT THE CROSS OF JESUS HER SON

The order in which we read texts influences what we see in them. By reading first the stories of Jesus' birth in the Gospels of Matthew and Luke, readers tend to see Mary as connected exclusively with the joyous strains of the angels'

songs and the astonishing gifts of the wise men. The scenes in John's Gospel
fade away. When we begin with John's Gospel, however, and attend to the
presence of Mary at the cross and her earlier anticipation of the crucifixion,
the cross looms even as we turn to Matthew and Luke.

That point is important both narratively and theologically. For the New
Testament writers, Jesus' death is not merely a bad ending to a promising
career, or a human mistake God corrects via the resurrection. Jesus' death is
inherently connected with his identity as God's Messiah. The one Matthew
identifies as "Emmanuel" or "God with us" is threatened even before his birth.
The one whom Gabriel announces as the heir to "the throne of his ancestor
David" will also be rejected. As bearer and even prophet of this Messiah, Mary
also can only be understood in light of his cross.

To consider Mary in light of the cross summons, first, images of the *mater
dolorosa*, the sheer fact of Mary's grief and the grief of all who acknowledge the
relentlessness of the human rejection of Mary's child. Yet more is at stake than
shared grief. Mary's association with the cross recalls for Christians the scandal at the heart of the gospel: that God's actions on our behalf meet ever and
again with misunderstanding and rejection. In Mary's "standing near the
cross" (John 19:25) Christians may find themselves alongside the suffering
world and its vulnerable God.

## NOTES

1. See her essay "'Pondering All These Things,'" in this volume, as well as *Also a
   Mother: Work and Family as Theological Dilemma* (Nashville: Abingdon Press,
   1994).
2. Although John never refers to her by name, here I will do so as a convenience
   and in recognition of the evidence elsewhere that Mary is the name of Jesus'
   mother. The exegetical discussion that follows draws heavily on my earlier
   work, *Mary: Glimpses of the Mother of Jesus* (Columbia, S.C.: University of South
   Carolina Press, 1995; Minneapolis: Fortress Press, 1999), 79–99.
3. For further discsussion, see Gaventa, *Mary*, 29–48.
4. For detailed discussion of these women, see Katharine Doob Sakenfeld's essay
   in this volume.
5. The word *lathra* appears in Matthew's Gospel only in these two adjoining
   passages.
6. On these roles, see further Gaventa, *Mary*, 49–78.
7. The NRSV translates "servants."
8. The wording used of her occurs also in the Septuagint translation of Genesis
   when Jacob worries about the troublesome dreams of his son Joseph (Gen.
   37:11). It appears again in the book of Daniel, when Daniel frets over the meaning of an apocalyptic vision (Dan. 7:28).

# PART 2

## *Living* Mary

# 5

# Mary, the Servant of the Lord

*Christian Vocation at the Manger and the Cross*

NANCY J. DUFF

> In the sixth month the angel Gabriel was sent by God to a town in
> Galilee called Nazareth to a virgin engaged to a man whose name
> was Joseph, of the house of David. The virgin's name was Mary.
> And he came to her and said, "Greetings, favored one! The Lord
> is with you." But she was much perplexed by his words and pon-
> dered what sort of greeting this might be. The angel said to her,
> "Do not be afraid, Mary, for you have found favor with God."
>
> *(Luke 1:26–30)*

"Greetings, favored one! The Lord is with you." When the church ponders
Gabriel's words to Mary and "what sort of greeting this might be," profoundly
different responses are given by Roman Catholics and Protestants. According
to the Roman Catholic tradition, Gabriel greets Mary as the "favored one"
because she is "full of grace," chosen by God before creation to bear the
Christ-child. As a result, Roman Catholics have built an elaborate theology
around her. Her numerous titles include "Mother of God" and "Queen of
Heaven." Seventeen festival days are devoted to her and fifty "hail Marys" are
included in the Rosary. Catholics often address Mary in prayer and call upon
her as intercessor, and some even consider her "co-redemptrix."[1] But while
Mary "found favor" with God and with the Roman Catholic Church, Protestants have virtually ignored her. Protestants regularly affirm their belief that
Jesus was "born of the Virgin Mary," occasionally include *Ava Maria* in a wedding celebration, and annually acknowledge Mary at Christmas, but they
rarely find Mary significant for contemplation in worship or spiritual formation. Protestants have devoted attention to the controversy over the doctrine

of the virgin birth (a debate over the literal interpretation of the Bible), but only occasionally refer to Mary in sermons, hymns, or prayers.

Ironically, this very absence of a "Reformed Mariology" provides a positive starting point for reflection on the biblical figure of Mary from a Reformed Protestant perspective. As Karl Barth observes, *because* Mary represents humanity to which the miracle of God happens, the grace of God that encounters her constitutes the focus of doctrinal attention, not Mary herself. An independent Reformed Mariology would shift attention away from the saving grace of God in Christ alone by suggesting that Mary contributed to her own salvation.

> [E]very word that makes her [Mary's] person the object of special attention, which ascribes to her what is even a relatively independent part in the drama of salvation, is an attack upon the miracle of revelation, because it is, after all, an attempt to illumine and to substantiate this miracle from the side of [humanity] or of [humanity's] receptivity.[2]

However, if one maintains the christological nature of claims about Mary, Barth insists that Mary should not "remain nameless or unnoticed." She is, in fact, "an indispensable factor in Bible proclamation" precisely *because* her importance lies in being one "who received and is blessed."[3] Barth even claims that Protestants should employ, rather than resist, the designation of Mary as "Mother of God." Reformed theology insists, however, that Mary, the mother of God, was not made perfect and holy in order to fulfill her vocation, for God's saving grace in Jesus Christ does not require human perfection.

For Protestants in the Reformed tradition Mary can be understood as "favored" only because for her, as for every child of God, God's saving grace is bestowed upon a sinner. This paper claims that Mary's presence at the manger and at the cross provides an instance of our own call to give witness to the reversal of power revealed in the incarnation of God in Jesus Christ. The reversal of divine power to which Mary gives witness neither requires nor produces perfection (in Mary or in any of us). In fact, the notion of perfection or ideal undermines the scandal of the manger and the cross. Finally, if Mary, who is the only biblical figure to bear witness to both the manger and the cross, is denied the authority of the ordained minister, the church courts the danger of severing itself from the divine power to which Mary gives witness. The first section of this essay addresses the christological function of Mary for Reformed faith. Claims for Mary's perfection are rejected because, if Mary deserves God's grace, the radical nature of God's grace breaking into this sinful world is undermined. The second section employs the Reformed doctrine of vocation for interpreting Christian discipleship, which Mary certainly embodies. Claims that Mary represents the "ideal" woman (or even the "ideal" disciple) are rejected because the notion of an "ideal" contradicts divine power revealed in the scandal of the manger and the cross.

## MARY, CHRISTOLOGY, AND SALVATION BY GRACE ALONE

According to John Calvin, Gabriel's words to Mary, "Greetings, favored one," provide "a commendation of the grace of God," directing Mary's attention to the goodness of God who favors her. It is the angel's salutation to Mary (a form of direct address, offering as it were a word of congratulation), not our subsequent and persistent salutation to Mary in prayer.[4] For Reformed theology the significance of Gabriel's greetings is not found in his addressing her as "favored one" but in his words that follow: "The Lord is with you." This brief proclamation constitutes a summary of the doctrine of the incarnation and, therefore, forms the heart of the birth narratives. God is with us. God is fully present in this world of "time and space and things" (as Paul Lehmann liked to say); the birth of Jesus means (as Shirley Guthrie reminds us) that God comes into "the real world of flesh-and-blood human beings."[5]

The church has, however, often encountered resistance to the claim that God—the maker and ruler of the universe—was incarnate, embodied, and fully present in this world. This resistance (which has been dubbed "docetism") has had disastrous consequences not only for christology (God's incarnational presence in the world is illusory if Christ is human in appearance only), but also for its implied devaluation of the physical, bodily nature of human life. As Christopher Morse notes, to thwart this docetic resistance to Christ's genuinely embodied presence in the world, the word "born," rather than the word "virgin," receives the *initial* emphasis in our confession of faith that Jesus "was born of the Virgin Mary."

> "Born of the virgin Mary" is but the beginning of a series of antidocetic affirmations in the Apostles' Creed entailing the disbelief of a phantom Christ, one in human semblance only, removed, as the Gnostics and Marcionites taught with their false understanding of spirit, from the materiality of physical existence. A fleshless Jesus would not be born of an actual woman's body.[6]

This antidocetic function of the affirmation that "Jesus was born of the virgin Mary" is lost when undue attention is given to the *biology* of the virgin birth. Fundamentalists and conservative evangelicals divert attention away from the christological function of statements regarding Mary by using the subsequent fulfillment of Gabriel's proclamation as evidence of the authority of scripture and its literal interpretation, rather than as pointing to the incarnation.

Consequently, as James Barr observes, the virgin birth becomes such a highly
formalized doctrine that it has no real content at all, that is, it functions primarily as a litmus test to identify "true believers" rather than an integrated
claim within systematic theology regarding the Word of God made flesh.[7]
Once this antidocetic function of the birth narrative is lost, so is the antidocetic function of Mary whenever she enters the biblical account. References
to Mary the mother of Jesus in the biblical narratives insist that the One who
is the Word (the One who was with God in the beginning and is God) is the
same Jesus of Nazareth who was born of a woman. In short, Jesus was this
Word made flesh. Beverly Gaventa observes that "as the Gospel's way of
insisting that Jesus had a human home, the mother of Jesus signals the scandal of Jesus' humanity. Through Mary, the Word becomes flesh and thereby
gives offense to the world."[8]

Once the initial emphasis of the affirmation, "*born* of the virgin Mary" is
understood, then (but only then) can attention rightly be focused on "born of
a *virgin.*" Far from giving biological (or as Morse says, "gynecological") proof
of the incarnation, the doctrine of the virgin birth proclaims that God makes
a way out of no way and brings into existence that which was not there before
(Rom. 4:17). It is no coincidence that Luke gives an account of the birth of
John the Baptist (who was born to a woman too old to conceive and bear a
child) in the same narrative that proclaims the conception and birth of Jesus
the Messiah to a young woman who is still a virgin. According to the angel
Gabriel, John the Baptist's birth is a sign of what God in Jesus Christ has done
for the world: "And now, your relative Elizabeth in her old age has also conceived a son; and this is the sixth month for her who was said to be barren. For
nothing will be impossible with God" (Luke 1:36–37).[9]

The doctrine of the virgin birth carries further significance in that the
absence of a human father in the incarnation challenges masculine conceptions
of power, a point not always acknowledged by theologians but one that serves
the feminist critique of patriarchy with surprising clarity and power. Karl
Barth (whose theology has never been called feminist!) makes this observation
when he says that the virgin birth is, in part, a word of judgment from God:
"[T]he male, as the specific agent of human action and history, with his responsibility for directing the human species, must now retire into the background,
as the powerless figure of Joseph."[10] Unfortunately, what Barth gives with one
hand he takes away with the other by relying on an essentialist understanding
of gender that ascribes to women the passive, receptive side of human nature.
"God did not choose man [humanity] in his pride and in his defiance, but man
in his weakness and humility, not man in his historical role, but man in the
weakness of his nature as represented by the woman."[11] Barth is *not* saying that
only men are prideful and defiant while only women are passive and weak. He

is, nevertheless, claiming that males best represent humanity's pride and defiance, while females best represent humanity's passivity and receptivity. One can, however, make Barth's point without resorting to an essentialist understanding of gender, as Christopher Morse demonstrates:

> Human history as we have told it has usually been the story of human males, the story of the power and accomplishments (often in the name of God) of statesmen, warriors, explorers, entrepreneurs, philosophers, and so on. But now in the most important event of all history the mighty male is excluded! It is a woman who is the agent of God's work in the world and gives us the first and prime example of the proper role of human beings in relation to God and God's work. Mary's modest "Let it be done with me according to your word" tells all of us, male and female alike, that our task is to bear witness to God's and not our own greatness, to be the servants and not the sponsors of God in the world."[12]

The task of bearing witness to God's greatness and not our own cannot be confined to the vocation of the "ideal woman" but must be understood, as Morse points out, as describing the vocation of men as well as women.

Once the christological function of all statements about Mary is recognized, Reformed Protestants can, as Barth says, not only turn attention to Mary but also embrace her identification as the "mother of God." Protestants wrongly reject this term as idolatrous because they incorrectly understand it to mean that Mary has an existence prior to God and somehow brings God into existence. This is not, however, the meaning of *theotokos* ("God-bearer") for Roman Catholics, nor should it be so understood by Protestants. Properly understood, *theotokos* constitutes a summary of the doctrine of the incarnation, for it maintains the Chalcedonian insistence that Jesus Christ is fully divine and fully human. In giving birth to this one who is fully human, Mary gives birth to the one who is also "fully God." This does not make Mary the *eternal* mother of God, nor does it deny the preexistence of the second Person of the Trinity. It does, however, stress both Christ's humanity (since Mary is his mother, he is born into human flesh) and his divinity (since he is fully divine, Mary is the mother of God).

To the surprise of many Protestants, Roman Catholics also believe that the veneration of Mary must serve the veneration of God in Jesus Christ. Protestants wrongly accuse Roman Catholics of worshiping Mary instead of Christ. The significant difference between Roman Catholic and Reformed thought about Mary is found (as is so often the case) in their respective understandings of grace and the human capacity to receive it. For Roman Catholics the holiness of Christ's presence in the world demands that Mary herself be holy in order to become the "mother of God," so that Mary has a *perfected capacity* to

receive God's grace. Hence, in Gabriel's words of greeting to Mary, the designation "favored one" is understood as a title describing Mary as "full of grace."
Mary's faithful acceptance of Gabriel's pronouncement that she will bear a son
despite the fact that she is a virgin is interpreted as an indication of Mary's holiness. Her response of faithfulness indicates "perfect co-operation with the
grace of God" as well as "perfect openness to the action of the Holy Spirit."[13]

Mary's perfect cooperation and her perfect openness are explained, in part,
by three major dogmas in Roman Catholic Mariology: Mary's immaculate
conception and subsequent sinlessness throughout her life, her perpetual virginity (both before and after the birth of Jesus), and her bodily assumption into
heaven. (1) Whereas Protestants tend to misinterpret the doctrine of *Mary's
immaculate conception* as another instance of virgin birth, the point for Roman
Catholics is not that Mary was conceived apart from human sexual activity but
that she was conceived without the taint of original sin; hence, Mary remained
sinless throughout her life. (2) Because Mary gave her entire self to God, she
committed herself to *perpetual virginity* even before Gabriel's pronouncement
and for the rest of her life, as did Joseph. (Biblical references to Jesus' siblings
are duly translated as "cousins.") (3) Being without sin, Mary did not experience death but was the first to be resurrected by the action of her Son, and so
was *bodily assumed into heaven.*

The Roman Catholic understanding of Mary's sinlessness, immaculate conception, and perpetual virginity arise from the notion that in order to be worthy of carrying the Savior in her womb, of giving birth to him, and serving as
his mother, Mary had to be higher than any creature or angel in moral and
spiritual virtue. Mary, therefore, becomes the mirror image of Eve; indeed, she
is often referred to as "the second Eve," for unlike her counterpart, Mary
resists temptation as she listens only to the Word of God delivered by the
angel. As a result of her obedience, Mary lives as Eve did before the fall. Hence,
she represents the restoration of the garden by the Second Adam through her
perfect obedience.

In contrast, for Reformed theology this emphasis on perfection contradicts
the doctrine of incarnation summarized in Gabriel's proclamation that "the
Lord is with you." That Mary was full of grace does not mean that she was cre-
ated without sin in order to be *worthy* of giving birth to the Son of God, for
God enters a world that is *un*worthy of the presence of God, a world that is sinful and broken.[14] If Mary must be perfect in order to be worthy of carrying the
Savior, the message is lost, for how could any of us be worthy of "carrying" the
Savior or being an "icon" of God (as Paul puts it)? Mary's perfection becomes
an extension of the docetism that denies the true bodily presence of God in
Jesus Christ, for it presents a field of holiness capable of receiving God rather
than the sinful and unworthy world into which God chooses to be present.

In spite of their rejection of Mary's perfection, Reformed Protestants have, nevertheless, sometimes allowed Mary to be understood as the ideal woman. Mary's passive acceptance of Gabriel's pronouncement, her obedience, and the absence of resistance or rebellion, as well as her role as mother, have at times been held up as the ideal model for women of faith to follow. This notion of Mary as an ideal woman or even an ideal disciple, however, is actually inconsistent with Reformed theology. God does not encounter Mary or any of us as ideals, nor does God transform us into ideals. We are like Mary, real human beings of flesh and spirit, body and soul, in need of the power of God as we seek to give glory to the One who saves and sustains us in grace. Mary, like all of us, was called not into perfection but into discipleship.

## THE DOCTRINE OF VOCATION AND CALL

In various biblical "call stories" we discover both reluctant and eager disciples. When God asks, "Whom shall I send?" Samuel responds heartily, "Here I am. Send me." Moses, on the other hand, pleads, "Not me! Send somebody else." While Abraham packs his bags and family without a backward glance, Jonah follows the divine call only when threatened by death in the belly of a whale. In the New Testament, Simon and his brother Andrew drop their nets and follow Jesus, and Zacheus climbs down from his tree and makes good on his fiduciary responsibilities. But the rich young ruler turns away full of sorrow. Therefore, when the angel tells Mary (a woman who has known no man) that she will bear a son, Mary's response of puzzlement ("How can this be?") and her ready acceptance of God's call ("Let it be with me according to your will") are not unique among biblical call stories. Although she does not show the reluctance of Moses, neither does she accept her call any more readily than Abraham or the fishermen. When we ponder Gabriel's words to Mary and "what sort of greeting this might be," we can consider the call of Mary in the same manner as the call of all the prophets and the disciples and, in fact, our own.[15] We find that Mary's vocation and ours is to glorify God in all that we do and to bear witness to God's greatness, not our own.

Often, however, Mary's response in faith to Gabriel's pronouncement has not been understood as God's gift of grace to all disciples, both men and women, but as the ideal response to be made by *women* of faith. Hence, even though Roman Catholics stress Mary's uniqueness and, therefore, her separation from the rest of humanity, she is thought to present an image of ideal womanhood; even though Protestants stress that Mary is the *same* as all other human beings, she represents not the ideal disciple but the ideal woman. In both cases Mary represents an ideal that is impossible to reach, not only because an "ideal" is by definition unreachable in real human experience but also because she represents the impossible contradiction of being simultaneously both virgin and mother. She has never experienced sexual intercourse, yet she is biologically the mother of Jesus. While one could argue that she represents, in one self, these two "ideal" states for women (virginity and motherhood), it is their *combination* that is presented as the ideal. This indicates, ironically, that Mary is both exception and model. Of course, the identification of either virginity or motherhood as the two ideal states for women is problematic even when they are not combined into an impossible singular state of being. While Christian theology and ethics rightly employs exemplary figures of the faith, these figures should never be presented as "ideals" towards which we are to strive, for so doing changes the nature of Christian moral action from giving parabolic expression of the reality of God's grace to futile striving for human perfection. Even the church's doctrine of Christ, which includes the image of sinlessness, rightly does not present Jesus as the ideal human being, an ideal for which we will perpetually strive and inevitably fall short. Scripture describes Mary, like all those called to be prophets or disciples, as a human being with a unique calling and exemplary faithfulness in obedience, not as an image of perfection. We are called in this world to real tasks, not ideal ones. When Mary is understood as the perfect model, we who are not perfect are doomed to endless striving toward that which we cannot achieve.

Similar problems arise when Mary's perfection is applied to the church, which Mary is often said to represent. One courts two dangers when using the image of Mary's perfection to represent the church. First, one forgets that the church is as sinful an institution as any other (an error that courts arrogance and self-deception). Second, one calls the church to live up to a perfection impossible in this world (an error that courts futility and perpetual guilt). The church never has room for arrogance, but neither does it give witness to God's greatness by engendering a sense of frustration and even shame at failing to reach perfection. Instead of arrogance or hopeless futility the church is defined by hope in the grace and promises of God. God's incarnate Presence in this world is not dependent on our perfection, nor does it produce (and, therefore, expect) such perfection. After all, Christ came to seek and to save the *lost*—not the perfect (Luke 19:10 RSV).

The doctrine of vocation provides one avenue for interpreting Christian discipleship while avoiding the notion of perfection or "ideal." In its most fundamental meaning the doctrine of vocation claims that every human life is called into the world for a divinely appointed purpose.[16] Whatever specific tasks we are called to pursue, the doctrine of vocation says that we are to glorify God in all that we do. One of the great gifts from the theology of the

Reformation is its insistence that the mundane as well as extraordinary tasks that are required of us in domestic, public, and ecclesial life can be done to the glory of God.[17] When we hear that Mary's soul "praises the Lord" and that her spirit "rejoices" in God her Savior, she reminds us that the chief end of humanity is to love God and *enjoy* God forever.[18]

In addition to glorifying God in all that we do, the doctrine of vocation recognizes that God's presence in this world, which brings into existence that which was not there before, calls us to provide a space where others can glorify God. When Mary proclaims that God has "scattered the proud" and "lifted up the lowly," she reminds us that God's incarnation in Jesus Christ opposes the powers and principalities in this world that destroy human lives (Luke 1:51, 52). When addressed by Gabriel, Mary is herself a poor, unmarried woman, whose pregnancy prior to marriage will threaten to make her an outcast. The *mother of God* is a poor woman, subject to political census taking but counting for nothing by those in power. The mother of God is forced by lowly circumstance to give birth in a stable. Romanticized images of the baby Jesus—undisturbed by the sounds of the animals that surrounded him—cannot muffle the cries of labor, conceal the pain and bloodiness of giving birth, or make acceptable the scandal of delivering a child in a place intended for the feeding and sheltering of animals.

Mary's presence in the biblical narrative gives witness to this scandal of the Messiah born in a manger. This One who will be great, the Son of the Most High, the Savior of the world: *this One* is a baby born in a place intended for housing animals. And because we know the whole story, we know that it is not a story of one of lowly birth who rises through the ranks to success and greatness. This Messiah was born in an animal stall and executed on a cross. The reversal of power demonstrated through the manger and the cross is anticipated by Mary's words in the Magnificat:

> He has shown strength with his arm;
> he has scattered the proud with the thoughts of their hearts.
> He has brought down the powerful from their thrones,
> and lifted up the lowly;
> he has filled the hungry with good things,
> and sent the rich away empty.
>
> (Luke 1:51–53)

Birth in an animal stall and death on a cross provide the threshold for God's radical presence in this world, and it is certainly not the portal one would expect for "the Son of the Most High." At this unlikely threshold we see Mary at the manger and will later see her at the cross; the same cannot be said of any other biblical figure. Perfection is an intrusion here; it has no place in this scene.[19]

Mary's perfection not only diminishes the doctrine of the incarnation and its reversal of power but subsequently puts the vocation of Christian women in jeopardy. Ironically, even though Mary represents perfect humanity in the Roman Catholic tradition, her perfection cannot recommend her (or any of her daughters, from generation to generation) to the ordained ministry. In her perfection Mary presents an image of the ideal woman, and women are not called to the priesthood. As a recent papal letter has decreed,

> If Christ—by his free and sovereign choice, clearly attested to by the Gospel and by the Church's constant tradition—entrusted only to men the task of being an "icon" of his countenance as "shepherd" and "bridegroom" of the church through the exercise of the ministerial priesthood, this in no way detracts from the role of women or for that matter, from the role of the other members of the church who are not ordained to the sacred ministry, since all share equally in the dignity proper to the "common priesthood" based on baptism.[20]

Although Mary herself represents the church and has been declared to be "as near to God himself as is possible for a created being," she is, nevertheless, excluded from being an "'icon' of Jesus' countenance as 'shepherd.'" Mary's subservience as a woman has overshadowed her parabolic witness to God's grace and power revealed in the manger and at the cross.[21]

According to the biblical narratives Mary *is* an icon of God's reversal of power revealed in the incarnation. Like Mary, the church is called to give witness to the manger and the cross; like Mary, each one of us is called to do the same. When Mary is thought to model faith only for women, and women are then denied the authority for assuming leadership in the church, a critical link is broken in Christian proclamation. If Mary represents an ideal exclusively for women, then the church and the men who lead it, the sacraments and those men ordained to administer them, will certainly exhibit some other form of power than that witnessed by the only biblical figure who was there at both the manger and the cross, that is, Mary, the mother of God.

And just as Mary was present at the manger and at the cross, the same can be said of us. As readers and hearers of the Word, we, too, are there at the manger and at the cross. We, too, are called to give witness to the One who has scattered the proud, brought down rulers, and lifted up the humble. If Protestants are persuaded to ponder Gabriel's words to Mary, "Greetings, favored one! The Lord is with you," and to give closer attention to the biblical figure of Mary, they will find that through Mary their attention is drawn more closely and more powerfully to Christ and to the vocation to give witness to the greatness of God Incarnate, who was born in a manger and died on a cross.

# NOTES

1. This latter designation has never received official Roman Catholic approval and remains highly controversial.
2. Karl Barth, *Church Dogmatics*, I/2, *The Doctrine of the Word of God* (Edinburgh: T & T Clark, 1978), 140.
3. Ibid., 140.
4. John Calvin, *A Harmony of the Gospels, Matthew, Mark and Luke*, in *Calvin's Commentaries*, vol. 1 (Grand Rapids: Wm. B. Eerdmans Pub. Co., 1972), 22.
5. Shirley C. Guthrie, *Christian Doctrine*, rev. ed. (Louisville, Ky.: Westminster John Knox Press, 1994), 235.
6. Christopher Morse, *Not Every Spirit: A Dogmatics of Christian Disbelief* (Valley Forge, Pa.: Trinity Press International, 1994), 153.
7. James Barr, *Fundamentalism* (Philadelphia: The Westminster Press, 1978), 175–6. "Since the virgin birth is known from only very few biblical passages, and since there is no compelling reason for believing in it apart from these passages, a person who says he believes in it is demonstrating his willingness to believe in a quite extraordinary event on the basis of scripture alone."
8. Beverly Gaventa, *Mary: Glimpses of the Mother of Jesus* (Columbia, S.C.: University of South Carolina Press, 1995; Minneapolis: Fortress Press, 1999), 129.
9. See Gaventa's reflections on Luke's account of Mary and Elizabeth in *Mary*, 51–59.
10. Karl Barth, *Dogmatics in Outline* (London: SCM Press, 1949), 99.
11. Ibid.
12. Morse, *Not Every Spirit*, 236–37.
13. Her response of faithfulness indicates "perfect co-operation with the grace of God" as well as "perfect openness to the action of the Holy Spirit." Pope John Paul II, "Our Lady Intended to Remain a Virgin," General Audience, July 24, 1996. Found on Catholic Information Network (CINB), August 8, 1996 (www.cin.org/jp960724.html).
14. See John Calvin, *New Testaments Commentaries*, 1.22.
15. Two scripture passages point clearly to Mary's connection with (rather than her unique distinction from) all others. In the first, when Jesus is told that his mother and brothers are outside waiting for him, he responds, "Who are my mother and brothers? . . . Whoever does God's will is my brother and sister and mother" (Mark 3: 31–34). In like manner, when a woman calls from a crowd, "Blessed is the mother who gave you birth and nursed you," Jesus says, "Blessed rather are those who hear the word of God and obey it" (Luke 11: 27–28).
16. The doctrine of vocation, as I have described it in other essays, also argues that there are no expendable, worthless human beings. The purpose into which we each are called is not calculated in terms of productivity, though there are situations in which we are meant to be productive, but neither can our divinely appointed purpose be compressed into mere biological existence. For all of us, at some point in our lives, our vocation includes dying. Hence, we neither destroy human beings because we believe their lives are worthless, nor do we believe that a person's divinely appointed purpose is fulfilled as long as he or she can breathe in and out.
17. This affirmation, however, is transformed into a burden whenever the emphasis is shifted from may to must, from permission to requirement, so that glorifying

God in all that we do becomes a law of Christian discipleship rather than an expression of joyful gratitude for what God has done for us.

18. In response to the question "What is the chief and highest end of man?" *The Larger Catechism* of the Westminster Standards answers, "to glorify God, and fully to enjoy him forever" (*Book of Confessions* [Louisville, Ky.: Geneva Press, 1996], 249).

19. As Beverly Gaventa points out, when the image shifts to Mary's perfection the scandal is lost. "The Protevangelium of James associates Mary with scandal, but it does so only to show, and with relentless insistence, that the scandal is a vicious lie" (*Mary*, 129).

20. Papal letter to women issued in preparation for the Beijing Conference, dated June 29 and released July 10, 2001, at the Vatican (http://www.vatican.va/archive/catechism/ccc_toc.htm).

21. As Beverly Gaventa points out, if Mary were not a *female* biblical character, commentators would not hesitate to describe her as a theologian, for she is portrayed as one who interprets and proclaims the Gospel, who reflects and gives witness to Christ, just as all disciples are called to do (*Mary*, 130).

# 6

# Proud Mary

*Contextual Constructions of a Divine Diva*

CHERYL A. KIRK-DUGGAN

With all of the Emily, Hosefina, Sita, Younghee, and Taylor female birth names in the world, millions of parents still name their infant daughters "Mary." As George M. Cohan once composed, "Mary, Mary, it's a grand old name." Tied to the Hebrew Bible name "Miriam," "Mary" is rooted in ideas of sorrow, trouble, rebellion, and disobedience. The name of Mary conjures up a myriad of images for the general public and has specific connotations for Roman Catholic believers. Protestants don't know quite what to make of her.

Who is this Mary, also known as the Madonna, the Holy Mother, the *Mater Misericordia*—immortalized in poetry, anthems, and spirituals; captured in clay, stone, wood, oils, and glass? Is Mary *theotokos*, the God bearer, and what does that say in 2002? If we took the Mary of the Gospels and transported her to our twenty-first-century world, how would that Mary fare? Would she be categorized as an unwed mother? Diagnosed as delusional or schizophrenic? Compared to the virtuous woman in Proverbs 31? Would Mary be placed in a convent or foster care? Is Mary so associated with the transcendent that we are afraid to speak too concretely about her? What about variations on Mary, like the Black Madonnas (of Marsat, France; of Einsiedeln, Switzerland; of Czestochowa, Poland) or Our Lady of Guadalupe? What are we to make of the varied cultural depictions and representations of Mary in art, literature, and film? For example, would Mary be viewed as a mirror to, or antithesis of, the protagonist in John Pielmeier's play *Agnes of God*?[1]

In evoking all of these images and questions about Mary, I am developing a working profile of a "Proud Mary" (in the words of Tina Turner, by the song of the same title).[2] Mary is, I believe, a sociocultural figure who symbolizes the embodiment of a vibrant, wise woman with maternal and earthy instincts. She is a collage: a representation of a continuum of personality traits in dynamic tension. Along these lines, I wonder, What can we learn by comparing the mysterious Mary of the Gospels to "Proud Mary"? Proud Mary is simultaneously young and old, wise and playful, committed to relationships and excellence, to love and compassion. She is a sensual, sexual being who is most intimate with God. Proud Mary works hard, has a sense of humor, and honors the earth and all of its fruits. She is artistic, has an abundance of common sense, is respected by her community, and is self-assured. I use the rock song "Proud Mary" as a lens for a Protestant reading of Mary because it mirrors both the biblical concern for women's oppression and the Bible's vision of who women really are.

In this essay I engage a wide variety of cultural, biblical, and theological images of Mary from a womanist perspective. After providing a brief overview of traditional Protestant and feminist readings of Mary and my view of womanist theological analysis, I then draw from Turner's lyrics in considering who Proud Mary might be. Next I set Proud Mary in conversation with biblical and theological understandings of Mary, constructing a prototype for Mary from the related Lukan and Matthean texts and in conversation with Leonardo Boff and Andrew Greeley. In dialogue with a Marian matrix devised by Pamela Thomas and Luke Buckles, I conclude with a constructive analysis of a biblical, theological, cinematographic Proud Mary by building on a relational womanist biblical and film analysis. I do this via consideration of a collage of maternal images in three films: *Eve's Bayou*, *Down in the Delta*, and *Soul Food*.

## PROTESTANT AND FEMINIST READINGS OF MARY

Many Protestant thinkers emphasize Mary's limited biblical presence, her secondary importance to Christ, and her failure to contribute anything to the divine grace. For Barth, Mary as virgin mother is the guarantor of christological dogma and orthodoxy—the virgin birth directs us toward the character of the incarnation. Barth attacks Roman Catholic Mariology because he understands it to focus on Mary and not on Christ. Tillich argues that Mary should not be elevated because her first child was not yet Christ, but Jesus of Nazareth. Jesus became the Christ—the New Being—after his resurrection. Tillich thus denies Mary's divine maternity, her alleged fullness of grace, and the virgin birth.[3] While some scholars expunge Mary, others, like Els Maeckelberghe, seek to explore, redefine, or salvage her.[4]

Maeckelberghe reviews a spectrum of feminist interpretations of Mary.[5] According to Maeckelberghe, Halkes, Ruether, and Fiorenza draw from Mary in developing ecclesiologies that seek to transform systemic sexism. Tine

Halkes prescribes Mary as an antidote to patriarchal religion. Rosemary Radford Ruether constructs a systematic, experiential treatment of Mary as a vision of new church. Elizabeth Schüssler Fiorenza explores Mary as a myth that can be life-guiding but often perpetuates a kyriarchal culture that oppresses women and proffers mind-body schizophrenia.[6]

Johnson, Gebara, and Bingemer focus on a hermeneutics of liberation and anthropology that elevates Mary to a sphere of prominence and freedom. Elizabeth A. Johnson explores Mary statements theologically toward new, accessible interpretations that can produce believing disciples, new faith, and liberation. Ivone Gebara and Maria Clara L. Bingemer, rooted in the experience of women and Latin America, construct a dialogical, theological anthropology that views Mary as the Mother of God and the Mother of the Poor.[7]

Daly, Ochs, Mulack, Goldenberg, and Kassel engage the concept of Mary as deity or archetype. Mary Daly sees Mary as archimage, the elemental creature and Great Original Witch in every one, as a strategy to refute the Catholic appropriation of Mary and the Protestant abolition of Mary. Carol Ochs, Christa Mulack, and Naomi Goldenberg construct or reject Mary in relationship to a variety of different readings of Goddess, a loaded term that has multiple and diverse elements under one rubric: a problematic analysis. Maria Kassel constructs a Jungian reading of Mary as female archetype. She represents a basic, universal human need, central for the psychological process of one rising to consciousness.[8]

Though these thinkers have diverse points of departure, they all work to remove layers of oppressive interpretation that muddy the Mary image. Womanist theory represents another way of seeing that can be used to illumine the symbol of Mary.

## WOMANIST THEOLOGICAL ANALYSIS: A LIBERATORY, REVOLUTIONARY MODEL

Womanist theory invites us to live in present time, as students of life and history, radically listening, discerning, seeing, knowing, and engendering excellence. Womanist thought, as theory and praxis, realizes the significance of critical thinking, perspicacity, and prayer. This analysis advocates unending intellectual and spiritual discourse to help people experience abundant and healthy lives.

Womanist theory is interdisciplinary and multifaceted, building on the lives, oral traditions, and writings of African-American women. Womanist theory is a strategy for naming, exposing, interrogating, and helping to transform the oppression of all people, especially those affected by gender, race, and class discrimination. Womanists support the struggle for freedom as a God-given gift and a right.

Womanist theory undergirds and frames womanist theological ethics. "Womanist," derived by Alice Walker from the term "womanish," refers to women of African descent who are outrageous, audacious, in charge, and responsible.[9] Womanist theological ethics is talking about God, in relation to human behavior, from the perspectives of women of African descent. Womanist theological ethicists critically assess our living and our value systems in concert with the Divine, analyzing and exposing injustices perpetrated by the abuse of power.

A womanist emancipatory theological ethics embraces hope and revolution toward engendering mutuality and community. Honoring the *imago dei* in all persons, womanist theological ethics builds on the vital goodness of humanity, focusing on liberation from personal, societal, and theological-ethical fragmentation. This way of seeing questions the status quo's criteria for assessing quality of life, critiques decision making, and asks how our assumptions affect and are affected by our social, political, economic, and cultural environment.

The cultural theory of bell hooks and critical social theory of Patricia Collins support such oppositional thinking and provide a framework for the subversive pedagogy and epistemology advocated by womanist theological ethicists. According to hooks, we must target discourse that diminishes ideas; destroys possibilities; and denigrates spirits, communities, individuals, and bodies. hooks uses "killing rage" as a form of powerful resistance: oppositional thinking that repositions us toward transformation and love. Because rage can be consuming, it must be tempered "by an engagement with a full range of emotional responses" to employ us in self-determination."[10] Killing rage, as both a destructive and creative force, gives us the choice to comply or resist, to be harmful or hopeful.

Seen through the lens of hooks's "killing rage," Patricia Hill Collins's notion of the intellectual subverts structures that ostensibly honor difference but actually perpetuate oppression. According to Collins, to be an intellectual is not tantamount to having a middle-class education or to working in the academy. Collins insists "[o]ne is neither born an intellectual nor does one become one by earning a degree. Rather, doing intellectual work of the sort envisioned within Black feminism or womanism requires a process of self-conscious struggle on behalf of Black women, regardless of the actual social location where that work occurs."[11] This subversive work requires that one (1) observe the connections between the dialectics of oppression and activism,

(2) live in the tension between experience and ideas, (3) celebrate knowledge as resistance, and (4) ask hard questions.[12]

## WOMAN, ROLLIN' ON THE RIVER: THERE'S SOMETHING ABOUT PROUD MARY

In Jungian terms, the Mary of scripture and tradition is an archetype created by men to personify the patriarchally devised tendencies of the feminine principle. Mary as a modern symbol for women, by contrast, is one who is not controlled and manipulated by others. She has tremendous self-respect and a healthy sense of sisterhood.[13] She is one who embodies a womanist sensibility, living life with passion and joy.

"Proud Mary," sung by Tina Turner, is a song that bears witness to the complexities of many women's daily lives. As the song unfolds, Proud Mary chooses to leave the city and her quite profitable job where she is oppressed by a dominant, patriarchal, Eurocentric system. Despite the comfort her job in the city may afford, the cost of oppression is too high. This womanist diva leaves the security of her position and goes to work near the river, a metaphor for the rhythms of life and community with reciprocity. The "Big Wheel," evoking the image of wheels on river boats, symbolizes the process of change over time. Proud Mary is pragmatic and optimistic. A self-assured woman, she thinks for herself and revels in the mysteries of life. She works hard in cities and places by rivers; she experiences pain but is not bitter. Proud Mary knows life on the river as a place where people will not be without, because those who live on the river are communitarian. They enjoy the opportunity of sharing and giving to others.[14]

Womanist analysis might engage these images by asking, Who lives on a river? What are the options for people who are not wealthy? Do these rivers have healing powers? What about the toxic waste dumps created by allowing waste to spew into our rivers and streams? Does Proud Mary have advantages that might frighten women of means?

The struggle to answer these questions provokes further reflection on who this Proud Mary is: She is a womanist who is concerned about human flourishing and the survival of people. She has a strong connection to nature and the earth. She is sentient of the seasons and cycles of her life. She fully embodies her physical, mental, emotional self and pulsates with vitality. The "Big Wheel" signifies her exuberance, sexuality, sensuality, and passion. She is outrageous and courageous. But she does not always make the right choices. And not everyone appreciates who she is. Paradoxically, the same river that is full

of life and supports the lives of others is one that can drown and destroy. Yet
Proud Mary is not fearful or complacent; nor does she take life for granted.
Proud Mary lives in the moment.

## WOMAN CHOSEN BY GOD, SHAPED BY HUMANITY

### Mary in Luke and Matthew

In the Gospels of Luke and Matthew, Mary's life is paradoxical: chosen to be
the mother of Christ, she is at the same time exploited as a poor Jewish woman
under imperialistic Roman rule. Mary was a refugee; the displaced immigrant;
a shrewd, hard-working woman. She suffered the persecution of Herod, fretted over Jesus' well-being and ministry, and watched his persecution. Her
strategy for confronting oppression unfolds within the Magnificat. Mary's
Magnificat is a personal, communal, socioeconomic, and moral statement that
praises God and celebrates freedom from injustice. Significantly, it recognizes
that God has direct interest in a woman, for God meets Mary in her humiliation and helps her and her child.[15] Interpreted through the lens of womanist
wisdom, Mary proclaims a cultural revolution favoring the poor, an economic
revolution where the poor can receive good things, and a political revolution
where the poor can access power. Culturally, Mary symbolizes the possibility
for all of low estate to be elevated by God and to be honored and blessed by
all generations (Luke 1:48). An economic revolution emerges as those who are
lowly are exalted and those who are hungry are filled with good things (Luke
1:53). Politically, just as God raised Abraham and gave him posterity forever,
the poor can also, by this birthright, have the same access to power. With
Mary's son, the poor participate in the lineage of David, Abraham, and Adam
and are the sons and daughters of God (Luke 3:23–38).

Who is this Lucan Mary? A womanist reading presses us to explore the
paradoxical, the less romantic, the experiences that smack of oppression. What
a scandalous blessing to be promised impregnation out of wedlock by the Holy
Spirit! Mary's questions and responses of joy around her pregnancy are certainly understandable. For Luke, this witness testifies to the salvific power of
God.[16] Jane Schaberg warns the reader, however, of the danger of reading the
Gospel of Luke as though it is unambiguously pro-women. Actually, she says,
the evangelist depicts women as keenly subordinate, despite Luke's unique stories about women. Granted, Luke features Elizabeth, Mary, Jesus' mother, and
Anna (Luke 1); the woman who anoints Jesus (7:36–50); women traveling with
Jesus (8:1–3); Martha and Mary (10:38–42); and women at the cross and empty
tomb (23:49; 24:1–12). But Luke also wants to limit the role of women in the

church's prophetic ministry. Elizabeth proclaims Mary as blessed and mother of her Lord; Mary converses with the angel Gabriel and prophesies in the Magnificat. Yet these two are prophets who are not heard; their prayers and study fail to yield decisive action or recognition; the Gospel is a plea for one to be fearless and confess, but it ultimately silences women.[17] Like most biblical stories about women, the Lukan stories about Mary and Elizabeth merely provide a framework for arguing that they were the right mothers for the right children at the right time.

Matthew must also be read with a hermeneutic of suspicion. As some scholars note, Matthew seems to challenge oppressive power structures even in the opening genealogy, associating righteousness with godly actions rather than with social position. The genealogy implies that neither marriage nor wealth is a prerequisite for salvation. Along these lines, Matthew frequently recognizes those who are not in positions of power but whose actions participate in divine purposes. Women are often noted, in Matthew, for their just actions and honor of God. This resonates with womanist sensibilities, where having the power to act for the good is highly valued. Yet Matthew still portrays Mary as passive. As much as Matthew speaks of tyrannical kings and deaths of Hebrew babies, he does not recognize Mary's sociopolitical identity and location as the mother of Jesus.[18]

## Mary in Boff and Greeley

Mary disappears from the Lukan and Matthean texts after Jesus' temple encounter at twelve years and the return from Egypt, respectively. Nonetheless, we assume that she continues to support Jesus in his ministry, trusting and respecting God. Many experience this ongoing relationship of Mary to God as evidence of God's historical activity, of God's *baselia* to come.[19] In the myth of Mary, then, the feminine experience of the divine—God's Wisdom and God's Presence—is familiar, covenantal, and relational.[20] Leonard Boff and Andrew Greeley develop a reading of Mary along these lines that contributes to our understanding of Proud Mary.

From a liberationist perspective, Boff understands Mary to be the mother of God incarnate; as such, she plays an integral part in divine salvation history. Mary as virgin mother is considered by Boff to be a perfect expression of God's freedom. Using the feminine as an organizing anthropological category, Boff upholds Mary as an archetype for Christian service. In Mary we witness a historicized eschatological feminine, able to give and receive.[21] For Boff, Mary's motherhood embraces (1) the divine will to reveal, (2) the divine will to become human, and (3) the human will to become God-like. Mary is a progenitor of Christ in agreeing to participate in the birth of Jesus.

With the vitality of her Magnificat, Mary becomes a liberative, prophetic voice. This Mary can cry with the oppressed, fully understanding that freedom and liberation are available to all. Her Magnificat is a prelude for God's holy, merciful rule, which allows humanity to trust and be in relationship, transforming the old to the new;[22] Mary, in short, symbolizes God.

Sociologist of religion Andrew Greeley offers four images of Mary that can move us to a fuller understanding of who Proud Mary is. First, along the same lines as Boff, he argues that Mary as "Madonna" manifests the gentle, reassuring side of God who inspires hope. Mary mothers us, protects us, and continues to give us life. In her close relationship to us, Mary also experiences ambiguity, the existential anxiety of the conflict between life and death. Second, Greeley associates Mary as "the Virgin" with the onset of creation; she is the primordial, nourishing principle, the wisdom-giving spiritual mother of possibility. Third, Mary as "Sponsa" is the focus of Yahweh's passionate love, the symbol for God's attraction to humanity. Mary as Sponsa invites us to graced, passionate goodness that lets us abandon our fears of nothingness for the freedom of experiencing responsible, joyous abandon in God. Fourth, Mary as the "Pietà" symbolizes a return to the womb at death. The Pietà—or "terrible mother"—also embodies the spaces of ambiguity and ambivalence. In psychology and history, the Pietà who protects her children as a violent, warrior-type mother is also one of reconciliation, where political methodology allows competition and reconciliation to stand in tension. This mother of sorrows stands with us in hope, as we face the terrifying, temporary life status on earth.

These various models for Mary move us to action, then contemplation. For Greeley, the Madonna causes us to enrich and protect the world. The Virgin persuades us to engage in sustained commitment to others. Sponsa encourages us to joyous celebration of the glories of the world. The Pietà is the powerful, fierce, protective mother who symbolizes our struggles for dignity, justice, and freedom against all evils of bigotry, injustice, and oppression.[23] We look for such a Mary in the world of film.


## WOMEN WONDERFUL AND COMPLEX:
## MARY ON SCREEN

"The secrets that hold us together can also tear us apart. . . . Memory is a selection of images, some elusive, others printed indelibly on the brain. The summer I killed my father, I was 10 years old." Opening with these words, *Eve's Bayou*[24] recalls Eve's childhood memories of growing up in a loving, gifted, but troubled extended family, descendants of slaves, and of her quest for her own truth. Kasi Lemmons's *Eve's Bayou*, set in Southern Louisiana Gothic bayou country, tells the Batiste's family story, headed by charming Doctor Louis. Married to beautiful Roz, Louis plays around with his women patients: "To a certain type of woman, I am a hero," Louis says. "I need to be a hero." One night at a party, Louis flirts with married, sexy Metty Mereaux. Unknown to him, his young, idealistic, impressionable daughter Eve sees them. Louis tells her not to tell. Traumatized, Eve shares this secret with her sister, Cisely, and the lying begins.

While Eve does not understand everything she sees, this story unfolds as her memories are filtered through the eyes of Cisely and her Aunt Mozelle, one with prophetic vision for all except herself. Other family members include Louis's matriarchal mother and son Poe. What happened the summer of 1962, when Eve's handsome father took one chance too many? What happened late one night between the father and Cisely, in a moment that was over before it began? What do you do when dangerous emotions build to the point of exploding, where no one is really responsible, but the things that happen can never be taken back? A womanist reading holds the ambiguity in tension with the quest for clarity and the need for truth telling.

The females in Eve's story provide complex characteristics ensconced in multiple memories and shaped by possibilities of misinterpretations—demonstrating both the potential and dysfunctional possibilities of a Proud Mary. The bayou is the metaphor for how secrets multiplied can end in tragedy. The secrets oppress and skew reality. The rich tapestry for creating a prototype for Proud Mary involves the joys and complications of personal and familial relationships. The persona of Proud Mary runs the gamut from a tough, matriarchal disciplinarian with hidden love to that of inner and outer beauty, smothered by allegiance to a philandering husband. She cares for her children and is intelligent but has become too distant. Mozelle, as Proud Mary, is a sensual, prophetic woman who takes time with the children and is assertive, earthy, and vibrant. Cisely, as a youthful embodiment of Proud Mary, symbolizes the confusion of adolescence, the instability of hormonal changes and a budding awareness of sexuality, and the need to be loved. Eve, a slightly younger, yet quite independent version of Proud Mary, exudes truthfulness, childhood innocence, and a creative curiosity. Amid typical sibling rivalry, Poe, the younger brother, is endearing to most and a pain to others.

A womanist reading of George Tillman Jr.'s *Soul Food*,[25] another family story released the same year as *Eve's Bayou*, juxtaposes physical and spiritual life and death. Set in urban Chicago, *Soul Food* connects mind, body, and soul. Among a loving, if dysfunctional, extended family, there is character, conflict, and growth. Soul food is a metaphor for the revitalization of the Joseph family's souls and for the strengthening of their relationships as they participate in the forty-year-old traditional ritual of going to Mama's every Sunday for dinner. When Big Mama Joseph, the family's matriarchal anchor, can no longer create this weekly feast, she calls on her three daughters to help. Teri, an icy, high-powered attorney, is tired of helping everyone financially. Teri's husband, Miles (also an attorney), wants to do music as a full-time career. Maxine, a happily married mom with husband (Kenny) and two children, is the most stable daughter. Our narrator and guide is their older son Ahmad, a twelve-year-old who has a special relationship with Big Mama. The film opens as the third grown daughter, Bird, is getting married. Her groom, Lem, has good intentions, but his prison record thwarts his ambitions. Warm, humorous moments contrast with dramatic segments of tension, hurt feelings, and misunderstandings. When Big Mama is hospitalized, things fall apart. Competition, infidelity, financial crises, jealousies, and broken dreams all erupt. Everyone forgets Big Mama's lesson: "One finger pointing blame can't make no impact. But five fingers balled up can deliver a mighty blow. This family has got to be that fist." After Big Mama dies, Ahmad steps in as the emotional heart of the family and is the only one that can get them back to Big Mama's house once again.

Once more we learn the family story through the eyes of a youth. How the family members each relate to Big Mama helps create a profile of Proud Mary. Big Mama celebrates family connections—serving love, intimacy, humor, and wisdom with her cuisine. She teaches us what happens when you love too much when she almost sacrifices her health for her family. The bond Big Mama has with Ahmad is one of cherished communication. Despite all her insensitivity around who owes her what, Teri really cares for her family; it is her insecurity that fuels her carelessness. Maxine helps keep the peace and openness; Bird brings an entrepreneurial spirit but has to learn to respect the boundaries and needs of others. The familial relationships depict the reality of good times and bad, the need to shield the dignity of others when they fall short. Individual and familial strengths and weaknesses, the import of dignity and caring, and the aesthetics of childlike innocence tempered by grandparental joy weave throughout. We celebrate the impact of sexuality, sensuality, and pride, the errors that emerge around vulnerability and misguided help, and the gifts of starting over. A womanist reading of a film that begins in Chicago but moves to the Mississippi delta follows the journey that seeks to mend broken, fragile spirits amid a reunion and reclamation of memory.

Maya Angelou's *Down in the Delta*[26] is a poignant, motivational story in which the Sinclair familial reconnections emerge, framed by new beginnings and the unearthing of deep-rooted family traditions. The two Sinclair families are both dealing with loss, disappointment, and illness. Grandmother Rosa Lynn, a hardworking, wise, gentle woman, heads the Northern household.

Her daughter, Loretta, is addicted to drugs and alcohol and has little education. Grandson Thomas is an energetic, smart, budding entrepreneur. Grand-
daughter Tracy is autistic. The Southern family consists of Earl, the keeper of
family oral history, and his wife, Annie, an Alzheimer's patient. Their son,
Will, and his family live in Atlanta. Rosa Lynn sees that Loretta is spiraling
into oblivion and that she must do something drastic. She sends Loretta and
the children away to live with Uncle Earl in Mississippi. To afford the cost of
passage, Rosa Lynn pawns a silver candelabrum—a family heirloom fondly
known as "Nathan." Nathan had served as collateral at a slave auction, many
years before, to purchase their great, great grandfather.

While the unfolding of the story is much too simplistic—Loretta goes to
Uncle Earl's without any resistance to her grandmother, for example—one
must note what the film reveals. The forces creating poverty, miseducation,
and prejudices; the diversity within all families; and the impact of a healthy
environment on personal well-being cannot be overstated. Once relocated,
Loretta works with her uncle at the family restaurant and learns about family
history since slavery. We learn of their story through Loretta's recovery,
inspired partially by the industrious nature of her young son, Thomas.

This intergenerational story resonates with Proud Mary, creating a collage
of inner beauty, strength, and good will. There is a connection to earth and
nature as a place of working and healing. For young and old, hope and dreams
are critical to sustaining a balanced life marked by family togetherness.
Loretta symbolizes fear, pain, miseducation, and a propensity to addiction.
We learn about the importance of persistence, rituals, and memory. Nathan
(the candelabrum) symbolizes overcoming—a link with the possibility for justice. Illness also becomes a reality that cannot be defeated. We learn that to
be ill is not a cause for shame and denial but for understanding and compassion. Humor remains good medicine when all the hope and faith in the world
cannot make an autistic child not be autistic. The tenacity of Thomas, Rosa
Lynn, and Uncle Earl prevails, and Loretta gets her life back in a way that
could have never happened in the desolate, urban sprawl of her drug-infested
neighborhood.

## WINNOWING THE MANNA:
## PROUD MARY UNVEILED THROUGH AN OPAQUE LENS

Will the real Proud Mary come forth? Thomas and Buckles have created a
four-fold Marian matrix[27] located within the mysteries of Christian belief
(incarnation, crucifixion, resurrection); theological virtues (faith, hope, charity); elements of human condition (being, character, journey); and goals of the

human quest (truth, wisdom, compassion). This model forms a helpful rubric for creating the composite of Proud Mary that emerges from this analysis.

Within the mysteries of Christian belief, Proud Mary is created in the *imago dei*. She is a spiritual being with a soulful essence, both gracious and gregarious. She knows deep and painful suffering though she is not a masochist. The pain comes from personal and familial crises. Sometimes it comes when she is abused or hurt from good intentions. Proud Mary daily experiences resurrection, as the Queen of Heaven, the queen of her household, the matriarch whose faith allows her to see each day as new. Her gift for being a young/old wise woman usually gives her a sense of purpose, grounded in hope.

From the perspective of theological virtues, Proud Mary is faithful. She believes when there is no proof. She believes in God/Spirit and in the spirit within humanity. She lives in hope as the big wheel of tragedy and triumph, of poverty or affluence, orders her ability to give of herself and her resources. She knows charity as she loves and helps those who are in need. She has a sense of aesthetics that allows her to be gracious amidst pain, to work hard, and to extend joy and compassion. Proud Mary wants to see the best in people and is sometimes disappointed. Though she may become disillusioned, her resilience affords her an ability to relate to the strength of others as she moves through the world: sometimes in defiance, other times as a matter of fact.

The elements of the human condition are those of her own reality. She is the fierce Pietà, the protective Madonna, the committed Virgin, the welcoming Sponsa; at once fragile and sturdy. She is simultaneously flawed and perfect, sensual and sexual, a public yet quite private person. Proud Mary knows the character of herself and especially of her children. She is a trustworthy leader and helpful companion. She is an independent spirit with a big heart. Proud Mary knows she is on a journey, crossing portals of the known and unknown. And she is there to journey with others, out of the hell of addiction, through labor pains, through graduations and weddings, at the dawn of birth and the sunset of death.

The goals of the human quest are written on Proud Mary's heart. As *theotokos*, Proud Mary dwells with Jesus, the New Being, as incarnated love. She knows a fundamental transcendence that radiates within and without. Her home may be humble, but the transcendental space she creates transforms it into a palace. She may be wealthy, but her humility puts one instantly at ease. Proud Mary may not be affluent in material things, but her spirit is opulent. Her gifts of discernment grant her ancient wisdom that allows her to have close, intimate relationships with lots of extended family. She embodies compassion. Proud Mary has a sympathetic consciousness that knows distress along with the desire to alleviate it. The collage of women and men from the Batiste, the Josephs, and the Sinclair families have this consciousness: an awareness of that "big wheel" of love that beyond anything else symbolizes God, faith, and possibility. Proud Mary knows that no one is ever alone. And like those on the river, she has the tenacity and the God-ness to know when to say "No" and the freedom to be "happy to give." Proud Mary is embodied in the lives of African American women. She is womanist: she not only survives but transcends. She makes out of rags quilts that get hung in the Smithsonian. She makes soul food that becomes haute cuisine. Admired by some, and feared by others, Proud Mary is who she is, without apology.

> Proud Mary, awesome:
> Spirit soaring, unbound; free
> Loves her family.[28]

## NOTES

1. *Agnes of God* is a story about the birth of a baby to an alleged virgin who is convinced she was never pregnant, thus never had a baby, and could not have murdered it.
2. See the title song of *Proud Mary: The Best of Ike & Tina Turner* (CD Emd/Capitol, B00000DRC5, 1991). The song was debuted at the Creedence Clearwater Revival in 1969, though composer John Fogerty did not himself perform it until November 3, 1991, at a Grateful Dead concert. Tina Turner, truly a Proud Mary, has immortalized and made this her signature song.
3. Thomas A. O'Meara, *Mary in Protestant and Catholic Theology* (New York: Sheed & Ward, 1966), 213–220, 233–238, 346.
4. See Els Maeckelberghe, *Desperately Seeking Mary: A Feminist Appropriation of a Traditional Religious Symbol* (Kampen, Netherlands: Kok Pharos, 1991).
5. Ibid., 13–34, 40–41.
6. Ibid., 13–20.
7. Ibid., 21–25.
8. Ibid., 25–34.
9. Alice Walker, *In Search of Our Mother's Gardens: Womanist Prose* (New York: Harcourt Brace Jovanovich, 1983), ix.
10. bell hooks, *Killing Rage: Ending Racism* (New York: Henry Holt, 1995), 19.
11. Patricia Hill Collins, *Black Feminist Thought: Knowledge, Consciousness, and the Politics of Empowerment*, 2nd ed. (New York: Routledge, 2000), 15.
12. Ibid., 22, 25, 29, 33.
13. Patricia Noone, *Mary For Today* (Chicago: Thomas More Press, 1977), 15, 154.
14. Fogerty, "Proud Mary."
15. Jane Schaberg, "Luke," in *The Women's Bible Commentary*, ed. Carol A. Newsome and Sharon H. Ringe (Louisville, Ky.: Westminster/John Knox Press, 1992), 275–292.
16. R. Alan Culpepper, "Luke" in *The New Interpreter's Bible: A Commentary in Twelve Volumes*, vol. 8 (Nashville: Abingdon Press, 1995), 52–53, 55–56.
17. Schaberg, "Luke" 275, 276, 278, 281.
18. Amy-Jill Levine, "Matthew," in Newsome and Ringe, *The Women's Bible Commentary*, 252–262.

19. Edward Schillebeeckx, *Mary, Mother of the Redemption* (New York: Sheed & Ward, 1964), xv, 3, 5, 27.

20. Rosemary Radford Ruether, *Mary—The Feminine Face of the Church* (Philadelphia: Westminster Press, 1977), 30.

21. Leonardo Boff, *The Maternal Face of God: The Feminine and Its Religious Expressions*, trans. Robert R. Barr and John W. Diercksmeier (San Francisco: Harper & Row, 1987), 9–13, 107–114, 116–121.

22. Ibid., 153–158, 190–196.

23. Andrew Greeley, *The Mary Myth: On the Femininity of God* (New York: Seabury Press, 1977), 5, 17, 106–114, 120, 133, 139, 142, 145, 157–168, 187–195.

24. *Eve's Bayou*, dir. Kasi Lemmons, Trimark Pictures, 1997.

25. *Soul Food*, dir. George Tillman Jr., Twentieth Century Fox, 1997.

26. *Down in the Delta*, dir. Maya Angelou, Miramax, 1998.

27. Fr. Luke Buckles and Pamela Thomas developed this model while teaching the course "Spirituality, Art, & Mary" at the Dominican School of Philosophy and Theology, Graduate Theological Union, Berkeley.

28. Verse by Cheryl A. Kirk-Duggan, ©2002.

# 7

# Ignored Virgin or Unaware Women

## A Mexican-American Protestant Reflection on the Virgin of Guadalupe[1]

### Nora O. Lozano-Díaz

According to Stephen B. Bevans, the contextualization of theology is imperative if it is going to be pertinent.[2] Since human beings have different stories,
contexts, and perspectives, it is clear that the work of theology cannot take
place in a vacuum. The last decades have witnessed an increased tendency to
acknowledge how the theologian's particular perspective affects the theological task. The corollary is that the classical notion of an objective, general, universal, unchanging theology has been accused of being oppressive, irrelevant,
and false. For theology to be life-giving, it needs to be grounded in a specific
context where a community can recognize it, relate to it, welcome it, and be
challenged by it.

Among the contextual theologies that have flourished in the last decades are
several feminist and women's theologies that affirm the need to take the experiences of women as a theological foundation.[3] As I ponder the foundations of
a Latina women's Protestant theology, I too avow the importance of incorpo-
rating Latina Protestant women's experiences as a theological source. These
experiences are grounded in a specific context: the Latino culture. Traditionally, Latino Protestantism has had a tense relationship with Latino culture. It
has dismissed many elements of the culture due to their connections with
Catholicism. This disregard for contextual experience suggests a need to
reevaluate the roots and motivations behind this reaction toward culture. Furthermore, this reevaluation necessitates review of the whole Protestant relationship to culture in order to challenge what is oppressive in it and to recoup
what is powerful and life-giving. As I explore the topic of the Lady of
Guadalupe, I present some preliminary thoughts toward this goal.

I want to identify myself as a Protestant woman who looks at life and theology from a bridge.[4] By looking from this bridge, as Leticia Guardiola-Sáenz describes it, I desire to recognize and honor the experiences that identify me as a Mexican as well as a Mexican-American woman.[5] In some areas of the border, the Mexican and U.S. lands stand united geographically by a bridge. These physical channels help me to imagine a cultural bridge where I can stand in order to incorporate my experiences in both of these cultures. The bridge I envision, then, distinguishes my Mexican and Mexican-American experience from other cultural and faith expressions.

## THE IGNORED VIRGIN

I grew up in a Mexican Protestant home. My parents have been active members in the Baptist church for as long as I can remember. As I was growing up in this Baptist home, the Lady of Guadalupe was not present in my immediate environment. Little by little, however, given her extensive presence in Mexico, I became aware of her existence. Early in my elementary school years I remember seeing the golden medals with the image of the Lady of Guadalupe that many of my classmates wore as a sign of devotion and protection. I remember hearing, on national television, slogans such as "*Todos los mexicanos somos Guadalupanos*" ("Every Mexican is a *Guadalupano*"). During my teen years, I learned about the apparition of the Lady of Guadalupe to Juan Diego thanks to a television show with one of my favorite actresses.

According to the Catholic story of how Roman Catholicism came to Mexico, the Lady of Guadalupe appeared in 1531 to an indigenous man called Juan Diego. She referred to herself as *Tlecuauhtlacupeuh*, which the Spaniards heard as "Guadalupe." She addressed Juan Diego as her son and told him that she was his mother. She asked Juan Diego to build a temple for her and promised to comfort all who suffer.[6] My Protestant family, however, told me that this story was only a superstition—that the apparition never happened.

Similarly, the Lady of Guadalupe was essentially ignored in my Protestant church. In fact, she is not acknowledged at all in the Protestant tradition. If Protestant people refer to the Virgin, they talk about the Virgin Mary, the biblical Mary who was the mother of Jesus. But even these references do not occur very often.

One reason for overlooking the Virgin Mary may be found in the way that Hispanic American Protestantism developed, for it has harbored since the beginning a radical anti-Catholic feeling:

> Against the baroque style and ostentation of the Catholic temples, the Evangelical halls were places without any decoration. The most that Protestants would allow was some biblical texts on the walls. Many of

them would consider it a sign of idolatry to hang a cross, even an empty one, or to have pictures with the image of Jesus. Against the Roman ritualism, the Evangelicals reacted by having a spontaneous worship service, many times an improvised one. . . . If the Catholic Church was bound with the State and the political powers, the Evangelicals preached indifference and abstention before all social and political matters. At other times they would proclaim an open opposition against any social or political participation.[7]

Given that the Virgin Mary is so central to Catholicism, she became also a casualty of this anti-Catholic perspective. The Protestants, in an effort to differentiate themselves from the Catholic Church, rejected and dismissed even the biblical Mary. They did this simply by ignoring her.

Protestant churches ignore the Virgin Mary in two primary ways: in the naming ritual and with a shunning silence. An examination of the *círculos femeniles* (women's church groups) reveals that no group adopts the name of Mary. One finds these groups embracing the names of other female biblical characters—Esther, Deborah, Martha, Mary (Lazarus's sister), Ruth, Sarah, Lydia, Rachel—or the groups are named after a local or foreign woman missionary.[8] Likewise, most Hispanic Protestant families would never name their daughters "Maria" or "Guadalupe." They would feel proud of the names of other biblical women but not that of Mary. The lack of reference to the Virgin Mary in traditional Protestant sermons and Bible studies symbolizes another way the Virgin Mary is ignored in Protestant churches. Sometimes she is mentioned during Christmas or Easter, but the rest of the year she is mostly ignored.

The effort of Protestant families and churches to ignore the Lady of Guadalupe, however, is finally futile. As soon as a Protestant family in Mexico gets on a bus to go home after church, for example, they are likely to see a small poster of the Lady of Guadalupe on the dashboard. Protestant children today have the same experiences I had growing up. They constantly hear that *"todos los mexicanos somos Guadalupanos."*

Much of what I have said in relation to Mexican Protestants is also true among Mexican Americans. A Hispanic Protestant woman from the barrio will find images of the Lady of Guadalupe in many of her neighbors' houses and in the windows of Hispanic stores. She will find images of Guadalupe in the graffiti on walls, on posters in the grocery store, or on the T-shirt of the store clerk. Protestant Mexican-American women will certainly see their favorite soap opera characters praying to the Lady of Guadalupe every time they face a problem. The image of the Lady of Guadalupe permeates all of Mexican culture in such a way that she is not only present but also plays a role in the lives of Mexican and Mexican-American Protestant women.

## UNAWARE WOMEN

Since the Lady of Guadalupe is a reality that affects the lives of Mexican and Mexican-American Protestant women, it is important for them to acknowledge her presence and how it affects them. To do so, they need a pertinent way to deal with her. Conceiving of the Lady of Guadalupe as an element of culture is a starting point for Mexican and Mexican-American Protestants. Given the fact that the Lady of Guadalupe has to do with belief, to argue over whether she really appeared to Juan Diego is not helpful. The important element from a Protestant perspective is that the Lady of Guadalupe, due to her extensive presence in society, has become a part of the Mexican and Mexican-American culture.[9]

Many Mexican and Mexican-American Protestant people, however, deny the idea that the Lady of Guadalupe has anything to do with Protestant women. They assert that, since the Lady of Guadalupe is a Catholic figure, she cannot influence the lives of Mexican and Mexican-American Protestant women. Yet the reality is different! She long ago became much more than a Catholic devotional figure: she became a cultural symbol that affects all people of Mexican descent.

A viable explanation for this unawareness or denial of the impact the Lady of Guadalupe exerts among Mexican and Mexican-American Protestants may be informed by reflection on the Protestant view of culture. Protestants have been taught to live primarily as citizens from heaven and not from earth.[10] Thus many Protestants have been encouraged to live their Protestantism outside their culture. This idea of living outside the culture relates to the anti-Catholic perspective mentioned above. Since the culture is seen as permeated with Catholic views, it is desirable, as much as possible, to withdraw oneself from it. In many cases, as soon as a person converts to the Protestant faith, he or she is required to stop dancing, smoking, drinking, playing cards, watching movies, seeing plays, and attending bull fights or horse races. The new believer is taught to see life dualistically: the church and the world exist as opposite and conflicting realities. Thus new believers are required to retreat from the world, from any political or social commitment,[11] and from the culture in general. Although this idea of a heavenly citizenship is a valid one, it is also true that while Mexican and Mexican-American Protestants dwell on earth, they are also citizens and members of an earthly culture: the Latino one. Even though some Protestants have tried to live outside earthly culture, this is not feasible. All human beings live in a culture, and despite the fiercest resistance, the culture affects them.

Mexican and Mexican-American Protestants live in a culture in which the Roman Catholic tradition is a key element. Thus, they are cultural Catholics who live in a cultural Catholic ethos. They live surrounded by Catholic symbols that affect their lives.[12] The roots of this cultural Catholicism are found in a history imbued with conflict and faith. In the sixteenth century, the American continent witnessed a violent clash between Spanish culture and the Aztec/Nahuatl cultures. The Spaniards were zealous Catholics who regarded Roman Catholicism not merely as religion but as a way of life. As the victors, the Spanish imposed their faith and lifestyle on the indigenous people. It is difficult to determine exactly how long it took for Roman Catholicism to become the authentic religion of the people or what elements from the Christian and indigenous religions coalesced in order that the people might accept the Catholic faith.[13] Nevertheless it is certain that the Catholic religion and way of life came to dominate in New Spain.

This Catholic ethos was the ground from which Mexican and Mexican-American Protestantism developed. Although Protestants began developing their own Christian values and lifestyles, they continued to live surrounded by Catholic culture. They became cultural Catholics, Protestants who lived their faith in a Catholic social environment.

These cultural dynamics, however, changed for Mexican and Mexican-American people. Mexican people continue to live in a predominantly Catholic environment, while Mexican Americans experience a third element in these dynamics: the dominant Anglo-Protestant culture. Mexican-American Protestants live their Protestantism inside an immediate Hispanic Catholic culture, yet this Hispanic Catholic culture exists in a predominantly Anglo-Protestant environment. This means that, on the one hand, Mexican-American Protestants are in tension in terms of religious beliefs with the immediate Catholic culture while in agreement with elements of the Anglo-Protestant culture. On the other hand, in most cases, Mexican-American Protestants are in agreement in ethnic terms with the Hispanic Catholic culture and in tension with the Anglo ethnic environment.[14]

Mexican and Mexican-American Protestants need to be aware of the contextual and cultural elements that shape their lives. Furthermore, they need to examine and evaluate these elements. In an effort to resist Catholic culture and maintain Protestant identity, when I was growing up, my siblings and I were not allowed to have a Christmas nativity scene or to participate in the *posadas* because they were Catholic traditions. We did, however, set up a Christmas tree and wait for Santa to bring us our toys. The Christmas tree and Santa Claus traditions are not Christian traditions, but we always followed them without question because they represent the Protestant way of celebrating Christmas that the missionaries gave us. This experience reminds me that Mexican and Mexican-American Protestants must not think in terms of rejecting culture but should consider how they are related to it. Furthermore,

Mexican and Mexican-American Protestants have the task and responsibility of examining their cultural experiences under the light of Jesus and his message of liberation and empowerment for all human beings. This examination entails the acceptance of what is life-giving in the culture and the dismissal of what is oppressive.

## THE LADY OF GUADALUPE: OPPRESSIVE OR LIBERATIVE?

The writer Octavio Paz has described the Virgin of Guadalupe as a symbol of passivity that is an illustration of the feminine condition.[15] In a collection of essays written by the Franciscan Friars of the Immaculate, the Lady of Guadalupe is presented as a sorrowful figure and as an example of perfection, purity, and submission.[16] Sandra Messinger Cypress mentions that, traditionally, the Virgin of Guadalupe has been seen as a saintly woman who has embodied attributes such as virginity, piety, helpfulness, forgiveness, goodness, and devoted and selfless motherhood.[17] Following these writers, one can conclude that the characteristics assigned to Guadalupe are not very liberating for women. These characteristics may be positive in some instances, but when they are abused they become oppressive. Yet these are the characteristics that have been emphasized for Mexican and Mexican-American women. They are at the heart of the cultural patterns of behavior that are normative for these women.

In the book *The María Paradox*, authors Rosa M. Gil and Carmen Inoa Vázquez describe how these characteristics affect the lives of Latinas. They refer to this view of the Virgin Mary as *marianismo*, which defines the traditional ideal role of women following patriarchal views of the Virgin Mary herself.

> *Marianismo* is about sacred duty, self-sacrifice, and chastity. This cultural phenomenon focuses on dispensing care and pleasure, not receiving them. The *marianismo* mentality fosters an environment in which women live in the shadows, literally and figuratively, of their men (father, boyfriend, husband, son), children, and family.[18]

The ten commandments of *marianismo*, according to the authors, are as follows:

1. Do not forget a woman's place.
2. Do not forsake tradition.
3. Do not be single, self-supporting, or independent-minded.
4. Do not put your own needs first.
5. Do not wish for more in life than being a housewife.
6. Do not forget that sex is for making babies—not for pleasure.

7. Do not be unhappy with your man or criticize him for infidelity, gambling, verbal and physical abuse, alcohol or drug abuse.
8. Do not ask for help.
9. Do not discuss personal problems outside the home.
10. Do not change those things that make you unhappy that you can realistically change.

Obviously *marianismo* is an outdated cultural structure that is oppressive for Mexican-American women. Gil and Vázquez highlight that the ultimate expression of *marianismo* is the noble sacrifice of self.[19]

*Marianismo* erodes the self-esteem of Mexican-American women. Although not every element of *marianismo* affects all Mexican and Mexican-American women in the same way and with the same intensity, I believe that all of these women are affected by *marianismo*. Consequently, they need to challenge these cultural stereotypes in order to discover and develop themselves and their self-worth. They must engage in this challenge in order to live fully as human beings made in the image of God.

One way to do this is to look for new readings of the Lady of Guadalupe. Traditionally, the readings of Guadalupe have been from patriarchally oriented views. New readings, therefore, need to come from a feminist liberative perspective that promotes freedom and espouses a holistic life for Mexican and Mexican-American women.

Among scholars who perceive the Virgin as a liberating figure, theologian Jeanette Rodríguez views the encounter between the Virgin and Juan Diego as a liberation event. After the encounter, Juan Diego was able to relate differently to God and the world around him. This liberation moment repeats itself today when Mexican-American Catholic women encounter the Lady of Guadalupe: it is a liberating event for them. Rodríguez stresses that Mexican-American Catholic women know only parts of the Guadalupe event and that they need to learn more about it so as to find in it more options for liberation and empowerment.[20]

Virgilio Elizondo is another Roman Catholic theologian who sees the Virgin as a liberating figure. He sees the apparition of the Lady of Guadalupe in 1531 as a life-giving event for the conquered indigenous people. By appearing to Juan Diego, an Indian man, the lowest of the low, the Lady of Guadalupe brought new hope and life to the indigenous people. She gave them back their dignity. Spaniards had raped many indigenous women, and the mestizo offspring of this violence were seen as a race of illegitimate children. Through her apparition to Juan Diego, the Lady of Guadalupe radically changed this. She legitimized the mestizo race by becoming its mother. Through the Virgin, the indigenous people went from degradation to pride; from rape to purity, dignity, equality, and freedom.[21]

Although the liberating endeavors presented by Rodríguez and Elizondo are valid ones, I believe that they do not address the particular concerns of Mexican and Mexican-American Protestant women. Both writers approach this liberative view of the Virgin through the lens of the Catholic faith and regard the Catholic faith as a central element of their articulations.[22] Since most Mexican and Mexican-American Protestant women do not put their faith in the Virgin, these liberating attempts do not represent an option for them. Second, as Catholic endeavors, these writings do not address the Protestant church's rejection of Mary.

This is not an excuse, however, to continue ignoring the Lady of Guadalupe and the influence she has on the lives of Mexican and Mexican-American women in general. As we saw earlier, the traditional image of Guadalupe has had oppressive effects for women; therefore, Mexican and Mexican-American Protestant women need to deal with her as a cultural symbol. Recognition of and struggle with the pervasive cultural symbol that is Guadalupe will enable these women to find liberation from this patriarchal model of womanhood.

But what is the relationship between a cultural symbol and a religious symbol? A symbol represents a reality of the senses that reveals a meaning related to but not limited to its form. It evokes and invites us to look beyond what is immediately apparent; to consider deeper or overarching meanings and realities.[23] Cultural symbols, therefore, reveal and signify aspects, habits, trends, mentalities, mores, and themes of culture. Wrestling with cultural symbols fosters a heightened understanding of cultural phenomena that exceed the symbol itself. A cultural symbol is widely present and visible in the whole life of a particular community. It may or may not have a religious background and does not necessarily require faith to be appropriated. It affects the whole population whether in a religious or a nonreligious way. On the other hand, religious symbols reveal something about a transcendent, mysterious reality that the senses cannot apprehend, bidding us to participate in a deeper understanding and relationship with this reality. Since they are rooted in a particular faith tradition, they have an effect only in the people who approach them through the eyes of faith.

The Lady of Guadalupe is a cultural symbol for the whole Mexican and Mexican-American population and a religious symbol only for the people who see and relate to her through their faith. An example of this is found in the flag that Miguel Hidalgo y Costilla used in the proclamation of the Mexican independence in 1810. This flag has, in the center, the image of the Lady of Guadalupe and as a background the official Mexican colors—green, white, and red. It is a national symbol that both Catholic and Protestants recognize as part of history. For Catholic people it also has religious significance while for Protestant people it has only cultural, historic meaning.[24]

If Mexican and Mexican-American Protestant women cannot approach the Lady of Guadalupe as a religious symbol, they can look at her through other liberating efforts approached from cultural and feminist perspectives. Such efforts represent attempts to rediscover the Virgin and to rectify the model that she presents for women.

In a powerful essay titled "Guadalupe the Sex Goddess," Sandra Cisneros, a Mexican-American writer, discusses how the traditional image of the Lady of Guadalupe as a pure and virginal mother negatively affects her relationship with her body and her sexuality. In searching for her own liberation, Cisneros finds that she needs a more liberating image of the Lady of Guadalupe. By looking at history, she finds indigenous perspectives and understandings of the Lady of Guadalupe that the church has tried to erase. Cisneros discovers Tonantzin, an Aztec goddess who is a feminine part of the Aztec supreme dual deity. Inside Tonantzin, Cisneros finds a pantheon of other mother goddesses of fertility and sex, such as Tlazolteotl, the patron of the sexual passion, and Coatlicue, the creative/destructive goddess who is not passive and silent but always gathering force around her. By rediscovering the Lady of Guadalupe's roots and meanings as an Aztec goddess who honored sexuality, Cisneros is able to reclaim a more holistic sexuality for herself and for all women of Mexican descent.[25]

As a Protestant woman, I believe that approaches that present the Lady of Guadalupe as a cultural symbol will make an impact in Protestant circles. This approach gives Mexican and Mexican-American Protestant women a way of dealing with the Lady of Guadalupe without having to embrace Catholic understandings of her.

For Protestant Mexican and Mexican-American women, however, the best resource to challenge the traditional image of the Lady of Guadalupe is the Bible, the book that holds greatest authority for them. Through an alternative feminist reading of the Bible that is both liberative and empowering, these women can recover and embrace the biblical Mary and confront the oppressive views of Mary and Guadalupe. If, traditionally, the Virgin Mary has been perceived as a passive woman, an alternative feminist reading of Luke 1:26–38 can suggest the opposite. The fact that she became a vessel to fulfill God's plan gives the idea of becoming a passive object. However, verse 38 suggests that she was in reality a subject. She decided out of her free will to take the mission that God had for her. She did not consult anybody about becoming a mother, not even her future husband. Thus this passage hints that Mary was an active and assertive woman who made her own choices.

Another characteristic that traditionally has been ascribed to the Virgin is submission. Luke 1:46–55, however, suggests that perhaps the biblical Mary did not have a very submissive mind. This passage presents Mary's song of praise to celebrate the merciful acts of God. The thinking reflected in this song gives the idea of a Mary who was well aware of social injustices and who celebrated the acts of God to reverse the social order in favor of the poor and oppressed.

A third characteristic of the traditional Mary is that the role of devoted motherhood was her only function in life. However, Acts 1:12–14 offers a glimpse of a Mary who also was busy with other activities. According to the passage, along with other women, Mary was a committed and active disciple of the Jesus movement, involved in the original group of disciples who started the church.[26]

These alternative views suggest a Mary different from the traditional one. They invite us to think about Mary as a subject with a strong will and social consciousness—a woman who was active, assertive, and involved with functions other than motherhood. This Mary and her liberating qualities can be a model for Mexican and Mexican-American Protestant women in their struggles to achieve liberation and justice because she provides them with a new biblical model of how to be a woman. Once these women grasp and experience the alternative options that this model presents, they will be able to use it also as a pertinent tool to confront and challenge the oppressive characteristics that have been ascribed to the Lady of Guadalupe. As a consequence, the traditional image of the Lady of Guadalupe as an oppressive cultural symbol will have less power to influence how these women live their lives.

## CONCLUSION

Protestant Mexican and Mexican-American women need to stop ignoring the Lady of Guadalupe. She long ago emerged as more than a Catholic devotional figure—she became a cultural symbol. As a cultural symbol defined and developed by a patriarchal culture, certain characteristics have been ascribed to the Lady of Guadalupe that influence women negatively. If Mexican and Mexican-American Protestant women ignore the Lady of Guadalupe, they will remain unable to rebuff patriarchal expectations of women as submissive, dependent, and passive. In consequence, oppressive models of womanhood will continue to dominate Latino images, conceptions, and culture. Unawareness and denial of the Lady of Guadalupe, therefore, constitutes complicit stagnation, not active transformation.

As Mexican and Mexican-American Protestant women acknowledge the importance of the Lady of Guadalupe and contribute to a different reading of her, they will benefit from their expanded understanding. They will realize a control and influence over important societal symbols. Participation in the defining and refining of cultural symbols will enable Protestant women to challenge and abandon oppressive images and models. Active engagement with the powers and symbols of culture will foster development of a better sense of self and generation of greater self-esteem. As these new readings emerge, Mary, Guadalupe, and Mexican and Mexican-American Protestant women alike will find liberation.

## NOTES

1. The original version of this paper was presented at the 1998 Annual Meeting of the American Academy of Religion. I want to thank the audience in that presentation for their helpful and engaging comments. Also, I am indebted to Leticia Guardiola-Sáenz and Ada María Isasi-Díaz for reading the first draft of this paper and providing helpful suggestions.
2. Stephen B. Bevans, *Models of Contextual Theology* (Maryknoll, N.Y.: Orbis Books, 1994), 1–10.
3. See María Pilar Aquino, *Our Cry for Life: Feminist Theology from Latin America* (Maryknoll, N.Y.: Orbis Books, 1993); Ada María Isasi-Díaz, *En la Lucha: A Hispanic Women's Liberation Theology* (Minneapolis: Fortress Press, 1993); Rosemary Radford Ruether, *Sexism and God-Talk: Toward a Feminist Theology* (Boston: Beacon Press, 1983); and Delores S. Williams, *Sisters in the Wilderness: The Challenge of Womanist God-Talk* (Maryknoll, N.Y.: Orbis Books, 1993).
4. Even though my particular identification is Baptist, I decided to use in this paper the general term "Protestant" because I believe that these reflections go beyond the Baptist Mexican and Mexican-American world. At least this is what I have found in my conversations about this topic with other Mexican and Mexican-American Protestant people. Although I believe that what I present here is a predominant position regarding the Lady of Guadalupe among Mexican and Mexican-American Protestant people, I recognize that there are exceptions to this picture. The Episcopal and Lutheran traditions are more open to the Virgin Mary/Guadalupe. However, they represent a minority among the Hispanic Protestant traditions.
5. Leticia Guardiola-Sáenz, "A Mexican-American Politics of Location: Reading from the Bridge," paper presented at the American Academy of Religion annual meeting in Philadelphia, 1995.
6. Franciscan Friars of the Immaculate, *A Handbook on Guadalupe* (Waite Park, Minn.: Park Press, 1997), 179–180 and 193–204.
7. Pablo Alberto Deiros, *Historia del Cristianismo en América Latina* (Buenos Aires: Fraternidad Teológica Latinoamericana, 1992), 722 (my translation).
8. For instance, Sara Alicia Hale, an American missionary who worked in Mexico, and Hortencia Morales, a Mexican missionary who worked in northern Mexico, are namesakes of such groups.
9. Donald Demarest, "Guadalupe Cult . . . in the Lives of the Mexicans," in Franciscan Friars' *A Handbook on Guadalupe*, 112–115.
10. Philippians 3:20.
11. Deiros, *Historia del Cristianismo*, 714, 722–723.
12. Ada María Isasi-Díaz and Yolanda Tarango, *Hispanic Women: Prophetic Voice in the Church* (San Francisco: Harper & Row, 1988), x.

13. Charles Gibson, *Los Aztecas Bajo el Dominio Español: 1519–1810* (México: Siglo XXI, 1978), 101–106.
14. Justo L. González mentions his experience regarding these dynamics in his book *Mañana: Christian Theology from a Hispanic Perspective* (Nashville: Abingdon Press, 1990), 22–26.
15. Octavio Paz, *El Laberinto de la Soledad* (México: Fondo de Cultura Económica, 1997), 94.
16. Franciscan Friars, *A Handbook on Guadalupe*, v, and Fr. Maximilian, F.F.I., "Our Lady's Submission to the Church," 205.
17. Sandra Messinger Cypress, *La Malinche in Mexican Literature* (Austin, Tex.: University of Texas Press, 1991), 6–7.
18. Rosa María Gil and Carmen Inoa Vázquez, *The María Paradox: How Latinas Can Merge Old World Traditions with New World Self-Esteem* (New York: G.P. Putnam's Sons, 1996), 7.
19. Ibid., 8.
20. Jeanette Rodríguez, *Our Lady of Guadalupe: Faith and Empowerment among Mexican-American Women* (Austin, Tex.: University of Texas Press, 1994), 159–165.
21. Virgilio Elizondo, *Galilean Journey: The Mexican-American Promise* (Maryknoll, N.Y.: Orbis Books, 1983), 11–13. See also Virgilio Elizondo, *La Morenita: Evangelizadora de las Américas* (Liguori, Mo.: Liguori Publications, 1981).
22. Elizondo, *La Morenita*, 79, 86; Rodríguez, *Our Lady of Guadalupe*, 6–17, 159.
23. Shawn Madigan, C. S. J., "Symbol," in *The New Dictionary of Catholic Spirituality*, ed. Michael Downey (Collegeville, Minn.: Liturgical Press, 1993), 953–955; also see "Symbol" and "Symbolism" in Peter M. J. Stravinskas, ed., *Catholic Dictionary* (Huntington, Ind.: Our Sunday Visitor Publishing Press, 1993), 463.
24. In conversations with other Hispanic scholars regarding these symbols, it became clear to me that Catholic and Protestant Hispanic people seem to have different worldviews that affect the way each group apprehends these symbols. For Hispanic Catholic people the categorization of cultural and religious symbols seems to be sharp, while for Hispanic Protestant people it seems to be less rigid.
25. Sandra Cisneros, "Guadalupe the Sex Goddess," in *Goddess of the Americas—La Diosa de las Americas: Writings on the Virgin of Guadalupe*, ed. Ana Castillo (New York: Riverhead Books, 1996), 46–51.
26. See Ivoni Richter Reimer, *Women in the Acts of the Apostles: A Feminist Liberation Perspective* (Minneapolis: Fortress Press, 1995), 231–233; Elisabeth Schüssler Fiorenza, *In Memory of Her: A Feminist Reconstruction of Christian Origins* (New York: Crossroad Books, 1985), 52–53; Elisabeth Schüssler Fiorenza, *Discipleship of Equals: A Critical Feminist Ekklesia–logy of Liberation* (New York: Crossroad Books, 1993), 114.

# 8

# "Pondering All These Things"

## *Mary and Motherhood*

### BONNIE J. MILLER-McLEMORE

One Advent season several years ago, eight-plus months pregnant, I looked upon a crèche scene of kings, shepherds, and Joseph and felt acutely Mary's Protestant isolation.[1] She literally faded away into the shadows hidden behind a bunch of men, including God incarnate. This pictorial memory partly captures women's position in the Protestant church: male clergy and God representations subsume Mary's role as mother and as a mediator of God.[2]

For many Protestants—and not just hypersensitive feminist mothers—Mary is almost completely invisible. She seldom appears pietistically in popular practices or liturgically in prayers or hymns. Artistic representations of the Madonna and child in stained glass or sculpture are rarer still. Mary stars briefly in annual Christmas pageants, if encountered at all, and gets occasional mention in Mother's Day sermons. But even these exceptions reflect Protestant ambivalence. This uncertainty about Mary is not unrelated to ambivalence about women and motherhood in general.

In this essay, I speak out of this silence by asking how a reconstructed Mary might better inform Protestant understandings of mothering. By "reconstructed" I mean a consideration of Mary from the perspective of feminist maternal Protestant theology. I will ask not only how reflection on Mary might influence motherhood but also how contemporary experiences of mothering might shape perceptions of Mary. These questions lead to an examination of two areas: the dynamics of Mary's Protestant disappearance and the implications of her reappearance. How has Mary informed Protestant understandings of motherhood? And what might a reconstructed Mary tell us?[3]

I will argue that abstinence from Mary in Protestantism went hand in hand with and even propped up the idealization of modern motherhood. I will suggest, in turn, that a Protestant revitalization of the centrality of Mary might help foster a more realistic view of motherhood. Fresh interpretation of her own concealment in scripture—her "pondering"—suggests that Mary herself weighed the complexities of mothering. How much more, then, might contemporary mothers rest easy with their own struggles?

## RECONSTRUCTING MARY

As philosopher Sara Ruddick observes, "[T]he passions of maternity are so sudden, intense, and confusing that we often remain ignorant of the perspective, the *thought* that has developed from mothering. Lacking pride, we have failed to deepen or articulate that thought."[4] "We know very little about the inner discourse of a mother," agrees literary theorist Susan Rubin Suleiman. "Mothers don't write, they are written." Yet, as long as we focus on "the-mother-as-she-is-written rather than on the-mother-as-she-writes [and thinks] we shall continue in our ignorance."[5]

Ignorance about the-mother-as-she-writes particularly plagues theology. Until recently, the reflective discipline of mothers has not been seen as a valid source of theological knowledge. While scholars in psychology, political science, literature, and other fields have begun to speak out of the experience of mothering, theologians have often remained wary.

With Mary, the silence around maternal thinking is compounded. And with Protestantism's evasion of Mary and mothers, the theological void is further deepened. We do not think of Mary as a maternal subject with religious or theological knowledge. And we do not think of using maternal wisdom as a way to understand Mary's theologizing. It's no wonder that when I went to work on this essay, my mind repeatedly went blank.

Ruddick's understanding of "maternal thinking" paves the way for fresh theological reflection on Mary. Drawing on Jürgen Habermas, Ruddick defines maternal thinking as a discipline that arises out of the social practice of mothering. This discipline involves the intellectual capacities, judgments, metaphysical attitudes, and values that are evoked, developed, and affirmed in the midst of mothering. In response to the "historical reality of a biological child in a particular social world," the mother "asks certain questions rather than others; she establishes criteria for the truth, adequacy, and relevance of proposed answers; and she cares about the findings she makes and can act on." In essence, she develops a "conceptual scheme" or "vocabulary and logic of connections" that orders and expresses the practice.[6]

A feminist maternal theology on Mary, therefore, draws on knowledge located within the practices of mothering. Maternal thinking has already shaped pivotal insights in feminist theology. When Valerie Saiving first put forth the revolutionary idea that women's sinfulness might not lie so much in pride and self-assertion as in self-loss and denigration, she drew heavily on her own experience of raising a young daughter in the midst of graduate study.[7] Other equally provocative challenges to Christian conceptions of the sacrificial meaning of the atonement, love as self-sacrifice, sexual ethics, and Christian vocation have evolved as a result of maternal thinking.[8]

Feminist maternal theology extends four core premises of feminist theology in new directions. The demand to give privileged voice to the marginalized is extended to mothers and children. Feminist maternal theology further challenges the demonization and idealization of women's bodies in the acts of bearing and raising children. It enriches debates about theological doctrines of love and sin by turning to the complex questions of love and sin between the unequal parties of adult and child. Finally, a feminist maternal theology stretches claims for justice and liberation to include children and mothers, for whom equality based on sameness with the adult male simply does not work. To think about Mary's motherhood from this perspective, therefore, means extending feminist theological convictions in a new direction.

Such imaginative theological speculation is not without historical precedent. Over the past two millennia, religious ideas about Mary have involved grand postulations on the part of the church and its mostly male theologians. Scriptural references to Mary are few in number (the Gospel of Luke makes the most mention, identifying her by name twelve times). But the legends and bibliographical citations are immense, with over two thousand books written about Mary in the twentieth century alone.[9] She is, in Shari Thurer's words, the ideal "blank screen, a perfect canvas for our projections."[10]

Mary's appeal as a blank screen is heightened, I believe, by the very fact that she is a mother. Pelikan wonders why she has retained such a "hold" on the Western psyche. His answer—that she has been "'first in the hearts'" of devoted religious practitioners, especially women—begs the question.[11] He never mentions the hold mothers have over their children, for good and for ill, and hence the hold Mary has over religious ideation. Speculation about Mary rests solidly on a whole host of conscious thoughts and unconscious longings. She gathers up all the free-floating desires that mothers evoke.

So a Protestant renaissance of thought is not out of order within this broader pattern of theological innovation. Maternal thinking about Mary is, however, relatively new. A Protestant feminist maternal reconsideration of Mary as mother allows for iconoclasm and reformation of another sort. Perhaps it is time that Protestants, who generally do not think all that much about Jesus even having a mother, also find inspiration, consolation, and liberation in Mary as mother.

## THE DYNAMICS AND IMPACT
## OF MARY'S PROTESTANT DISAPPEARANCE

Protestant feminist exploration of Mary's motherhood immediately encounters two doctrinal and practical suspicions: the Protestant rejection of Mary as intercessor and religious icon and the feminist rejection of Mary as a symbol of "ultimate womanhood" and perfect motherhood. These theological misgivings deserve both respect and reconsideration. In order to reconstruct Mary as mother, two movements are needed. We need to understand the Protestant suspicion and glean from it the best insights while leaving behind the worst. Likewise, we need to understand and move through the feminist resistance to Mary and romanticized, subservient motherhood.

### Protestant Apprehensions

Beverly Gaventa puts it bluntly: "[I]f there is one thing Protestants agree on—across the theological spectrum . . .—it is that *we* do not talk about Mary." She describes the reluctance she experienced first-hand when her offers to speak on Mary in a variety of settings elicited the following response: "'Oh. I don't think that would attract a very large audience. We're mostly Protestants here.'"[12] Even recent fascination with other biblical and saintly women throughout history has not sparked similar interest in Mary.

What is this Protestant apprehension all about, and what might be some of its inadvertent consequences? Rosemary Radford Ruether identifies three aspects of Protestant thought that fed the decrease in Marian devotion: the Reformation idea of the Bible as fundamental source of God's Word; the radical definition of justification by faith alone; and the exaltation of Christian marriage and rejection of the sanctity of virginity.[13] Pelikan also notes the first two factors. Protestant Reformers used slogans of *solus Christus* and *sola Scriptura* to attack the "entire chain of mediating powers—the sacraments, the church, the saints" and ultimately, Mary.[14] There was simply no biblical basis for the proliferation of stories about Mary. And no saint, even the Mother of God, mediated grace.

Ruether, however, is attentive to an additional factor of particular relevance here: the abolition of monasticism, which had multiple consequences. Hand in hand with the demise of monastic life went a drastic change in the status of celibacy and virginity. Chastity no longer promised a closer walk with God. Instead, the Reformers named marriage and parenthood valid religious vocations. Luther himself extolled the married state and declared God's smile evident in the meanest of child-rearing tasks when done in faith.[15] These affirmations drained the impulse behind religious beliefs, such as the Immaculate Conception and the Perpetual Virginity of Mary. Procreation and sex did not defile women. Nor did abstinence from sex make Mary special. Mary and Joseph became just another "normal married couple."[16]

Yet, while the exaltation of the virgin ideal had its problems, so did the glorification of marriage and motherhood. Although motherhood was recognized as a religious vocation, women's subservience was all the more strictly enforced. Moreover, motherhood became the only legitimate calling for women. Through vows of celibacy, medieval women had avenues of relative freedom and power and were able to pursue scholarship, retain property, and live in community with other women. To be sure, the Reformation elevated the family's status and gave women roles as religious companions of their husbands. But it also confined them more strictly to their households, under the authority of husbands, ministers, and magistrates.[17]

Protestants no longer exalted Mary. They elevated instead the virtuosity of submissive wives and selflessly loving mothers. With the diminishment of Mary's role came the embellishment, idealization, and domestic confinement of mothers—the angel "in the home"[18]—and the idolization of God the Father. Fathers, husbands, and clergy, in turn, assumed the role of mediating God's word in relationship to women, wives, and children.

This is not a wholly fair portrayal of Reformation theology. Ruether herself, in some of her swift generalizations about Protestant subordination of women, waxes less than generous. Pelikan rightly observes, "It would be a mistake, and one into which many interpretations of the Reformation both friendly and hostile have all too easily fallen, to emphasize these negative and polemical aspects of its Mariology at the expense of the positive place the Protestant Reformers assigned to her in their theology."[19] The Reformation slogan that best epitomized Protestant views of Mary was *sola fide*. While Mary no longer served as an intercessor, she could act as a model of faith. Mary heard the Word and responded, matching her faith in the great drama of salvation, Luther notes, to that of Abraham himself.[20]

Nevertheless, holding up Mary as a model of faith became increasingly difficult as corresponding creed and ritual diminished. So, while some Reformers, such as Zwingli, continued to teach the "right kind of Marian piety" and none of the Reformers denied Mariology entirely, those more anxious about eradicating papist expressions of Marian devotion, such as Calvin, won the day.[21] Feasts of Mary vanished, use of holy pictures were banned, and Protestant churches, with the exception of the Anglican Church, gradually lost interest in her. As a well-socialized Protestant today, when I searched for models of faith in motherhood, I simply never considered Mary.

## Feminist Apprehensions

The feminist movement is also partly responsible for the growing neglect of Mary. By and large, feminists question the Christian portrayal of the Virgin Mary as a holdover from patriarchy. Elizabeth Schüssler Fiorenza, for example, asserts that the "Mary myth" has its "roots and development in a male, clerical, and ascetic culture and theology" and "serves to deter women from becoming fully independent and whole human persons."[22] Ruether argues that the "Mariological tradition functions in patriarchal theology primarily to reflect and express the ideology of the patriarchal feminine."[23]

What are the chief complaints that support such feminist opposition? In an essay on Mariology and feminism (an addition not often found in most feminist theological anthologies, by the way), Sarah Coakley uses a fairly standard division of feminism—liberal, radical, socialist, and postmodern—as a way to group distinct concerns about Mary. While the liberal emphasis on equal opportunity does not "readily combine with Mariological themes," more reflection on Mary appears, not surprisingly, in the radical feminist reclamation of female biology and motherhood. Both approaches, however, tend to criticize more than reconstruct. Liberal feminists worry about the ways in which Mary personifies the obedient female kneeling subserviently before Christ. Radical feminists see Mary as "an impossible ideal as Virgin *and* mother, and thus a crushing exemplar for real mothers."[24] Doctrines of the Immaculate Conception and the Assumption, aimed at transcending the entrapment of sex and death, hold up a narrow ideal. They perpetuate a dualistic perception of women as either death-wielding temptresses and sources of sin or disembodied, sexless divinities. Mary Daly is the most scathingly outraged. She casts Mary as a rape victim and sees traditional Mariology as a projection of "*male* femininity." In the 1950s, as women were "badgered into housewifery," it was "no coincidence" that the Assumption became official Catholic doctrine. As women went "down," Mary went "up."[25]

On occasion, however, legitimate concerns about Mary as a beacon of true womanhood turn into thoughtless rhetoric. For example, in her *Report on the Family*, Shere Hite makes sweeping assumptions about the "icons of Jesus, Mary and Joseph." On the first page she blames family crises on the sorry attempt to imitate the "holy family." The church "has as its basic principle, at its heart, the political will of men to dominate women."[26] Beyond this unquestioned assumption and the use of religious imagery as a straw horse, Christianity receives little further attention. She simply ignores the plurality of Christian traditions and, equally disturbing, the existence of feminist theologians.

Yet in their concern about matricide and advocacy for female god imagery, feminist theologians themselves have not paid enough attention to Mary. Seldom have they considered the Protestant annihilation of Mary or explored a reconstructed Mary as a partial solution to these issues. In *Remembering Esperanza*, for example, Mark Kline Taylor identifies matriphobia and matricide as the operative dynamics behind sexism. He advocates a cultural-political theology that grants *"a privilege for those excluded or absent from the conversation."*[27] Yet his constructive response turns neither to women's experience, except in a remote way through his memory of Esperanza, nor to Mary's experience. Instead, he proposes Christ as mother—*Christus mater*— arguing that "to take seriously the Christ in our time is to take seriously the mother."[28] Taking Mary's motherhood seriously is never entertained as a means to revalue maternal theological powers or combat sexism.

Likewise, Catherine Keller mounts a scathing, insightful exposition of the development of matricidal myths, psychologies, theologies, and philosophies over the centuries of Western civilization. Fearful of maternal power, Greek myth and biblical creation stories turn their fury on the mother. The "covert slaughter of the mother is this culture's bond of reenactment."[29] Yet her work also avoids any discussion of Mary's Protestant matricide or Mary's resurrection as part of revisioning divine incarnation.

In these and other works, Protestant feminist theologians do recognize the need for women to know themselves as representatives of God and, equally important, for men to have the "chastening experience of being unlike the Goddess." Barbara Andolsen sees such a theological move as absolutely necessary to grounding her view of Christian love as mutuality. But she remains dubious. It is, she argues, "questionable whether any religion which unselfconsciously incorporates a female aspect of the deity would remain Christianity." Despite efforts to reinterpret the Trinity in more inclusive terms, "it will be extraordinarily difficult for Christianity to embody in its symbols a belief that women are full human beings and hence are equally capable of serving as symbols of divine power."[30]

Feminist theology, however, is not without rich resources on Mary. Daniel Migliore includes feminist and liberation theologies alongside collaboration in biblical studies as one of the "two most important developments" since Vatican II.[31] It is particularly unfortunate that Pelikan's 1996 historical survey fails to include any commentary on feminist theology's contributions, beyond the briefest reference. He completely misses what Coakley describes as a "wide range of Mariological options . . . already at least fragmentarily in play" in feminist theology.[32]

In liberal feminism, Ruether, for example, sees Mary as an exemplar of autonomy, choice, and empowerment. "Luke goes out of his way," she says, "to stress that Mary's motherhood is a free choice," made without consultation with Joseph.[33] Here Mary's motherhood is not her exclusive self-definition.

Her vocational obligations extend to her role as witness and cocreator. Others have taken up this approach, even if not under the explicit auspices of feminism. Patrick Miller, for example, identifies Mary as Christianity's "first theologian" who offers "the first christological reflection" of the church, musing about what Jesus would become and about what would become of him.[34] As Gaventa notes, in Luke's Gospel Mary assumes three interconnected roles of disciple, prophet, and mother, and ignoring any of them "flatten[s] Mary's character and reduce[s] her to a single feature or one function."[35]

Socialist and postmodern feminists venture still further. In a different mode, Ruether and, more recently, Brazilians Ivone Gebara and Maria Clara Bingemer proclaim Mary "mother of the poor," liberating the economically and politically oppressed.[36] And postmodern feminists, such as Julia Kristeva, have taken particular interest in Mary as part of their claim that it is motherhood, more than womanhood, that is repressed in patriarchal society. "Wholesale rejection of Marian mythology by mainstream feminism leaves a gap" that needs to be filled. Motherhood needs fresh discourse and symbols that will correct distorted perceptions of the maternal "other."[37]

In *Because of Her Testimony*, British feminist theologian Anne Thurston argues that the sanitized, desexualized ideal of the Virgin Mary falsely represents women's maternal experience. The "sanitizing of the birth of Jesus—removing all physical and sexual connotations—has closed off whole areas of possible theological reflection."[38] Time could hardly be riper for reconsideration of Mary as mother, both to enrich the Christian tradition and to empower women as mothers.

## THE IMPLICATIONS OF MARY'S PROTESTANT REAPPEARANCE: PONDERINGS

If Mary's erasure went hand in hand with the idealization of modern motherhood, a revitalization of Mary's theological importance might foster a richer view of motherhood. Even in a postmodern context of ambiguity and pluralism, people need ideals by which to live. Children and adults alike seek ideals as a means to soothe, comfort, and sustain the self. People will worship gods; the important question is what kind.[39]

The religious figure of Mary as mother is not an altogether bad place to project hopes and dreams. It is certainly an improvement over popular fascination with questionable public figures, like Madonna and Princess Diana, and over projecting on ourselves or on our own mothers the domesticated virtues of modern motherhood, especially if religious ideals remain open to critique and reform. A fuller grasp of Mary as a maternal example opens up space for a more generous understanding of the plight of contemporary mothers.

Lacking postbiblical traditions and church teachings on Mary, Protestants are left with Scripture. As Gaventa observes, "[I]f Protestants are going to talk about Mary . . . we must begin in a Protestant-like way. That is to say, we must *begin* with scripture."[40] Similarly, lacking nonpatriarchal traditions about Mary, feminists are left with human and maternal experience. If feminist theologians are going to provide fresh insight on Mary, they must begin in a feminist-like way—with experience. What then might we learn about mothering in Scripture and experience from Mary as mother?

## Mary's Ponderings

Compared to the lore surrounding Mary over the centuries, the Scripture references are few. And the passages on Mary's "pondering" hide as much as they disclose. More has been said on her words, the Magnificat, than her musings. Nonetheless, fresh insights can be gleaned from Luke's portrayal of Mary in the second chapter.

Mary's "pondering" appears in two passages, first as a part of the birth narrative (Luke 2:19) and later after the twelve-year old Jesus stays behind in the temple (Luke 2:51b). The shepherds tell Mary that angelic hosts announced her child as the Savior, the Christ, and amid the wonder of others, she "kept all these things, pondering them in her heart" (RSV). And later, upon returning to Nazareth to watch an "obedient" son grow in "wisdom and in stature" after his three-day disappearance, Mary "kept all these things in her heart" (RSV).

I never paid much attention to these passages until I became a mother myself. With children in tow, the words, Mary "kept all these things in her heart" literally jumped off the page. Long before this book's editors invited me to write about Mary's motherhood, I had underlined these two passages. And when I flipped through my book *Also a Mother* in search of inspiration, there on the first page, staring me in the face, was the word "ponder." The book basically "ponders" the dilemmas of mothering. It especially ponders the virtues of the good mother/good worker, tested regularly in the fire of trivial yet revelatory moments of child care.

Why this maternal attraction to and even unconscious adoption of Mary's own pondering? As a mother, perhaps I felt able to identify with Mary—albeit partially and in a carefully contained Protestant feminist way. I doubt that I would have recognized, much less admitted, this indulgence without the pressure to write on the subject. Frankly, I have been in awe of Mary's pondering for a long time. I have, so to speak, wanted this conversation with her. I have wished, as I think many in Catholicism also desired, that she could talk back. I have wondered if Mary's experience as mother even remotely resembles my own.

The author of Luke deserves credit for the brevity of his portrayal of Mary's thought. In these two instances, he does not put words into her mouth. He thereby avoids turning her into "the-mother-as-she-is-written" and retains something of the mother as she speaks. He uses similar phrasing earlier in characterizing Mary's response to her angelic visitation, where Mary pondered or "considered in her mind what sort of greeting this might be" (Luke 1:29b, RSV). One can almost imagine his constraint as he searched for the right way to keep her dignity as speaking subject intact.

Other equally compelling readings, of course, have been given. Biblical scholar Jane Schaberg sees Luke's restraint here as simply another instance of his view of women as "models of subordinate service, excluded from the power center of the movement."[41] Mary is speechless, she argues, because that is her proper role as dependent "listener," pondering what is not understood in "silence."

Silence, narrowly defined as muteness or speechlessness, does not do justice to the intent of Luke's words.[42] Calling this "silence" is to cast her pondering, as Gaventa remarks, "in sentimental and trivializing terms." If the gospels had depicted John the Baptist or Peter pondering over Jesus, the "church would long ago have dubbed these as moments of theological reflection."[43] Maybe it is time to consider them thus.

While a strand of passive, ingratiating submission can certainly be deduced from these texts, we can also untangle other threads. Certainly, as Schaberg herself points out, in chapter 1 women play more powerful roles than in the rest of the Gospel, with speeches by Elizabeth and Mary that go unadulterated by men.[44] Schaberg's simplistic interpretation of Mary's role in chapter 2 as mere listener seems limited by comparison. Others, such as Miller, join Schaberg in mistakenly naming Mary's musing as simply "silence."

Seen in a more positive light, perhaps pondering was Luke's version of what Ruddick calls "maternal thinking." Ruddick identifies three interests around which the practice of maternal thinking evolves: the desire for the preservation, the growth, and the acceptability of the child.[45] Such interests cross over differences of class and race, even though they take different shape in other contexts. They also, undoubtedly, shaped Mary's pondering. Ironically, when Ruddick spells out the capacities and virtues that mothers develop in pursuit of these interests, such as "humility" and "attention," we actually hear echoes of Mariology. "Whilst owning nothing conscious to Mariological traditions," Coakley observes, Ruddick's tough-minded philosophical analysis of parenting "nonetheless returns to central Marian themes."[46] Ruddick provides, however, a reworking of these virtues from the mother's internal frame of reference.

The dictionary offers several definitions for "ponder": to weigh in the mind, to deliberate about, to muse over, or to think or consider, especially quietly, soberly, and deeply. It offers a list of synonyms: meditate, ruminate, and muse.

Pondering is prolonged consideration. It is often inconclusive. Meditate implies a focusing of one's attention to understand more deeply. As one author notes, the very tone of the word "ponder"—its "heavy, slow sound"—"reinforces the idea of introspection." The word "lacks the implied resolution of words like 'assess' or 'analyze.'"[47] The sonorous effect of the word is magnified by its location in the "heart" rather than in the mind. This location does not negate thinking, as in the conventional opposition between the thinking mind and feeling heart, but rather deepens the wisdom found within and through one's passions. Keeping thoughts in one's heart means keeping them at the center or core of one's being. Finally, "ponder" involves a certain acceptance of realities that go beyond our understanding. At such a point, the only response is appreciation and perhaps amazement. This play on the text's vocabulary hints at three aspects of mothering that deserve elaboration as powerful activities of mothering implied by Luke's words: attention, anguish, and amazement.

## Attention

To describe the capacity of attention and the coinciding virtue of love, Ruddick turns to Simone Weil. As a Christian theologian, Weil actually sees the realization of attention as a "miracle" rather than a "discipline."[48] One cannot command attention by sheer will power or muscular concentration. It evolves out of the mere joy of the work. Attention requires a kind of patient, anticipatory "waiting upon truth," a holding openness. Prayer itself consists of attention.

Human activities can nonetheless hone our attention. Weil points to school studies, but the practice of mothering serves as well. "Every time that a human being succeeds in making an effort of attention with the sole idea of increasing his grasp of truth," she says, "he acquires a greater aptitude for grasping it, even if his effort produces no visible fruit."[49]

Most fundamentally, Weil sees attention as a way of looking that asks genuinely of the other, "What are you going through?"[50] The ordinary mother, then, who comes to ask, "What are you going through?" without rushing to give the answer, embodies maternal attention. For Ruddick, maternal attention means regarding children as fully real, without seizing or using them. Elsewhere she talks about an attitude of "holding" governed by the "priority of keeping over acquiring, of conserving the fragile, of maintaining whatever is at hand and necessary to the child's life."[51]

In her attentive pondering, Mary models a certain kind of Christian spirituality of presence, what I have attempted to describe elsewhere as "contemplation in the midst of chaos."[52] Contemplation is not simply something monks do in solitary settings. Mary attends to God precisely within the confused, messiness of her life. She prays in the midst of tensions and questions, fixing her attention so that she might see things otherwise hidden and make God's purpose manifest in the daily toil. Mary, then, "is not the one to whom we pray," as Migliore recognizes, but the one *with* whom we pray, as a sister in Christ and God's mother, unceasingly, in the midst of our work and loves.[53]

There is much about mothering that makes attentive love challenging—the "intensity of identification, . . . the daily wear of maternal work, . . . indignities of an indifferent social order, and the clamor of children themselves."[54] Ruddick believes it requires effort and self-discipline; Weil sees it as a gift. In either case, the attentive focus of the Lukan Mary offers some sort of vision or sign of hope and guidance as mothers respond every day to some of the many temptations that Ruddick enumerates—"indifference, passivity, . . . anxious or inquisitorial scrutiny, domination, intrusiveness, caprice, and self-protective cheerfulness."[55]

## Anguish

One of the hazards that Ruddick does not explicitly mention but that is present in the Lukan text, read from the end of the story backwards, is maternal anguish. Mothering involves loss. It demands a constant giving up and letting go. From the moment of conception, a woman physically experiences a life that is both herself and not herself. Art historian Anne Higonnet captures some of the sentiment well:

> There is, arguably, no identification at once more intense and more vexed than the identification a parent feels with her or his child, perhaps especially so in the case of the mother, whose child begins biologically as a part of herself, and whom she feeds as an infant with her own body. If, moreover, . . . identification reacts defensively against loss, then again, identification would be a crucial issue for parents, who must inevitably begin losing their children as soon as they are born.[56]

Fearfulness and excessive control naturally tempt mothers. To stem these temptations, mothers must learn to sit easy with a certain amount of anguish.

When Mary ponders, she meets up with her own anguish. From the beginning, as Gaventa notes, Mary lingers over and contends with a son that is "profoundly hers and yet not hers at all."[57] In the second passage, observes Migliore, this tension spawns confusion, anxiety, and doubts when Jesus does not follow his parents, tempting Mary to strive to contain Jesus' mission.[58] A mother can even "experience her children's own liveliness," notes Ruddick, as an "enemy of the life she is preserving."[59]

Mary's distress runs deeper still because of the distinctiveness of Jesus' "liveliness" and the impossibility of maternal preservation. The author of Luke knows the end of the story as he tells the beginning, and hence he ties Mary's pondering to her deeper intuition about Jesus' mission. Not insignificantly, he places the story of Simeon's oracle between the two pondering passages, reminding readers of the suffering to come. Simeon warns Mary, "[T]his child is destined for the falling and rising of many in Israel . . . and a sword will pierce your own soul too" (Luke 2:34–35). Here, Luke names the pain that the death of Jesus will cause her.[60]

Many mothers experience what psychologists have described as "disenfranchised grief," grief over loss that is denied social and religious legitimacy.[61] Unfortunately, interpretations of Mary as the perfect example of self-sacrificial love conceal her real distress. Calvin himself corrects views of Mary's interrogation of Jesus for his twelve-year-old thoughtlessness ("[W]hy have you treated us like this?"—Luke 2:48a) as a case of selfish pride. She was "pushed not by pride," he observes, "but by *three days* of sorrow."[62] Interpreting Mary's remark as self-serving puts her, and, in turn, all mothers who appear insufficiently self-effacing into the position of disenfranchised griever who must do grief work in secret without social support.

Mary's response to Jesus in the temple discourages such a reading. As Gaventa discerns, the NRSV—"[Y]our father and I have been searching for you *in great anxiety*"—fails to "capture the poignancy of the word Luke selects (*odynoun*)." A better translation of verse 48b is "Behold, your father and I have been looking for you *in anguish*." The emotional claim that Mary makes here "is the real and present terror of parents who do not know where their child is."[63]

Contemporary society has a rather truncated, hackneyed phrase for parental anguish—the "empty nest syndrome." This oft-used term confines loss to the final stage of a child's official departure and is oblivious to the infinitesimal leave-takings that occur daily and at each life stage, including the terror at moments when our children vanish from sight without warning. Society unfortunately renders maternal anguish a "syndrome" or abnormal affliction that one ought to get over rather than recognizing it as an inherent and ongoing part of all parenting, as these passages imply.

## Awe

Ultimately, awe is intrinsic to parenting. The attention and anguish of Mary's pondering also contains a certain amount of awe—sheer amazement about what she sees and hears. Mary's pondering in Luke 2:19 is sandwiched between two exclamations of wonder at Jesus. In Luke 2:51, her meditation follows the amazement of the teachers in the temple at Jesus' answers. While Gaventa stresses the contrast between the verbal cries of marvel and Mary's stillness, I cannot help but see contagion.[64] How could Mary not join in praise as she has already done in her testimony to Elizabeth?

Here Mary seems even more as Miller describes: "one whose maternal response outran those of any other mother while also being like those of any mother."[65] If I attend well to my three sons, daily I am astonished and dazed—by spontaneous humorous comments, by their sheer persistence in the face of daunting challenges, by shoes larger or shoulders taller than mine, or by small acts of gratitude and love returned to me unasked for and unexpected. Simplistically put, I am amazed by their growth. How much more then was Mary dazzled by the grace of God within her own life—touching her skin, changing her life—that words themselves could not suffice? The passage on Jesus in the temple points to this fact by placing as bookends, at the beginning and end, testimony that Jesus grew in wisdom and in favor before God. The translation that Mary "*treasured* all these things" in the NRSV rather than "*kept* all these things in her heart" in the RSV points more directly to the sureness of Mary's wonder.

Without romanticizing either pregnancy or delivery, there is much about bearing the gift of new life, from quickening to the travail of labor to birth, that goes beyond words. No wonder Luke only reports that Mary pondered these things. What was Mary thinking? It was simply too much to put into words, although, as we have seen, there is more to say about her pondering than this. The miracle of birth and, indeed, the miracle of Christ's birth, all have to be "carefully weighed," as one definition offered by *Webster's Collegiate Dictionary* puts it. And as the second Lukan passage attests, this experience of amazed yet focused musing repeats itself regularly in the activity of parenting throughout the years to come.

## CONCLUSION

With Mary, Protestants experience powerfully the presence of an absence. That is, Mary is most present in her absence.[66] For, as Jaroslav Pelikan concludes in his history of Mary over the centuries, the very lack of attention given Mary in Protestantism remains in a curious way a "part of the unbreakable hold that she has continued to have on the imagination of the West."[67] This presence of an absence is twofold. It entails the absence of woman as God-mediator and even as God-representative. And it entails the eclipse of women and mothers as publicly, religiously valued. Probing behind Mary's pondering disturbs this absence. Disturbing the absence by pondering over Mary's pondering opens up space to revalue maternal thought and to consider women as willing and able negotiators of God's grace and purpose.

Mary had "an inauspicious beginning" in Scripture, but Scripture left plenty of room for invention.[68] Readers cannot know literally and historically whether

Mary experienced attentive love, anguish, or awe in her deliberation. We cannot even know definitively whether the author of Luke intended to convey such an impression. But we can know that if Mary gave birth to Jesus and did the work of mothering, she likely experienced all these sentiments and much, much more. She knew Jesus first, foremost, and most profoundly. And we can move from a renewed sense of the complexity of Mary's motherhood to enriched Christian aspirations about the responsibilities and challenges of mothering today. In the very midst of her mothering—not when she got away from it all—Mary engaged in Christian reflection and prayer. In this and other ways, her pondering suggests fresh ways of embodying faith in the act of mothering.

## NOTES

1. See Bonnie J. Miller-McLemore, *Also A Mother: Work and Family as Theological Dilemma* (Nashville: Abingdon Press, 1994), 129.

2. This is not to say that churches that have honored Mary have done better. Indeed, churches that esteem her most—Roman Catholic and Eastern Orthodox—are sometimes the least receptive to women in positions of religious leadership. Nonetheless, Protestants do well to revisit the question of Mary and the impact of her neglect. How one interprets Mary's place in Christian faith matters.

3. For the sake of this discussion, I bracket more common theological debates about Mary's motherhood—Mary mediating God as the Mother of God, *theotokos*, or God-bearer. My focus on the ordinary aspects stands in contrast to the focus on the "mystery of Mary's motherhood" in essays such as Frederick M. Jelly's "The Concrete Meaning of Mary's Motherhood" (*The Way* 45 [Summer 1982]: 30–40), which explore the meaning of *theotokos*.

4. Sara Ruddick, "Maternal Thinking," in *Mothering: Essays in Feminist Theory*, ed. Joyce Treblicot (Totowa, N.J.: Rowman & Allanheld, 1983), 213.

5. Susan Rubin Suleiman, "Writing and Motherhood" in *The (M)other Tongue: Essays in Feminist Psychoanalytic Interpretation*, ed. Shirley Nelson Garner, Claire Kahane, and Madelon Sprengnether (Ithaca, N.Y.: Cornell University Press, 1985).

6. Ruddick, "Maternal Thinking," 214; Sara Ruddick, *Maternal Thinking: Toward a Politics of Peace* (Boston: Beacon Press, 1989), 24.

7. Valerie Saiving, "The Human Situation: A Feminine View," *Journal of Religion* (April 1960): 108; reprinted in *Womanspirit Rising: A Feminist Reader in Religion*, ed. Carol P. Christ and Judith Plaskow (San Francisco: Harper & Row, 1979).

8. As a wonderful example directly related to the subject matter of this essay, see Beverly Roberts Gaventa's comments on the differences between her reading and John Dominic Crossan's reading of the same birth narratives in Matthew and Luke ("The Challenge of Christmas," *The Christian Century* [December 15, 1993]: 1270–71). For other general examples, see Christine E. Gudorf, "Parenting, Mutual Love, and Sacrifice," in *Women's Consciousness and Women's Conscience: A Reader in Feminist Ethics*, ed. Barbara Hilkert Andolsen, Christine E. Gudorf, and Mary D. Pellauer (San Francisco: Harper & Row, 1985), 175–191;

Sally Purvis, "Mothers, Neighbors and Strangers: Another Look At Agape," *Journal of Feminist Studies in Religion* 7:1 (Spring 1991): 19–34; Cristina Traina, "Maternal Experience and the Boundaries of Christian Sexual Ethics," *Signs: Journal of Women in Culture and Society* 25, no. 2 (Winter 2000): 369–405, and "Passionate Mothering: Toward an Ethic of Appropriate Parent-Child Intimacy," *Annual of Christian Ethics* 18 (1998): 177–96; and Cynthia L. Rigby, "Exploring Our Hesitation: Feminist Theologies and the Nurture of Children," *Theology Today* 56, no. 4 (January 2000): 540–554.

9. Jaroslav Pelikan, *Mary Through the Centuries: Her Place in the History of Culture* (New Haven, Conn. and London: Yale University Press, 1996), 225.

10. Shari L. Thurer, *The Myths of Motherhood: How Culture Reinvents the Good Mother* (Boston: Houghton Miffflin Co., 1994), 107.

11. Pelikan, *Mary Through the Centuries*, 216–17.

12. Beverly Roberts Gaventa, "'All Generations Will Call Me Blessed': Mary in Biblical and Ecumenical Perspective," *The Princeton Seminary Bulletin* 38, no. 3 (1997): 251, emphasis in text.

13. Rosemary Radford Ruether, *Mary—The Feminine Face of God* (Philadelphia: Westminster Press, 1977), 70–72.

14. Pelikan, *Mary Through the Centuries*, 155.

15. *Luther's Works*, ed. Jaroslav Pelikan and Helmut Lehmann, 55 volumes (St. Louis: Concordia Publishing House, 1955–1986), 45: 40–41.

16. Ruether, *Mary—The Feminine Face of God*, 71.

17. Rosemary Radford Ruether, "Church and Family II: Church and Family in the Medieval and Reformation Periods," *New Blackfriars* (February 1984): 84.

18. This allusion is to Coventry Patmore's poem, "Angel in the House" (1856).

19. Pelikan, *Mary Through the Centuries*, 157.

20. Martin Luther, "Sermon on Luke 2:41–52," *Luther's Werke*, 12:409–19, cited by Pelikan, *Mary Through the Centuries*, 160–61.

21. George H. Tavard, *The Thousand Faces of the Virgin Mary* (Collegeville, Minn.: Liturgical Press, 1996), 107, 126–27.

22. Elizabeth Schüssler Fiorenza, "Feminist Theology as a Critical Theology of Liberation," in *Churches in Struggle: Liberation Theologies and Social Change in North America*, ed. William K. Tabb (New York: Monthly Review Press, 1986), 57, 59, cited by Pelikan, *Mary Through the Centuries*, 4.

23. Rosemary Radford Ruether, *Sexism and God-Talk: Toward a Feminist Theology* (Boston: Beacon Press, 1983), 149.

24. Sarah Coakley, "Mariology and 'Romantic Feminism': A Critique," in *Women's Voices: Essays in Contemporary Feminist Theory*, ed. Teresa Elwes (London: Marshall Pickering, 1992), 101.

25. Mary Daly, *Gyn/Ecology* (London: The Women's Press, 1979), 85; and *Pure Lust* (London: The Women's Press, 1984), 74, 128, cited by Coakley, "Mariology and 'Romantic Feminism,'" 102 (emphasis added by Coakley).

26. Shere Hite, *The Hite Report on the Family: Growing Up Under Patriarchy* (New York: Grove Press, 1995), 359.

27. Mark Kline Taylor, *Remembering Esperanza: A Cultural-Political Theology for North American Praxis* (Maryknoll, N.Y.: Orbis Books, 1990), 60, 64, 104–110. Emphasis in text.

28. Ibid., 195.

29. Catherine Keller, *From a Broken Web: Separatism, Sexism, and Self* (Boston: Beacon Press, 1986), 78.

30. Barbara Hilkert Andolsen, "Agape in Feminist Ethics" *The Journal of Religious Ethics* 9, no. 1 (1981): 80–81.
31. See below, p. 118.
32. Coakley, "Mariology and 'Romantic Feminism,'" 110. For another overview of feminist options, see Els Maeckelberge, *Desperately Seeking Mary: A Feminist Appropriation of a Traditional Religious Symbol* (Kampen, Netherlands: Kok Pharos, 1991), ch. 1. For a book-length feminist attempt to recast Mary, see Maurice Hamington, *Hail Mary? The Struggle for Ultimate Womanhood in Catholicism* (New York and London: Routledge, 1995).
33. Ruether, *Sexism and God-talk*, 153.
34. Patrick D. Miller, "The Church's First Theologian," *Theology Today* 56, no. 3 (October 1999): 293–94.
35. Beverly Roberts Gaventa, *Mary: Glimpses of the Mother of Jesus* (Columbia, S. C.: University of South Carolina, 1995; Minneapolis: Fortress Press, 1999), 73.
36. Ruether, *Sexism and God-talk*, 155, 158; Ivone Gebara and Maria Clara Bingemer, *Mary, Mother of God, Mother of the Poor* (London: Burns & Oates, 1989), 14, 161.
37. Coakley, "Mariology and 'Romantic Feminism," 104, 110.
38. Anne Thurston, *Because of Her Testimony: The Word in Female Experience* (New York: Crossroad Books, 1995), 27.
39. See Bonnie J. Miller-McLemore, "Ideals and Realities of Motherhood: A Theological Perspective," in *Mother Troubles: Rethinking Contemporary Maternal Dilemmas*, ed. Julia Hanigsberg and Sara Ruddick (Boston: Beacon Press, 1999), 290–92.
40. Gaventa, "'All Generations Will Call Me Blessed,'" 253, emphasis in text.
41. Jane Schaberg, "Luke," in *The Women's Bible Commentary*, ed. Carol A. Newsom and Sharon H. Ringe (Louisville, Ky.: Westminster/John Knox Press, 1992), 275.
42. When Martin Marty tries to summarize Miller's argument (see note 34, above), he does not, in fact, seem able to make much out of Miller's exegesis of the "silence" and so skips over to Miller's comments on the hymn of praise (*Context* [January 15, 2000]: 6).
43. Gaventa, *Mary*, 130.
44. Schaberg, "Luke," 282.
45. Ruddick, "Maternal Thinking," 215. See Jürgen Habermas, *Knowledge and Human Interests* (Boston: Beacon Press, 1971).
46. Coakley, "Mariology and 'Romantic Feminism,'" 171.
47. Kathleen Hansley, "Supernatural Beings," *Christian Century* (April 5, 2000): 393.
48. Simone Weil, "Reflections on the Right Use of School Studies with a View to the Love of God," in *Waiting on God*, trans. Emma Craufurd (New York: Harper & Row, 1951), 114; Sara Ruddick, *Maternal Thinking: Toward a Politics of Peace* (Boston: Beacon Press, 1989), 122.
49. Weil, "Right Use of School Studies," 107.
50. Weil, "Right Use of School Studies," 113, 115.
51. Ruddick, "Maternal Thinking," 217.
52. Bonnie J. Miller-McLemore, "Contemplation in the Midst of Chaos, " in *The Vocation of the Theological Teacher*, ed. Gregory Jones and Stephanie Paulsell (Grand Rapids, Mich.: Wm. B. Eerdmans Pub. Co., 2001), 48–74.
53. See below, p. 129.
54. Ruddick, "Maternal Thinking", 223–24.

55. Ruddick, *Maternal Thinking*, 120.

56. Anne Higonnet, *Pictures of Innocence: The History and Crisis of Ideal Childhood* (New York: Thames & Hudson, 1998), 200.

57. Gaventa, "The Challenge of Christmas," 1273.

58. Migliore, "A Reformed Theological Perspective," 350.

59. Ruddick, "Maternal Thinking," 216.

60. Gaventa, *Mary*, 65.

61. Kenneth Doka, ed., *Disenfranchised Grief: Recognizing Hidden Sorrow* (New York: Lexington Books, 1989), cited by Lucy Bregman, *Beyond Silence and Denial: Death and Dying Reconsidered* (Louisville, Ky.: Westminster John Knox Press, 1999), 111.

62. John Calvin, *Commentarius*, col. 106, my emphasis, cited by Tavard, *The Thousand Faces*, 121.

63. Gaventa, *Mary*, 68.

64. Ibid., 61.

65. See below, p. 126.

66. I owe this way of putting this to my friend and colleague Paula Cooey.

67. Pelikan, *Mary Through the Centuries*, 222.

68. Thurer, *The Myths of Motherhood*, 107.

# PART 3

*Bearing* Mary

# 9

# Woman of Faith

## *Toward a Reformed Understanding of Mary*

### DANIEL L. MIGLIORE

Unlike Roman Catholic theology, Reformed theology has never given much attention to Mary, the mother of Jesus. Indeed, the two most recently adopted confessions of the Presbyterian Church U.S.A. ("The Confession of 1967," and "The Brief Statement of Faith," 1991) do not even mention her name. Nor is there any reference to her in the new children's catechism recently approved by the General Assembly for use in Presbyterian congregations.

The reasons for this eclipse of Mary in Protestant theologies in general and Reformed theologies in particular are not difficult to identify. The profuse growth of Mariology in the Middle Ages met with strong criticism at the time of the Reformation. Since the Reformers held with Scripture that there could be only one mediator between God and humanity (1 Tim. 2:5), exaggerated Marian titles and exuberant Marian devotion seemed to them to threaten the clarity of the gospel message of salvation by grace alone, through faith alone, in Christ alone.

The Reformers were, of course, deeply respectful of Mary. They accepted the patristic designation of Mary as *theotokos*, "the bearer of God," a name whose primary import both for the patristic church and for the Reformers was christological rather than mariological. Luther often spoke of Mary as the "blessed Mother of God" and wrote a beautiful treatise on the Magnificat (1521). Calvin discussed the stories of Mary with characteristic insight and balance in his commentaries on the Gospels, saying that Mary should be held in high regard. He referred to her not only as the holy Virgin but also as our teacher in the faith, remarking that even the apostles were her students in certain matters.[1] For Calvin, however, Mary was accorded appropriate honor not by bestowing high-sounding titles on her but by following her simple obedience and her witness in praise of the grace of God.

Despite the respect and honor the Reformers gave to Mary, she virtually dropped out of Protestant theology and piety in the increasingly polemical post-Reformation period. In the nineteenth and twentieth centuries, several developments served to widen the chasm between Roman Catholic Mariology and Protestant avoidance or suspicion of the subject. Prominent among these were the promulgation of the Marian dogmas of the Immaculate Conception (1854) and the bodily Assumption (1950); the sharp increase of Marian devotion in popular Catholicism associated with special apparitions of the Virgin at sites like Lourdes, Fatima, Guadalupe, and Medjugorjes; and the periodic debates within the Roman Catholic Church about the appropriateness of designating Mary as coredemptrix and mediatrix of all graces.

Today, however, the place of Mary within the gospel tradition is being reappraised by both Catholic and Protestant theologians. After vigorous debate, the Vatican II Fathers decided not to treat Mary as an independent theological theme but as a subtheme of the doctrine of the Church. Since Vatican II, the two most important developments in thinking about Mary have been the collaborative biblical studies of Protestant and Catholic scholars[2] and the revised image of Mary presented in feminist and liberation theologies.

According to feminist theologians, Mary has often been portrayed in ways that provide religious legitimation of stereotypically subordinate roles for women. A new picture of Mary, more faithful to Scripture and more adequate to the situation faced by the church today, must be sought. As Mary Hines observes, "Mary herself is in need of liberation from past interpretations."[3]

Taking these recent developments into account, my thesis is that Reformed theology should make its own distinctive contribution to contemporary rethinking of the significance of Mary for Christian faith and theology. With the new attention to the role of women in Scripture and in the life of the church, the time is ripe for a new look at Mary. A full account of the story of redemption and of the nature of Christian discipleship will have to speak with theological clarity about this woman. It is therefore appropriate to ask, What would a new understanding of Mary look like from a Reformed theological perspective?

## SOME PROMINENT IMAGES OF MARY

Before addressing this question directly, it may be helpful to review briefly a few of the more prominent images of Mary in the theology and piety of the Roman Catholic and Protestant churches.[4]

Still immensely influential is the traditional Roman Catholic picture of *Mary as the queen of heaven*. As the perpetually virgin mother of God, Mary has been crowned queen of heaven, and she is entitled to a devotion superior (*hyperdu-*

*lia*) to the devotion (*dulia*) given to the other saints. Having ascended to glory, she reigns at the right hand of God. This regal image of Mary has been reinforced in the modern era by the dogmas of the Immaculate Conception and the bodily Assumption of Mary. Since Mary is seen as a symbol of the church, these dogmas tend to support an ecclesiology that ascribes to the church the capacity to be coredemptrix with Christ and the authority to reign with him over the rulers and emperors of the earth. Unchecked, the Mariology of the queen of heaven readily provides symbolic support for ecclesiastical triumphalism.

A very different image of Mary emerges in Protestant orthodoxy. Here the interest in Mary is largely confined to the miracle of the virgin birth. As a result, the particular gospel contours of the figure of Mary tend to disappear behind the image of the *virgin mother of Jesus*. While Calvin did not think it was necessary to hold to the perpetual virginity of Mary and counseled against impious speculation on the matter, Luther, Zwingli, and other Reformers insisted that Mary remained a virgin even after the birth of Jesus. This view was endorsed by Bullinger and inscribed in the Second Helvetic Confession (1566), one of the confessional documents in the Presbyterian *Book of Confessions*.

At the dawn of the era of modern Protestant theology, Friedrich Schleiermacher challenged the assumption of orthodoxy that there was a necessary link between the virgin birth and the divinity of Christ. In a characteristically succinct formulation, he argued that "the being of God in Christ cannot possibly be explained by the fact that no male activity had any share in His conception."[5] Schleiermacher further contended that the idea of a supernatural conception should not be allowed to rob Jesus of his full historicity; that the notion of Mary's perpetual virginity is completely without basis; and that a responsible doctrine of the supernatural conception of Jesus should carefully avoid any disparagement of human sexuality. While challenging the assumptions of Protestant orthodoxy, however, Schleiermacher failed to offer an alternative picture of Mary to that of traditional doctrine and conventional piety.

An alternative image was provided in liberal Protestant theology after Schleiermacher. For liberal Protestantism Mary became the *model of motherhood* and *the archetype of the ideal woman*, who displays the gentle feminine virtues that are essential to the civilizing of men and nations. A striking example of such a view of Mary is found in a sermon entitled "The Virgin's Character," delivered in London in 1867 by Stopford A. Brooke, a prominent Church of England clergyman.[6] Brooke lauds Mary's "gentle maidenhood" and her "noble womanhood." He speaks of her as the ideal expression of the nature God has assigned to woman, which is to bless and serve others and to influence them by her own selfless love, stainless honor, and chivalrous aspirations. The mission God has given women, perfectly realized in Mary, is to lead men and nations toward a life of virtue and noble sacrifice for others.

According to Brooke, "The regeneration of society is in the power of women. . . . The hearts of men, the lives of men, are in their hands." Brooke can even speak of the "patriotism" of Mary, her forgetting of herself in her love of country.

> This is what we want in England—women who will understand and feel what love of country means and act upon it; who will lose thought of themselves and their finery and their pleasure in a passionate effort to heal the sorrow and to destroy the dishonour, dishonesty, and vice of England; to realize that as mothers, maidens, wives, and sisters, they have but to bid the men of this country to be true, brave, loving, just, honourable, and wise; and they will become so, as they will become frivolous, base, unloving, ashamed of truth and righteousness, if women are so. . . ."[7]

In Brooke's view, the influence of noble women over men and nations is clearly evident in the "mighty music" in the song of the Virgin Mary. Brooke's picture of Mary is of a piece with the uncritical accommodation of Protestant liberalism to the norms and values of bourgeois western culture.

With the rise of Karl Barth's theology of the word of God and its attack on the theology of Protestant liberalism, the way was prepared for a radically different approach to Mary. In his *Church Dogmatics*, Barth reclaims the importance of the "miracle of Christmas" and the significance of the virgin birth as the indispensable sign of that miracle. For all its doctrinal rigor and insight, however, Barth's reflections on Mary remain almost entirely focused on her role in the event of the birth of the Savior. Mary is seen by Barth as *the purely receptive participant in God's salvific action.*

Barth rejected both the Roman Catholic and the liberal Protestant views of Mary with which he was familiar. When Emil Brunner dismissed the doctrine of the virgin birth as encumbering Christian faith with a mythical biological theory, Barth charged Brunner with biological reductionism and concluded that "Brunner's denial of the virgin birth is a bad business."[8] On the other hand, Barth refused to go the way of Roman Catholic Mariology, well known to him in the writings of his Basel friend, Hans Urs von Balthasar, on the grounds that it displaced the centrality of the humanity of Jesus Christ. As Barth wrote in the preface to *Church Dogmatics*, IV/2, "The content of this book might well be regarded as an attempted Evangelical answer to the Marian dogma of Romanism—both old and new. I have nowhere mentioned this, let alone attacked it directly. But I have in fact shown that it is made superfluous by the 'Exaltation of the Son of Man' and its anthropological implications."[9]

In recent decades a picture of Mary very different from all the preceding portrayals has developed especially within Roman Catholic liberation theology.[10] This revisionist Catholic view of Mary concentrates on her humble status and her song of praise at the time of the annunciation. From the liberationist perspective Mary is seen as a *prototype of the liberation struggle of poor people*, and especially of poor women, against injustice and oppression. In her song of praise, Mary proclaims that God "has brought down the powerful from their thrones and lifted up the lowly; he has filled the hungry with good things, and sent the rich away empty" (Luke 1:52–53).

In some versions of the liberationist portrayal, it appears that Mary's faith makes possible God's entrance into history and that God is therefore dependent on humanity in the ongoing struggle against injustice. While such a view is understandable as a reaction against many traditional portrayals of Mary, it runs the danger of replacing the witness of Mary to God's grace with a witness to the redemptive power of revolutionary faith and action in history.

These diverse pictures of Mary should give us pause. While each may possess an element of truth, all tend to be onesided or even reductionist. Thus is violence done to the full reality of Mary. It is instructive to recall an incident that occurred in St. Peter's Cathedral in Rome some years ago. The magnificent *Pietà* by Michelangelo was attacked by a man with a hammer, and before the assailant could be stopped, he struck and seriously damaged the face and arm of the figure of Mary. This episode offers a kind of parable of the violence that has been done to Mary in the Christian church, a violence that has distorted her image almost beyond recognition.

We have made Mary the queen of heaven, clothed her in purple robes, put a crown on her head, and elevated her high above the earth. We have made her the perfect lady, praised her untouched virginity, and sent forth our knights in shining armor to prove our allegiance to her. We have made her the ideal woman, extolled her self-effacement, her passivity, her silent acceptance of her duty, and her obedience to her husband, and we have expected all Christian women to approximate this idea. We have made her the total mother, exhausted her significance as a human being and a servant of God in the biological processes of childbirth and child-nurture, and have presented her in this form as the Christian standard for all women to follow. We have enlisted her as a revolutionary leader of our liberation struggles.

Our distortions of Mary have deep historical, psychological, and religious roots. Our violations of her are also violations of ourselves. Our fantastic pictures of Mary are expressions of our fantastic self-images, our secret daydreams of true womanhood and true manhood. In theological terms, both the Roman Catholic glorification of Mary and the Protestant neglect and cultural accommodation of her have contributed to an anthropocentric twist of the gospel of God's sovereign grace. If there are doctrines that seem especially vulnerable to a Feuerbachian critique of theology as mere self-projection, Mariology would stand near the top of the list. While Protestants find reason for

complaint in the excesses of Catholic Mariology, Catholics are dismayed by
the Protestant neglect of Mary and the unrelieved masculinity of Protestant
faith—with its exclusively male symbols, its all-male liturgical language, and
its all-male models of Christian life. Given these alternatives, is it any wonder
that the secular world forges its own images of the true woman and the true
man, without benefit of guidance from the biblical witness and the gospel that
stands at its center? Is it any wonder that modern American culture smiles contemptuously at both the Virgin Queen of medieval Mariology and the bourgeois Protestant ideal of female gentility, only to offer for its own part a
pathetic potpourri of images of womanhood that features figures like Miss
America, Madonna, and Thelma and Louise?

## MARY AS A WOMAN OF FAITH

What would a new picture of Mary look like, from a Reformed faith perspective? It would have to be a picture of Mary as witness to the sovereign grace
of God, and it would have to be based not in fantasy but on the scriptural witness. Mary is inseparable from the gospel story. Her name and faith are woven
into the fabric of the gospel and into the warp and woof of classical Christian
creeds. From a Reformed perspective, a new understanding of Mary would go
hand in hand with a rediscovery of the gospel and a transformed understanding of who we are as Christian men and women.

Scripture does not tell us enough about Mary to write a biography. We don't
know how she looked, how old she was when Jesus was born, or what thoughts
she had about her firstborn son as he grew to maturity and began his ministry.
We don't even know when and where and how she died. The Gospel writers
were not interested in supplying us with material for a biography of Mary any
more than they were in giving us material to write a life of Jesus. Yet Mary
stands before us in the Gospels as a woman of faith. The faith of Mary is portrayed—with economy, beauty, and stunning realism—in several clusters of
Gospel stories.[11]

### Mary's Consent to God's Election

The first and most familiar New Testament reference to Mary is the story of
the annunciation. The angel Gabriel tells Mary that the Lord is with her and
that she has found favor with God. God elects Mary to play a very special role
in the drama of redemption. She will conceive and bear a child who will fulfill
God's promises to Israel and who will usher in the reign of God that will never
end. Perplexed and startled by this strange news, Mary nevertheless responds

in simple trust: "Here am I, the servant of the Lord. Let it be with me according to your word" (Luke 1:38).

Mary's pilgrimage of faith thus begins in simple trust in the grace of God. In her courageous openness to the working of God in the world for its salvation, Mary is presented to us as an exemplary witness of faith. Strictly speaking, however, the story of the annunciation is told not in praise of Mary but in praise of the surprising, unmerited, electing grace of God. Mary is favored and chosen by God (Luke 1:28).

It is curious that Reformed theologians have not given more attention to the place of Mary in the doctrine of election.[12] Her election, of course, is not to be seen as competing with the election of Jesus Christ from the foundation of the world. Rather, Mary's election serves the divine purpose whereby the eternal election of the Son of God is historically realized. As a daughter of the elect people of Israel, Mary is herself elected and called to a special vocation. This is the meaning of the announcement of the angel that Mary has found favor with God and that she will give birth to the Son of the Most High.

It is, therefore, God's electing grace and not a biological miracle as such that stands at the heart of the New Testament stories of the virgin birth. To confess that the Savior was conceived by the Holy Spirit and born of the Virgin Mary is to give all praise and glory to God. The point of the story is not to demean procreation through the sexual act but to speak of the coming of the Savior as the sheer gift of God. Barth is surely right in arguing that it is not sexual activity per se that must be excluded as a vehicle of God's saving activity; it is the presumption of the overly self-confident, achievement-oriented, autonomous human being that is excluded. Only humanity in its willing receptivity and openness to God's sovereign grace can be a fitting servant of God in the work of salvation.[13]

Barth's way of stating this point, however, is problematic. He contends that in human history and culture up to the present, it is the human male who represents the arrogant claim of humanity to be utterly self-determining, independent of God's grace, and capable of redeeming self and history apart from God. While some feminist theologians might applaud this apparent subversion of patriarchy in Barth's exposition of the virgin birth, they would also no doubt note the dangers of gender stereotyping in Barth's interpretation. If the virgin birth is the indispensable sign that the male must be excluded from the event of the incarnation because it is the male who represents human achievement, creativity, and independence, the question arises whether the female is permitted to have a role only because she represents, in Barth's words, "non-achieving, non-creative," purely submissive humanity?[14]

Mary's response—"Here am I, the servant of the Lord. Let it be with me according to your word"—is reminiscent of the replies of Abraham, Moses,

Samuel, and Isaiah to the summons of God. It is a free, strong, and courageous response to the sovereign, electing grace of God addressed to her and has nothing to do with what is commonly understood by words like passivity and servility. Mary does not submit to coercion; she freely consents to the working of God's grace in and through her. That her consent is not made without deliberation and struggle is hinted by Mary's question, "How can this be?" Far from being a mere puppet, Mary makes an active, conscious, and free choice to participate in God's destiny for her. Mary elects God's election of her. *Mary exemplifies Christian faith and discipleship in her trustful hearing of the word of God and in her free and glad consent to the electing grace of God.*

## Mary's Solidarity with the Poor

A second element in the Gospel portrayal of Mary is contained in her song of praise. Mary's hymn gives voice to her solidarity in need with all poor and broken people yearning for God's redemption and renewal of the groaning creation. As a young, unwed, mother-to-be, Mary is certainly one of the poor. In both the Matthean and Lukan nativity narratives, she is described as extremely vulnerable.[15]

In his sermons on the Magnificat, Calvin underscores the point that Mary declares that she possesses no virtue that would account for God's favor to her. She is small, poor, and of lowly estate, yet God reaches out to her. Mary avoids all self-glorification and praises the unconditional grace of God.[16]

As Calvin's sermons and commentaries on Marian texts show, the theme of the unconditionality of God's grace and the theme of God's special love for the poor are not mutually exclusive. Mary's song is a powerful expression of God's solidarity with the poor and the weak. While it would be a mistake to think of the poor as inherently more virtuous than others, it is nevertheless true that the theme of God's special concern for the poor runs throughout the Bible. Moreover, the poor are more likely to be waiting for the inbreaking of the new world of God's justice than those who live in the captivity of relative affluence and self-satisfaction. It was not Karl Marx but Jesus who said, "It will be hard for a rich person to enter the kingdom of heaven" (Matt. 19:23). That will always remain a disturbing saying for those who by material standards are the rich, the successful, and the powerful of the earth. Perhaps that is why many Christians of every age are less disturbed by the image of Mary the queen of heaven than by the biblical Mary who astounds us first by her free and glad consent to God's electing grace and then by her bold and passionate expression of God's solidarity with the poor and downtrodden of the earth.

In her soaring song of praise to God, Mary bears witness to the justice and mercy of God. Her humility before God is coupled with courage to declare

God's judgment on injustice and oppression and to announce the coming of God's justice and mercy that turns the order of this world upside down. In pointing to the radicality of Mary's song, both Calvin and contemporary liberationists are right. Her song is indeed a song of the dawn of a revolution, but the revolution she announces is spiritual as well as political. It comes not from us but from God.

Neither in the biblical portrayal of Mary's passion for justice expressed in the Magnificat nor in the classical Reformed emphasis on the sovereignty of grace does radical trust in God lead to passivity or complacency. On the contrary, acknowledgment of salvation by grace alone goes hand in hand with the passionate cry for justice and a transformed world. This passion for justice remains anchored in God; it is not transferred to revolutionary ideologies. Nevertheless, zeal for God's honor and the manifestation of God's justice in all the creation ignites a real rebellion—a spirit of resistance against all forces of injustice and all the powers and principalities that oppose God's redemptive purposes. *Mary exemplifies Christian faith and discipleship in her praise of God's surprising and unmerited grace and in her fearless announcement of God's righteous concern for the poor.*

## Mary's Fallibility

A third group of Gospel stories adds another dimension to our understanding of Mary as a woman of faith. The astonishing realism of the biblical picture of Mary reaches its peak in this third group of stories. They describe Mary's confusion and her need for deeper understanding. According to the Reformed tradition, the church is always in need of reformation and correction by the word of God. Mary is exemplary of the church not despite but because she is portrayed in Scripture as being a person of faith who must learn the meaning of Christian discipleship through obedience and who must remain open to reform.

In the Gospel of Mark we are told of an occasion when Mary and the brothers of Jesus sought to see him while he was preaching. When he was told of their presence, his response was to say that those who had chosen to follow him were his true mother, brothers, and sisters. "Whoever does the will of God is my brother and sister and mother" (Mark 3:35). We are not told why Mary and other relatives of Jesus sought him out. Did they want to take him home? Had he been separated from them for so long that they were worried? Had they perhaps heard of his controversial ministry? Were they upset and even fearful for his life? We know nothing of these things. Nevertheless, it would be to dehumanize Mary to suggest that we must think of her as never experiencing anxiety, confusion, and fear about the ministry of her son and the dangers that accompanied it.

The Gospel writers (Mark, in particular) seem remarkably free of the compulsion to cover up the confusion and questionable motivations of the disciples of Jesus during his ministry. James and John wanted to sit on the right and left hands of Jesus when he became king (Mark 10:37). Peter, after a lot of bravado, denied Jesus three times on the night of his arrest and trial (Mark 14:66–72). Judas, one of the twelve, betrayed him with a kiss (Mark 14:44–45).

On what grounds could we assume that Mary was immune to this confusion, anxiety, and doubt about the risky and disturbing ministry and proclamation of Jesus? To be sure, we have no basis for imputing to her any of the baser motives that the Gospel writers ascribe to the inner circles of Jesus' disciples. Nevertheless, Mary naturally would have wanted and expected a special relationship with Jesus. To this extent, she would have shared the same confusion and uncertainty, the same struggle to understand, experienced by all followers of Jesus then and now. What disciple does not think, at least on occasion, that Jesus belongs especially to him or her? The Gospel portrayals of the disciples and friends closest to Jesus warn us not to make him the leader of our closed circle. Jesus calls us out of ourselves and our little circles of family, kin group, and nation. He summons us into a community beyond the common boundaries based on family, race, gender, nationality, culture, or social class. This call is enshrined in the words of Jesus: "Whoever does the will of God is my brother and sister and mother" (Mark 3:35).

Aware of the possibility that Mary as well as Jesus' intimate disciples might become objects of uncritical adulation and devotion, the early church preserved a few stories that warned against this tendency. One story reports that when a woman in a crowd shouted to Jesus, "Blessed is the womb that bore you and the breasts that nursed you," Jesus responded, "Blessed rather are those who hear the word of God and obey it" (Luke 11:27–28). Calvin comments,

> We see that Christ thought next to nothing of what the woman praised. And surely what she thought was Mary's special glory was far inferior to her other graces. For it was a better thing to be born again by the Spirit of Christ than to conceive the flesh of Christ in her womb, to have Christ spiritually living in her than to suckle him at her breast. The height of the holy Virgin's bliss and glory was to be a member of her own Son and to be numbered by his heavenly Father among the new creatures.[17]

According to another story, when Mary urged Jesus to perform a miracle at a marriage feast, he said to her, "Woman, what concern is that to you and to me? My hour has not yet come" (John 2:4). This is perhaps the most difficult of all the New Testament texts about Mary. Does it have the force of a reprimand? Calvin will not go that far, but he does speak of Mary's "unseasonable zeal" and thinks that Christ addresses his mother like this "so as to transmit a perpetual and general lesson to all ages, lest an extravagant honour paid to his mother should obscure his divine glory."[18] Or is Jesus' question to Mary a call for reflection about the necessary change that must come in the relationship between mother and son now that the ministry of Jesus has begun? Unless Mary understands and accepts that change, she too might become a hindrance rather than a help in the ministry of Jesus.

In a similar vein, Luke tells the story of Jesus as a young boy, conversing with the teachers in the temple. When his parents who had been looking for him expressed anxiety and irritation, Jesus responded that they should have known he must be in his Father's house. "They did not understand," is the evangelist's laconic comment (Luke 2:50).

These stories do not constitute a put-down of Mary. Rather they are a reminder to us all of the confusion and temptation that are a part of the life of faith. They remind us that the church and individual Christians must live a life of continuous repentance and readiness to be reformed by the word of God. They lead us to recognize in Mary not only a special witness to God's grace, not only one who testifies powerfully to God's world-transforming justice and mercy, but also one who struggles, as do all followers of Jesus, to overcome the temptation to try to lead Jesus rather than being led by him, to want privileged access to him, to have a too provincial and too narrow understanding of the reign of God that he proclaims. From a Reformed perspective, it is neither embarrassing nor dishonoring of Mary to see in her confusion and need of redirection a reminder of our own confusion and need. *Mary exemplifies the reality of Christian discipleship that all followers of Jesus and the church as a whole must be* "semper reformanda": *always being reformed by the Word of God.*

## Mary's Call to Ministry

We find a fourth element in the Gospel picture of Mary in the passion narratives. Mary, together with a few other disciples, stands under the cross of Jesus. As he hangs on the cross, Jesus looks to Mary and to a beloved disciple, traditionally identified as John. He says to Mary, "Woman, here is your son," and to the beloved disciple, "Here is your mother" (John 19:26–27).

Rich with symbolism as John's Gospel is, it is unlikely that the evangelist wanted this scene at the cross to be understood as expressing only Jesus' concern to entrust his mother and one of his disciples to their mutual care. It is instead a vivid picture of the church and its ministry of reconciliation and service in the name of the crucified Lord.

Mary's vocation is not exhausted in her giving birth to the Son of God. She is given the further dignity of ministry in the name of the Son that she bore. The self-giving love of God in Jesus Christ creates a new and inclusive family of human beings. This community is not created and is not sustained by what Dietrich Bonhoeffer called "cheap grace." The grace of God is costly to God. Christian discipleship, too, exacts a cost. Christians are called to community marked by mutual, self-giving love and the bearing of one another's burdens. True community requires the willingness to let our self-centered lives die and to find new life in solidarity with all our fellow creatures, experiencing both their need of redemption and their sufferings as our own.

Mary and all other disciples gain their Christian identity not in splendid solitude but as they take part in this costly and painful process of unexpectedly acquiring new brothers, sisters, parents, and children—even as God has welcomed and loved us all in Jesus Christ. At the foot of the cross, Mary and the beloved disciple are called to the ministry of friendship and reconciliation. A right reading of this story of Mary and the beloved disciple under the cross provides powerful biblical authorization of the ordination of men *and* women to ministry. The Christian ministry of men and women has its basis in the commission of the crucified Lord and takes its signature from his self-giving love. *Mary exemplifies Christian faith and discipleship in her location at the foot of the cross and in her call to ministry with and for others.*

## Mary's Spirituality

A fifth and final New Testament reference to Mary that must be mentioned is found in the Book of Acts, where we read that all of the followers of Jesus came together after his resurrection and ascension and devoted themselves constantly to prayer for the coming of God's enlivening and empowering Spirit. Among the disciples were certain women, "including Mary the mother of Jesus" (Acts 1:14).

As a pious Jew, the life of prayer would have been a familiar practice of Mary. Luke portrays her as a woman familiar with the practice of prayer and meditation. Twice he tells us that Mary pondered the words and events of Jesus' birth and boyhood and treasured them in her heart (2:19; 51b).

Together with other members of the community of faith after the resurrection, Mary prays and waits for the coming of the life-giving Spirit of God. Mary's spirituality is a spirituality of common prayer, of sharing with others in the disciplines and practices of Christian life. The commission that she and the other disciples had received from the crucified and risen Jesus could be acted on only in a context of common, prayerful waiting on God. This waiting is not quietistic; it is not mere passivity. It is a persistent, hopeful, and active waiting for the coming of God's Word and Spirit.

Prayer that waits, that is persistent, and that is practiced in common is the prerequisite of the effectual ministry of the church. Such prayerful waiting on the Word and Spirit of God characterizes Reformed faith and theology at its best in the practices of worship, proclamation, sacraments, Christian education, and the social outreach and service of the church in the world.

Mary and the early church understood active ministry to commence again and again in waiting on God and in the prayer, "Come, Creator Spirit." For Reformed Christians, Mary is not the one *to* whom we pray. Rather, she is our sister in the faith and our Lord's mother *with* whom we constantly pray and actively wait for the new coming of God's Word and Spirit in our midst, to enliven, empower, guide, and gladden us in our praise and service of the free, sovereign, gracious God. *Mary exemplifies Christian faith and discipleship in her prayerful waiting for the coming of God's renewing and empowering Spirit.*

## SUMMARY

Within a Reformed faith perspective, the biblical stories of Mary are testimonies to the grace of God in Jesus Christ by the power of the Holy Spirit. They are stories of Mary as witness to God's sovereign, electing grace. They are stories of the zeal of this woman of faith for the coming of God's righteousness and mercy to transform the whole creation. They are stories of Mary's and our need for continuous reform by the word of God. They are stories of what it means to live faithfully as women and men ordained to ministry under the cross of Christ, commissioned by him to bear one another's burdens and to serve God's work of reconciliation. They are stories of a woman who prays and waits with the whole people of God for the coming of God's Word and Spirit to empower us for ministry and mission.

Why not let Mary be what the Bible describes her as being: a woman of humble yet courageous faith from whom we might learn to praise the sovereign grace of God, cry out against injustice, and acknowledge our daily need for repentance and forgiveness? Why not join with Mary in receiving our commission to ministry from Christ at the foot of his cross, and in hoping and praying without ceasing for the coming of God's Word and Spirit to renew the church and empower it for service?

In a Roman Catholic church in Guernavaca, Mexico, renovated after Vatican II, a large crucifix hangs over the main altar. On the left wall—toward the front, yet still clearly in the nave—there is a simple, modest, unadorned figure of Mary. She does not draw special attention to herself. She stands among the people of God, and her eyes are turned to the cross.[19] That is, I would venture to hope, a picture of Mary that Christians of the Reformation heritage, in solidarity with their Roman Catholic sisters and brothers, might happily make their own.

# NOTES

1. John Calvin, "Evangile selon Saint Luc, 1, 26 à 30," reprinted in *La revue reformee* 28 (1956): 3–4.
2. See Raymond E. Brown et al. eds., *Mary in the New Testament* (Philadelphia: Fortress Press, 1978).
3. Mary Hines, "Mary," in *The New Dictionary of Catholic Spirituality*, ed. Michael Downey (Collegeville, Minn.: Liturgical Press, 1993), 635–45.
4. For a comprehensive survey of interpretations of Mary, see Jaroslav Pelikan, *Mary Through the Centuries* (New Haven, Conn.: Yale University Press, 1996).
5. Friedrich Schleiermacher, *The Christian Faith* (Edinburgh: T &T Clark, 1928), 403.
6. Stopford A. Brooke, *Sermons Preached in St. James' Chapel* (London: Kegan Paul, Trench, 1881), 83–94.
7. Ibid., 93–94.
8. Karl Barth, *Church Dogmatics* I/2 (Edinburgh: T & T Clark, 1956), 184.
9. Karl Barth, *Church Dogmatics* IV/2 (Edinburgh: T & T Clark, 1958), ix.
10. See, for example, Tissa Balasuriya, "Mary and Human Liberation," reprint of *Logos* 29, nos. 1 & 2 (March/July, 1990).
11. For an excellent recent study of the New Testament texts pertaining to Mary, see Beverly Roberts Gaventa, *Mary: Glimpses of the Mother of Jesus* (Columbia, S.C.: University of South Carolina Press, 1995; Minneapolis: Fortress Press, 1999).
12. This theme is not absent, of course, from the writings of Calvin and Barth, but neither develops it at length. "The *fiat mihi* of Mary is preceded by the resolve and promise of God. It confirmed his work, but it did not add anything at all to it. It confirmed the election of Israel and Mary, but it did not give it either its truth or power" (Barth, *Church Dogmatics* IV/2, 45).
13. Barth, *Church Dogmatics* I/2, 191.
14. Ibid., 191.
15. See Gaventa, *Mary*, 130.
16. Calvin, "Evangile," 22.
17. John Calvin, *Matthew, Mark and Luke*, vol. 2, Calvin's New Testament Commentaries, ed. David T. Torrance and Thomas F. Torrance (Grand Rapids, Mich.: Wm. B. Eerdmans Pub. Co., 1978), 54.
18. John Calvin, *The Gospel According to St. John*, part 1, 1–10, Calvin's New Testament Commentaries, ed. David W. Torrance and Thomas F. Torrance (Grand Rapids, Mich.: Wm. B. Eerdmans Pub. Co., 1978), 47.
19. Lukas Vischer makes reference to this church in his essay, "Maria—Typus der Kirche und Typus der Menschheit," in *Oikumenische Skizzen* (Frankfurt: Verlag Otto Lembeck, 1972), 123.

# 10

## What Mary Has to Say about God's Bare Goodness

LOIS MALCOLM

Mary is a complex figure. She has taken on many forms within the Christian tradition (e.g., virgin, queen, bride, mother, intercessor)[1] and many names (e.g., *theotokos*, "The Mediatrix," "The Model of Faith," "The Queen of Heaven").[2] She is, in David Tracy's sense of the term, truly a classic and embodies a classic's two main criteria: permanence and excess of meaning.[3] This paper unravels a strand of that permanence and excess by interpreting what could be identified as the first instance of Protestant Mariology: Martin Luther's *Commentary on the Magnificat* (1521).[4]

Luther's commentary brings to the fore what would come to be an identifying feature of Protestant theological reflection on Mary: its emphasis not on her role as a mother but on the way she (like Abraham, Job, and others before her) is an exemplar of faith. Although this reading has its drawbacks (for example, what is distinct about Mary's being a mother or even a woman tends to be lost), it nonetheless opens the way for a different kind of Mariology. This faith-focused Mariology resonates more closely, perhaps, with the Mary of the Magnificat (Luke 1:46–55) and the broader apocalyptic, prophetic, and egalitarian traditions it draws from. But its apocalyptic and prophetic thrust is not what is most interesting about this commentary. What is most interesting is its depiction of how we, like Mary, might perceive God's goodness (even when hidden and unfelt) and defend the "right" and the "truth" (even when it appears not to prevail).[5]

## MARY'S EXPERIENCE OF TASTING
## GOD'S "BARE, SWEET GOODNESS"

The key theme of Luther's commentary is Mary's "experience" of being "over-shadowed" by the Spirit.[6] Most of the commentary is devoted to describing precisely what this experience is.[7] Luther makes clear, for example, that Mary speaks on the basis of her experience, an experience the Holy Spirit used to enlighten and instruct her. "Experience," he notes, is the "school" of the Spirit. We cannot understand God or God's Word without having received such understanding "immediately" from the Holy Spirit, "without experiencing, proving, and feeling it" for ourselves (299). It is because Mary herself "experienced" the Spirit's power that she is able to speak with such "strong ardor" and "exuberant joy":

> My life and all my senses float in the love and praise of God and in lofty pleasures, so that I am no longer mistress of myself; I am exalted, more than I exalt myself, to praise the Lord. (302)

Indeed, she breaks out into sighs and groaning: "[H]er words flow forth in such a way that the spirit comes seething with them." And these words "live." They have "hands and feet." They are "fire, light, and life." And not only her "words" but her "whole body and life" with all its members "strive and strain for utterance." She has experienced being "saturated with the divine sweetness and Spirit." Like the psalmist, she has "tasted" God's sweetness *before* she has "seen" God (Ps. 34:8).[8] This has given her true insight into God's nature. Thus, she has much to teach us about "God's work, method, nature, and will," a work that can only be interpreted as an "art" (331).

So what did Mary experience? The "deep insight and wisdom" she experienced was that God is a God who does nothing but "exalt those of low degree" and "put down the mighty from their thrones"—in short, "break what is whole" and "make whole what is broken." When God acts, what was "nothing, worthless, despised, wretched, and dead" is made "something, precious, honorable, blessed, and living." In turn, "whatever is something, precious, honorable, blessed, and living" is made to be "nothing, worthless, despised, wretched, and dying." Mary experienced this kind of action when God chose her to be the "Mother of God" despite her "insignificance, lowliness, poverty, and inferiority." Why does God work in this way? To make clear that it is *God's work* at play here—God's action of creating out of nothing—since "no creature can produce anything out of nothing" (299–300).[9]

What Mary experienced was a reversal: the lowly were exalted; the mighty were brought down. Yet this status inversion embodies more than a simple reversal. Mary's exuberance in verse 48 results not merely from the fact that

God lifted her up from a "low estate." What is significant is that God "regarded" her. At issue is the theme of *perception*—and not only *what* is being seen but *who* is doing the seeing. Even before Mary has seen God, God "sees" her and thus enables her to taste God's "sensible sweetness" (303). As the one who creates out of nothing, God is able to look into the "depths" and not the "heights." By contrast, the "eyes of the world" only look above them. "We experience this everyday," Luther observes. Everyone strives after what is "above" them—"honor, power, wealth, knowledge, a life of ease, and whatever is lofty and great." And with them are many "hangers-on," gladly yielding to them, eager to be at their side and share in their exaltation (300). No one wants to look into the "depths" of "poverty, disgrace, squalor, misery, and anguish." From these "all turn away their eyes"—"take to their heels, forsake and shun them." God alone looks into the "depths" of need and misery and is "near" to all in the "depths" (300).

And now Luther explains the core reason why being "seen" by God when one is in the "depths" is so important. If being seen by God when one is in the depths says something about the character of God's power and action—that God is a God who creates out of nothing—then it also says something about the character of human experiences of God. It is precisely when we have been "seen" by God in the "depths"—when God has "regarded" us there and "lifted" us up—that we truly are able to "trust" and to "love and praise God." There is something about the excessiveness and sheer gratuity of God's love for us even and *precisely* when in the "depths" that causes "the heart to over-flow with gladness" and "leap and dance with great pleasure" (300). The Holy Spirit is present precisely in these moments, teaching "such an exceedingly great knowledge through this experience" (300). It is for this reason, Luther avers, that God lays upon us "Christ's cross" along with "countless sufferings and afflictions." Indeed, for this reason he goes on to say, quite controversially, that God permits some to sin precisely so that they will more fully experience the love of God.

## SUFFERING AND GOD'S APOCALYPTIC ACTION

But why this focus on suffering? Is this merely a macabre interest in pain? We arrive here at a deep theme in Luther's theology, his theology of the cross, which is embedded in the cross-mysticism of medieval monasticism evident in such figures as Bonaventure, Bernard of Clairvaux, and in much popular lay piety of the late medieval period.[10] Luther's own twist to this tradition is most succinctly articulated in the *Heidelberg Disputation* (1518), where he contends that "sufferings and the cross" depict the "love of God" which "*creates* what is pleasing to it" (in contrast to the "love of [human beings]" which "comes into being through attraction to what pleases it").[11] In "suffering and affliction" we perceive what is "visible" of God, what Luther calls "God's backside" (referring to Exod. 33:23).[12] Why? Because it is precisely situations of distress or chaos that are the loci of God's creative activity, which "creates out of nothing" (Gen. 1:2).

We can note that for the ancients, the "nothing" God creates out of was not understood to be simply a void, as the traditional English translation of the Hebrew word *tohû wabohû* usually implies (e.g., when Gen. 1:2 is translated as "without form and void"), but something more like "disorder, injustice, subjugation, disease, and death."[13] This is analogous to Luther's sense of God's "creative power," which creates out of the "nothing" of suffering. It is in the "visible" situations where God appears "hidden"—where it seems that all we can see is God's "back side" in our experiences of affliction—that we know God is present. Why? Because only *God* could redeem such situations and not merely our own good intentions, no matter how noble or pious they may be.

The logic at work here is analogous to that found in 1 Corinthians where the "foolishness" and "weakness" of "Christ crucified" is contrasted with human "wisdom" and "power" (1:18–31). As with that of Paul in 1 Corinthians, this language has a strong critical function. "Theologians of the cross" (that is, theologians of "suffering and affliction") are best able to "say what a thing is" (Thesis 21). They are able to smoke out false and apparent works—as opposed to merely overt sins—in contrast to "theologians of glory" who tend toward duplicity by calling a "good thing bad and a bad thing good" (Thesis 21). The latter tend to rely on the more sophisticated but nonetheless more duplicitous "invisible" fabrications of human attempts to manipulate God that may "appear" to be wise and good but, in fact, do just the opposite: "puff up, blind, and harden" (Thesis 22).

Yet this logic focuses not on suffering itself but on the *activity* of God.[14] What is unique about God's power and wisdom is precisely that it creates what is pleasing to it (bringing life out of death, hope out of despair, healing out of disease, justice out of injustice, order out of chaos, and so on) rather than simply responding to what it is attracted by (which is what creatures tend to do). Thus the focus in this logic and language is on the distinct character of *God's* power and wisdom, which may appear as foolishness and weakness to us but in fact has the power to create out of nothing and which cannot be manipulated despite the sophistication of our efforts.

The distinct character of this divine power—this "strength" that scatters the proud, brings down the powerful, and sends the rich away empty—is especially evident in the Magnificat. An apocalyptic perspective is at work in both this theology of the cross and the Magnificat itself. Apocalyptic discourse refers not only to a literary genre or a socioreligious movement but also to a theological perspective, a way of perceiving divine plans within mundane reality.[15] Such a perspective is oriented toward God's ultimate saving and judging activity in the future. Nonetheless, apocalyptic discourse also presupposes that some—those chosen by God—can actually perceive that ultimate salvation and judgment even now. Thus, "epistemology" is key to apocalyptic discourse: how we *perceive* present events in terms of that future. J. Louis Martyn speaks about the "epistemology of apocalyptic discourse" as involving not only a seemingly hopeless depiction of the human situation in human terms, but the conviction that God has given the elect a true perception of this situation in view of its future transformation.[16] The Greek word group *apokalypsis/apokalypto* can be translated "unveiling"/"unveil" (*apo* as "out from" and *kalypso* as "veil").

In line with the Magnificat, Luther uses language that reverses one's initial expectations of things (the low are brought high, etc.) in order to bring about a shift in perception among his readers. Luther employs a set of paradoxical statements that enact—or "perform"—an epistemological shift.[17] They enact for their readers or hearers a true perception of *present* events in light of God's *future* transformation of them.[18] Luther organizes his actual exegesis of the Magnificat around three sets of contrasts: wisdom, power, and wealth (using Jer. 9:23, 24 as a lens for interpreting the paradoxical statements in Luke 1:46–55). The following chart displays these contrasts.

| Jeremiah 9:23 | Luke 1:51–53 | Commentary on the Magnificat |
|---|---|---|
| "[D]o not let the wise boast in their wisdom" | "scattered the proud in the thoughts of their hearts" (v. 51b) | "poor in spirit" versus "wisdom" (all "spiritual possessions" that bring popularity, fame, good report: e.g., intellect, reason, wit, piety, virtue) |
| "[D]o not let the mighty boast in their might" | "brought down the powerful from their thrones, and lifted up the lowly" (v. 52) | "oppressed" versus "might" (e.g., authority, nobility, friends, high station, honor) |
| "[D]o not let the wealthy boast in their wealth"[19] | "filled the hungry with good things, and sent the rich away empty" (v. 53) | being "rich" versus the lack of life's necessities (e.g., good health, health, beauty, pleasure, wealth) |

136

This apocalyptic epistemology, therefore, entails two different perceptions of things. God's creative activity affects different people in different ways. It "comforts" the lowly but "terrifies" the mighty. Luther's language is strong: You must fear if you are mighty and take comfort if you are lowly, he observes. Indeed, the higher you are, the more you must fear, and the lowlier you are, the more you must take comfort. This point is significant in and of itself because it makes clear that the activity of God truly affects people differently. In sum, those who are in affliction hear not a word that keeps them in their affliction but a word of comfort that has the power to bring them out of it. By contrast, those who are self-satisfied—or oppress others—hear a different type of word.[20]

## PASSIVITY AND THE LOGIC OF DOUBLE-NEGATION

Here we move to our second major theme in this reading of the Magnificat: that what is at stake in this experience of God's power is not simply the experience of being raised or being brought low. What is interesting about Mary's exalting God because God "regarded her low estate" is that he regarded *her*. What is important here is being "seen" by God, being "regarded" by "God's eyes." Only when we know that we are "seen" by God's eyes—eyes that have the power to penetrate even to our "depths"—can we "taste" God's sweetness and "trust." We can then "love and praise God" regardless of whether we are high or low.

Indeed, Luther contrasts two types of "false" spirits with Mary's outlook in the Magnificat: (1) those who magnify themselves and (2) those who magnify God only during times of tangible blessing. Self-magnifiers are "smooth and slippery" persons who are so satisfied with God's gifts that they no longer have any regard for the giver. The fair-weather faithful are only able to praise God when things go well for them. When they suffer oppression or find themselves in the depths they are plunged into despair.

At issue, then, in this experience of God's power is not simply the vindication of the righteous and the oppressed. Following a theme in German mysticism that describes the soul as a "virgin mother" whose "detached love" is united with God, Luther describes how Mary experiences God's "bare" goodness, a goodness she "tastes" whether she is raised or brought low. Mary differs from "impure and perverted lovers" (those who seek their own advantage in God, who seek only after the gifts that God can give them).[21] Rather she is able to love and praise God's "bare" goodness," which at times may be "unfelt." Impure lovers of God only have an eye out for the good *things* God has done for them. They can only hold God in high esteem and be filled with joy when those good things are given to them. But as soon as God "hides" God's face and "withdraws the rays" of God's goodness, "leaving them bare and in misery," their "love and praise" ends. They are unable to love and praise "the *bare, unfelt goodness* that is *hidden* in God" (309, my italics). As a result, they are unable to preserve "an even mind in plenty and in want, in wealth and in poverty" (cf. Phil. 4:12).

Mary, by contrast, keeps an "even mind" in both types of situations. She loves and praises God's goodness just as much when she does not feel it as when she does. She is neither seduced by good gifts when they are given nor plunged into despair when they are taken away. This is why she, like Job, is a model of faith. She loves and praises God "evenly" and "rightly." She is not tempted when overwhelming honors are "heaped on her head." She clings only to God's goodness, "which she neither sees nor feels." In fact, she "overlooks the good things she does feel, and neither takes pleasure nor seeks her own enjoyment in it" (311). Mary seeks only the "bare goodness of God"—even when it is unfelt. Indeed, this is the only way to "equanimity" and an "even mind"— regardless of whether one has wealth or poverty, power or weakness.

But this "apocalyptic epistemology" does not simply have to do with the *negation* of wealth, power, and wisdom. Rather, a "double-reversal" is at work here.[22] The point is *neither* to have wealth, power, or wisdom *nor not* to have it (and have poverty, weakness, foolishness). The point, rather, is to continue trusting God's "bare goodness" regardless of one's circumstances. Thus, Luther makes fun of those who "carry water to the well"—who affect "humble" clothing, faces, gestures, and words with the intention of being "regarded by the mighty and rich, by scholars and saints, even by God himself" (314–315). Conversely, he points out, someone like Queen Esther did not have "lofty things" removed from her sight but remained "truly humble" despite her wealth and power.

In all of this Luther is asking, "[A]re you putting your trust in God or in God's gifts?" This question echoes Augustine's ancient theme that the "direction of one's love" determines the validity of one's action, not the specific action itself; thus one can do whatever one wills as long as what is done follows from the love of God. It also echoes Bernard of Clairvaux's depiction of the highest form of love: loving God simply for God's sake and not for any other ulterior purpose. As stated most succinctly in the *Heidelberg Disputation* (1518) (and, much later, in Nietzsche's *Genealogy of Morals*), there is a critique in this of the sophisticated means we employ to "appear" wise, spiritual, and righteous while actually seeking to use our apparent spiritual superiority (or, conversely, our very spiritual "weakness") to manipulate or establish power over others. Luther notes, for example, that in "things divine, the smart alecks and proud sages usually make common cause with the mighty and persuade them to take sides against the truth" (344).

Luther has no patience for false wisdom, presenting a stinging critique of those who think they are "in the right" (332–339).

> No rich or mighty man is so puffed up and bold as one such smart aleck who feels and knows that he is *in the right*, understands all about a matter, is wiser than other people. Especially when he finds he ought to give way or confess himself in the wrong, he becomes so insolent and is so utterly devoid of the fear of God that he dares to boast of being infallible, declares God is on his side and the others on the devil's side, and has the effrontery to appeal to the judgment of God. If such a man possesses the necessary power, he rushes on headlong, persecuting, condemning, slandering, slaying, banishing, and destroying all who differ with him, saying afterward he did it all to the honor and glory of God. . . . Oh, how big a bubble we have here! How much Scripture has to say about such men, and how many grievous things it threatens them with! But they feel them less than the anvil feels the smith's hammer. (332–333)

You can never gain a hearing with such people, Luther exclaims. They *must* have their way. It is impossible that they should be wrong or give way. They simply assert, "We are in the right," and that is the end of it "in spite of everyone else, though it be the whole world" (333–334).

At this point in our reading of Luther, certain suspicions might emerge. Does Luther's critique of those who believe they are "in the right" imply a negation of the right and the truth? Does it support passivity in the face of evil, discouraging the defense of righteous causes and fighting for the good things of life? Has the logic of double-negation so spiritualized this reading of the Magnificat that it stands in opposition to what the Magnificat actually says: that those who have been politically and economically oppressed will be vindicated?

The nuance of this double-reversal is brought to the fore in Luther's discussion of what it means to "defend the right." Everything depends, Luther observes, on a "proper understanding of being in the right" (334). Yes, we are to defend the truth and the right—and even suffer for it. This is what the martyrs have done throughout the ages. But we are not to defend our righteous causes or our causes for truth by means that negate the very right or truth we are seeking to defend. That would be to turn "the right" into a wrong.

A similar point can be made regarding more tangible human rights—say, the defense of one's spouse, child, friends, body, property, money—things that are good in and of themselves and created and given by God. If an enemy were to deprive you of these gifts, Luther asks, or if you were to lose them simply by chance, do you have just cause "to rage and storm and to take them again by force or to sulk impatiently until they were restored to you?" (334–335). These gifts are good in and of themselves; they are God's creatures. They are to be defended, even for Luther, to the point of using physical resistance, if necessary.[23] In other words, we confess that "the right, your reason, knowledge, wisdom, and all thoughts are right and good" *in and of themselves*. For the world to go on, these things must remain. The act of God in this apocalyptic logic creates these very goods and does not destroy them; it does not endorse some otherworldly future unrelated to the actual goods we need for our survival and flourishing in this life. But once the defense has been made—the "goodness" of these creaturely goods "confessed"—one must be ready to "let such things go and be ready at all times to do without them" and instead "cleave to God alone." This does not mean that we do take them back, or that we convince ourselves they are actually *not* good. We are simply compelled to regard them with "equanimity," confessing that they are "good and not evil" (335).

## MOTHERHOOD OR THE REIGN OF GOD?

We have addressed two possible objections so far: that this reading might endorse suffering and that it might endorse passivity. There is, however, yet a third issue that this commentary raises. What comes to the fore in this first Reformation reflection on Mary is the fact that Mary's femaleness and her motherhood are not in and of themselves *theologically* significant to the reflection. For Luther, the Holy Spirit's "overshadowing" of Mary has to do primarily with God's activity of judging and saving; the fact that that act entailed her being chosen to be the "Mother of God" is not central to its theological point. That she as a lowly maiden was chosen for this great act simply exemplifies how God chooses people in humble circumstances to do great things. Of course, this ties Mary in with the great apocalyptic and prophetic traditions of the Hebrew and Christian Scriptures that depict a new heaven and new earth where justice and mercy will reign for all people, and indeed all creation. It links her to Jesus' own Spirit-inspired preaching of the reign of God, where good news is brought to the poor, the captives released, the blind given sight, and the oppressed liberated (Luke 4:18–29). Ultimately, it links her to the scene at Pentecost where people are filled with the same Spirit even though they speak different languages—and where Joel's prophesy is said to be ful-filled: that both sons and daughters prophecy, young and old see visions, and even male and female slaves are given the power to prophesy in the Spirit (Acts 2:17–21; cf. Joel 2:28–32). But the central theme with such associations is not Mary's being a mother or even her being a woman but her being a witness to the way God acts and to what God does when God acts.[24]

By contrast, most Roman Catholic teaching about Mary, even teaching that emphasizes how she is an "exemplar" of faith, stresses the theological significance of her being a mother and a woman. For Hans Urs von Balthasar, a noted Roman Catholic of the twentieth century, Mary's experience of being "overshadowed" is profoundly rooted in "her maternal feelings and experience, joys and especially sorrows."[25] This is what constitutes, in a very concrete and material way, her act of faith—her "spiritual and physical readiness" for God, her "superabundant fruitfulness." Indeed, everything about this act of faith is "drenched in the blood of human experience," that is, blood from the "womb." The Spirit's overshadowing her—the "lightning flash" of this "miracle"—is an experience that begins with all that is *natural* about her as a mother. On the one hand, her being a mother exemplifies the faith of Abraham and that of all Christians, much like the Reformation reading. But this faith also, precisely because it bears and gives birth to the Son, encloses within itself all future Christians—bringing them forth from Mary's womb, just as Jesus was brought forth from her womb. There is, then, according to von Balthasar, a "physical substratum" of spiritual solidarity that unites the church across space and time that comes not only from the Eucharist, and Christ's tangible presence there, but from the actual physical unity of Mary and Jesus as mother and child. Thus, while Mary exemplifies the faith of all Christians, she nonetheless has a unique vocation that distinguishes her from all other Christians.

Such theological attention to the "concrete and irreducibly unique facts" about Mary's being Jesus' mother tends to be lost in Protestantism. For inheritors of the Reformation, all talk of Mary serving as a "physical substratum" between Jesus and the church smacks of idolatry. We need no other mediator, Protestants argue, but Christ. But idolatry is not their only issue. As Douglas Farrow has pointed out, the ascendance of devotion to Mary in the Middle Ages was accompanied by an increased emphasis on the role human merit plays in achieving salvation; indeed, attention to Mary's very role as mother suggests a focus on her activity rather than on God's.[26]

Interestingly, the Reformers' desire for the spiritual equality of all believers led them to "level" all vocations before God. All believers are now priests; Mary is yet another believer—a priest who gives witness to God's activity. But have the inheritors of the Reformation—and their secularized counterparts—lost something in their rejection of Mary's *sacred* status precisely as mother and woman? Julia Kristeva, a French psychoanalyst, wonders whether the demise of the Mary cult has left us without a satisfactory way of speaking and thinking the very sacrality of being mother or woman.[27] Certainly American society, in particular, has difficulty recognizing the value of mothering, locating it as part of the "shadow work"[28]—the invisible work—of the economy, work that is done but not fully or explicitly recognized for its true value.[29]

We have reached the limit of this Reformation reading of Mary. Yes, it links Mary with God's action of raising the lowly and bringing down the mighty—the act that ushers in a future reign we can participate in even now. Yes, in the context of this "now" and "not yet" reign, distinctions based on age, gender, ethnicity, and class no longer serve as means for establishing power over one another. This very shift in focus to the reign of God should open up a space for the equality of men and women, a space not allowed by traditional Mariologies that link Mary's very motherhood and gender to a more subordinate and receptive role for women in church and society.[30] But herein also lies the problem with this reading. Its very shift in focus leaves a vacuum, seen in the search undertaken by Protestants and others for traces of feminine imagery for God.[31] Although this reading of Luther opens up the space for one type of reflection on Mary's identity, it does not fully encapsulate the fecundity of her power as a "classic" within the Christian tradition.

Nonetheless, Luther's insights do link Mary to another set of classic biblical traditions. They link Mary not with motherhood or even womanhood per se but with the judging and saving act of God that creates a new world of justice and mercy. In this world, the righteous are vindicated; life is created out of death; order out of chaos; joy out of suffering; and distinctions among human beings are no longer used as markers of power. The key insight of Luther's reading of the Magnificat, however, is that though this reign will only be fully consummated in the future, it is a reality we can perceive now—even in circumstances that seem to contradict it. Indeed, precisely in such situations do we come to grips with the reality of this power that can create out of nothing. But what we confess is not simply the experience of its presence or the gifts it gives us but God's "bare" goodness. The lesson that Mary and other exemplars from Abraham to Job teach is that God's bare goodness, even when hidden or unfelt, gives the equanimity not only to defend the right or the truth (even our right to creaturely goods) but to face whatever may come with an "even mind."[32]

## NOTES

1. Taken from the titles of the chapters in Marina Walker, *Alone of All Her Sex: The Myth and Cult of the Virgin Mary* (New York: Knopf, 1976).

2. Taken from some of the titles in Jaroslav Pelikan, *Mary Through the Centuries: Her Place in the History of Culture* (New Haven, Conn.: Yale University Press, 1996).

3. David Tracy's definition of "classic" is found in the *Analogical Imagination: Christian Theology and the Culture of Pluralism* (New York: Crossroad Books, 1981).

4. Parenthetical page references in the text of this essay will be to the "Commentary on the Magnificat," in *Luther's Works*, vol. 21 (Saint Louis: Concordia, 1956).

5. For other recent Lutheran treatments of Mary, see the essays on "Mary" in *Dialog* 31 (Fall 1992): 245–271 (edited by Carl Braaten, with essays by F. M. Jelly, F. C. Senn, R. W. Jenson, and R. W. Bertram). See also H. George Anderson, ed., *The One Mediator, the Saints, and Mary* (Minneapolis: Augsburg Books, 1992), especially the essay by Eric Gritsch, "The Views of Luther and Lutheranism on the Veneration of Mary," 235–248.

6. Luke 1:35: "The Holy Spirit will come upon you, and the power of the Most High will overshadow you." Note that in Exodus, God's presence is often depicted as a light hidden in a cloud to "overshadow" human beings (see Exod. 16:10; 24:15–18; 40:34–35; also Luke 9:34). See also Gen. 1:2 where the Spirit of God sweeps over the face of the waters.

7. This reading develops more fully an initial reading of Luther's *Commentary on the Magnificat* in my essay, "The Hidden God Revisited: Desecularization, the Depths and God's Sort of Seeing," *Dialog*, forthcoming.

8. Note Luther's translation of Psalm 34:8: "Oh, taste and see that the Lord is sweet; blessed is the man that trusts in Him" (302–303).

9. An apparent allusion to the old axiom *"Ex nihilo nihil fit."*

10. For a discussion of this period, see Bernard McGinn, *The Growth of Mysticism* (New York: Crossroad Books, 1994).

11. See Gerhard Forde's translation of Thesis 28 of the *Heidelberg Disputation* (1518) in *On Being a Theologian of the Cross: Reflections on Luther's Heidelberg Disputation (1518)* (Grand Rapids, Mich.: Wm. B. Eerdmans Pub. Co., 1997), 112. On the theology of the cross, see also Walter von Loewinich, *Luther's Theology of the Cross* (Minneapolis: Augsburg Books, 1976) and Mary Solberg, *Compelling Knowledge: A Feminist Proposal for an Epistemology of the Cross* (Albany, N.Y.: SUNY Press, 1997).

12. See Thesis 20 of the *Heidelberg Disputation*: "But rather the one who perceives what is visible of God, God's 'backside' [Exod. 33:23], by beholding the sufferings and the cross," in *Martin Luther: Selections from His Writings*, ed. John Dillenberger (New York: Doubleday, 1961), 502.

13. See Jon Levenson's "Preface" to *Creation and the Persistence of Evil: The Jewish Drama of Divine Omnipotence* (Princeton, N.J.: Princeton University Press, 1994), xxiv–xxv.

14. See also L. Ann Jervis's discussion of suffering in Paul ("The Promise of Affliction: Paul's Preaching on Suffering," *The Character of Scripture: Moral Formation, Community, and Biblical Interpretation*, ed. W. P. Brown [Grand Rapids, Mich.: Wm. B. Eerdmans Pub. Co., forthcoming]).

15. Richard E. Sturm, "Defining the Word 'Apocalyptic,'" in *Apocalyptic and the New Testament: Essays in Honor of J. L. Martyn*, ed. Joel Marcus and Marion Soards (Sheffield: Sheffield Academic Press, 1989), 24. See also Paul D. Hanson's "Apocalypticism," in *The Interpreter's Dictionary of the Bible*, supp. ed. (Nashville: Abingdon Press, 1976), 29–30.

16. J. Louis Martyn, "Apocalyptic Antinomies in Paul's Letter to the Galatians," *New Testament Studies* 31 (1985): 424, n. 28; reprinted in *Theological Issues in the Letters of Paul* (Nashville: Abingdon, 1997), 111–123.

17. J. Louis Martyn, "Epistemology at the Turn of the Ages: 2 Corinthians 5:16," in *Christian History and Interpretation: Studies Presented to John Knox*, ed. W. R.

Farmer, C. F. D. Moule, and R. R. Niebuhr (Cambridge: Cambridge University Press, 1967), 264; reprinted in Martyn, *Theological Issues*, 89–109. My analysis of Luther has been informed by Alexandra Brown's depiction of Paul's "performative" enactment of an epistemology of the cross in *The Cross and Human Transformation: Paul's Apocalyptic Word in I Corinthians* (Minneapolis: Augsburg/Fortress, 1995).

18. On "performative utterances," see Austin Searle, *How to Do Things with Words* (Cambridge, Mass.: Harvard University Press, 1962).

19. Jer. 9:24 continues, "[B]ut let those who boast in this, that they understand and know me, that I am the LORD; I act with steadfast love, justice, and righteousness in the earth, for in these things I delight, says the LORD."

20. For a treatment of these issues, see Daphne Hampson, *Theology and Feminism* (Oxford: Basil Blackwell, 1990), and Sarah Coakley, "Kenosis and Subversion: On the Repression of 'Vulnerability' in Christian Feminist Writing," in *Swallowing a Fishbone? Feminist Theologians Debate Christianity* (London: S.P.C.K., 1996), 82–111. See also the classic, Rosemary Radford Ruether, *Sexism and God-Talk* (London: SCM, 1983).

21. See, e.g., Amy Hollywood, *The Soul as Virgin Wife: Mechtild of Magdeburg, Marguerite Porete, and Meister Eckhart* (Notre Dame, Ind.: University of Notre Dame Press, 1995).

22. See Michel Corbin's analysis of "redoubling negation" in "Négation et transcendance dans l'oeuvre de Denys," *Revue des sciences philosophiques et théologiques* 69 [1985]: 41–76. See also Bernard McGinn's discussion of Dionysius in *The Foundations of Mysticism*, vol. 1 (New York: Crossroad Books, 1991), 157–182. For an analysis of this pattern in Anselm, Søren Kierkegaard, Emmanuel Levinas, Jacques Derrida, among others, see Mark C. Taylor, *Nots* (Chicago: University of Chicago Press, 1993). Of course, the relationship between Luther and Dionysius is a complex one. Luther's own statements on Dionysius differ during his lifetime. Eberhard Jüngel's comparison of the two in *God as Mystery of the World*, trans. Darrell L. Guder (Grand Rapids, Mich.: Wm. B. Eerdmans Pub. Co., 1983) is somewhat oversimplified.

23. See Luther's discussion of the conditions for the use of force in the defense of such "tangible rights" (332–339). For a more extensive discussion of this theme, see his treatise "Secular Authority: To What Extent It Should Be Obeyed" (1523).

24. One could argue, of course, that such a reading is much closer to the actual role Mary plays in the New Testament texts where she is mentioned, where attention consistently seems to be deflected away from her or her role as mother and onto Jesus, his identity, and the reign of God he ushers in.

25. The following is based on Hans Urs von Balthasar's discussion of Mary in *The Glory of the Lord: A Theological Aesthetics*, vol. 1, trans. Erasmo Leiva-Merikakis (San Francisco: Ignatius Press, 1982), 338–343.

26. For a recent articulation of these criticisms, see Douglas Farrow, *Ascension and Ecclesia: On the Significance of the Doctrine of the Ascension for Ecclesiology and Christian Cosmology* (Grand Rapids, Mich.: Wm. B. Eerdmans Pub. Co., 1999).

27. See, e.g., Julia Kristeva's "Stabat Mater," *The Portable Kristeva*, ed. Kelly Oliver (New York: Columbia University Press, 1997), 308–330.

28. Ivan Illich, *Shadow Work* (London: M. Boyars, 1981).

29. For a nuanced discussion of these themes, see Don Browning, Bonnie J. Miller-McLemore et al., *From Culture Wars to Common Ground: Religion and the American Family Debate* (Louisville, Ky.: Westminster John Knox Press, 1997).

30. See, for example, Marina Walker's influential critique in *Alone of All Her Sex*.
31. See, among others, Virginia Ramey Mollenkott, *The Divine Feminine* (New York: Crossroad Books, 1987).
32. For a historical discussion of the concept of the "natural right" and its relation to medieval understandings of "natural law," see Brian Tierney, *The Idea of Natural Rights* (Atlanta, Ga.: Scholars Press, 1997).

# 11

## Mary and the Artistry of God

It's a simple flat disk, two inches in diameter, with a knowing, man-on-the-moon face painted on one side. The artist gave it to me as a gift. "This piece," reads the tag, "is hand-built porcelain, burnished with a quartz stone then painted and kiln fired. Finally, it is stained, then waxed and polished. It is a centuries-old technique."[1] "She sure put a lot of work into this," I think to myself, rubbing my thumb across the smooth finish.

My brother Mark sits at my parents' kitchen table twenty hours a day, eight days in a row, editing his film. I have been told (by people who know) that he is brilliant at what he does. "How's it going?" I ask him, one morning. It is six a.m., and I have come downstairs to find him not working and not sleeping. "I'm finished," he says. "Want to see it? It won't take long—it only runs about four minutes."

My friend, eight-and-a-half months pregnant, gingerly crosses the room and lowers herself into a chair. Success! She smiles—she had made it through another week of teaching; she'd prepared the house; the dinner party is happily underway. One of her guests comes toward her. "You must feel too human, these days," he comments. "I, of course, can't presume to understand . . . but I imagine it must be like being sick. A reminder that the body, with all its foibles, can't always be transcended! I bet you're anxious to be done with it." My friend, a thoroughly unassuming individual, stares at him, dumbfounded. "Actually," she finally says, "I feel really creative . . . almost, well . . . almost God-like."

In the story of the annunciation, Gabriel does not present Mary with options. Rather, the angel comes to tell her about something wonderful she and God will do together. To speculate about how many women might have "turned down" the request before Gabriel visited Mary or to emphasize that Mary could have "opted out" of the plan is to slight the disturbing fact that the Lukan story neither leaves open the possibility of Mary's refusal nor credits her for making the right decision.[2] Mary's participation in the event is never in question. It is sometimes argued, in an attempt to reconcile God's sovereignty and humanity's volition, that God "foreknew" what choice Mary *would* make. But such an argument is still suspiciously deterministic. And we (post)moderns are not fond of determinism. For us, to be fully human is to be free, and to be free is to have choices.[3]

Recently, some New Testament scholars have associated the absence of options offered to Mary regarding the conception of Jesus Christ with emotional and sexual violation.[4] Others, unhappy with this thesis, have tried to argue that Mary had more options than, at the text's face value, seem to appear.[5] Some writers, implying that Mary was destined to be the God-bearer regardless of her response, praise her for freely submitting to the will of God.[6]

In this essay I suggest that to get caught in the debate about whether Mary had a choice is to risk perceiving her as a secondary player rather than an essential participant in the incarnational event. To argue either that Mary could have opted out or that she could not have is to relate human actions to God's actions contractually or instrumentally rather than covenantally.[7] The repercussions of such approaches are spiritually disastrous, impeding us from recognizing the character of our creaturely participation in the work of God and therefore from enjoying fully our relationship to God. An alternative approach considers the incarnation as an *essentially* cooperative effort between Mary and God. It is impossible to conceive of the incarnation apart from either God's or Mary's involvement. The Word's self-emptying (*kenosis*) is realized in Mary's God-bearing (*theotokos*) and vice versa; human creativity is included in the creative work of the Creator become creature. The polisher of the moonfaced-disk, the bleary-eyed editor, the expectant mother gingerly lowering herself into a chair: all are created to be more than *contributors to* the artistry of God. Scandalously enough, they are claimed as *participants in* the life of God by way of the One who has entered into existence with us. As is the case with Mary, the question is not whether we will choose to take part in God's plan but whether we will embrace who we are as carriers, bearers, irreplaceable participants in the life of the unnamable God, who calls us by name by becoming a particular human being, called by a particular name.

I develop this thesis first by reflecting theologically on "artistry" as one way of understanding the character of Mary's relationship to God. I then highlight how scandalous it is to say that God became flesh and that Mary bore God, showing that it is precisely in braving the impossibility of these scandals that one becomes an artist who participates in the work of God. Finally, I briefly suggest how we, like Mary, enter into this impossibility. In what sense are we, also, bearers of the God who has entered into existence with us?

## TOWARD A THEOLOGY OF ARTISTRY

I have suggested that our preoccupation with "choice" and our insulated understanding of "freedom"[8] inhibit us from understanding the character of the divine/human partnership as reflected in the Lukan story of the annunciation and advanced by way of the church's confession that Mary bore God.[9] Theologians including Augustine, Luther, Barth, and Lehmann have pleaded with us not to identify freedom with having unbounded options. People are most free, they argue, when they recognize that there is only one *real* option: to love and enjoy God as creatures created by God. Augustine explains that a Christian acting freely always chooses for this good.[10] To be fully human, then, is not simply to have multiple options or even to make a commendable choice, but to make the only choice that genuine freedom allows: the choice to be who one is created, and called, to be.

Because it is difficult to understand how a choice can be made when there is only one real option, a person's involvement in the work of God is often talked about in terms of his or her "submission to" God's sovereign will. Thinking in terms of "submission" rather than "choice," however, can also lead to a misunderstanding of the character of creaturely involvement in the work of God. Mary did not pause to consider her options in the course of her conversation with Gabriel; neither did she abdicate her freedom for the sake of conforming to God's will. Either of these scenarios implies that Mary is added on to the divine plan rather than an integral part of the plan itself. In actuality, Mary does not stand at arm's length from God, assessing whether and how she will respond to what God is saying. She responds to Gabriel's message, rather, out of the context of her relationship with God. She already participates in the creative work of the God who favors her and will enter into her.

"Here am I, the servant of the Lord; let it be with me according to your word," says Mary (Luke 1:38). This declaration to the angel is better understood in terms of the creative claiming of her person than "her unquestioning acceptance of the will of God."[11] The plan of God, for Mary, is not something alien to herself to which she is being called courageously to submit. The plan, in fact, quite literally presumes symbiosis with her person, since she will both physically receive into her being the person of God and contribute to the God-human her humanity.

Mary is not being asked, then, to put herself to the side and take a "leap of faith."[12] On the contrary, the Lukan story gives no indication that the angel is posing a challenge, laying out a proposal, or simply informing Mary of what will inevitably take place, regardless of how she feels about it. The matter of having a choice or not being offered a choice does not come into play at all. Instead, the angel addresses Mary in a manner consistent with who she herself claims to be: a servant of God who celebrates God's inclusion of her.

The argument that the roles of Mary and God are inextricably intertwined in the event of the incarnation should be carefully scrutinized by those who do not want to blur the distinction between God and humanity. One reason the question of whether Mary had a choice might have developed is, in fact, that it keeps God and Mary comfortably distinguished. Certainly, in articulating the event of the incarnation in terms of the simultaneity of the divine self-empty-ing and the human God-bearing, one must take pains to guard against the mis-conception that Mary is God or that God can be identified with creaturely efforts. While God is present with us, working in and through us, God is first distinct from us, transcendent to us. God, as Creator, created all things out of nothing (ex nihilo); any creating that creatures do begins with raw materials that have already been created. Creation took place without the assistance of crea-tures. Creaturely creativity, by contrast, relies on the providential involvement of the Creator. Without attentiveness to the distinction between God and humanity, it is nonsensical to talk about the cooperation between God and humanity, for cooperation by definition involves discreet participants. What leads us to stand in amazement at Mary's participation is that she is both *not* God and essential to God's salvific work. How can it be that one who is not God can bear God? That we are somehow included in the Word's becoming flesh?

If Roman Catholics have been guilty of veering toward merging Mary and God, Protestants have erred on the side of underemphasizing the intimate character of their relationship to the point of denying the *theotokos*. Articulat-ing how it is that Mary participates in the life of God while at the same time remaining distinguished from God is, however, no easy matter. The concept of artistry offers a suggestive way of envisioning who Mary is (and, ultimately, who we are) in relationship to God. This is true (1) because artists do not think of their creative endeavors in terms of choosing or not choosing and (2) because artists do not understand their creations to be either extensions of themselves or unrelated to themselves. Let me explain this understanding of artistry in more detail before going on to explore how it helps us understand how Mary participates, as artist, in the creative work of God.

Artists seem consistently to indicate that there are both intrinsic energies (indistinguishable from themselves) and extrinsic energies (distinct from themselves) that press upon them to enter into the creative mode. For example, I recently asked Carol Adams (a prolific writer)[13] what writing was like for her. She said she felt "physically pained" when she did not make the time to write. She explained that she believed it was necessary, as a writer/artist, to "keep a regular date with your subconscious," sitting down and working at the same time each day. Adams described instances in which she would feel the intrinsic urge to write, yet not know exactly what she was going to write. On one occasion, she wrote a guide to meditation that she never imagined herself writing, attributing the impetus to an external energy, distinct from herself, which she identified as the Holy Spirit.[14] Along the same lines, while author Justin Korman Fontes does not identify a transcendent contributor to her creative work, she does explain that the "process" of getting story ideas is often " . . . mysterious, and not something I question."[15]

Stephen King, the well-known writer of horror novels, also believes he is relating to something distinct from himself in his artistic endeavors. He does not encourage planning out plot lines, he explains, because he believes the writer/artist is not so much formulating a story as he or she is recovering one. King likens stories to "relics . . . part of an undiscovered pre-existing world." "The writer's job," he explains, "is to use the tools in his or her toolbox to get as much of each one out of the ground intact as possible."[16] The characters in the story, if they are respected, will guide the writer in the unfolding of the plot. Faithful to this work, King is driven to sit at his desk every morning of the year until eight pages are written. Clearly, though King believes that the artist is drawn by extrinsic energies, he does not think for a minute that the preexistence of the stories means the artist is any less creative, a mere passive vessel.

Artists other than writers similarly describe the tension they experience in their creative work between intrinsic and extrinsic energies. One of my students—a poet and painter—turned in a pastel study as part of a final project. The drawing was beautiful but unfinished. When I saw the student on campus the next day, she begged me to get the project back to her as quickly as possible. "I can't stand it!" she said. "I've just got to finish it." As we talked about her anguish, it became clear not only that she had prematurely handed over something of herself but that she had unwittingly set my possession of her work as a barricade between herself and an extrinsic idea that demanded her participation.

Mark, a filmmaker, experiences similar pressures when he creates. "People ask me why I choose certain ideas for my films," he says. "They don't understand that I *have* to work with certain ideas. I determine what language I will use to express them, but I don't pick and choose the ideas." As he explains this, my mind flashes back to my classmate Noelle, sitting in the Princeton Seminary cafeteria and frantically writing on a napkin. "A song just came to me," she'd say. "Sorry . . . I just have to write it down! But *how* to capture it?"

The idea that people of faith participate in the work of God the way an artist engages in the creative enterprise has been suggested before. Timothy Gorringe, for example, uses the analogy of the director guiding actors in a play to better explain the workings of divine providence. Relaying the discovery of director Peter Brook, Gorringe explains that God, like a good director, does not choreograph the movements of the play from a distance. Rather, God enters the stage with us, working with us in developing our persona and shaping the expression of our lines. Just as the director creates by inviting and integrating the creativity of the actors, so creatures participate, as creators, in the artistry of God.[17]

Similarly, Madeleine L'Engle draws a connection between humanity's relationship to God's work of grace and the artist's relationship to her art. Quoting H. A. Williams, she notes, "Justification by faith means that I have nothing else on which to depend except my receptivity to what I can never own or manage."[18] Since "[f]or the Christian writer," this is "what the creative process is all about,"[19] L'Engle believes she is called to "have more faith in the work than I have in myself."[20]

Like L'Engle, all of the artists I have mentioned resist thinking of their art as something which they "manage," "achieve," or "choose." Instead, they describe it as that which calls them to participation. Neither do these artists understand themselves to be noncreative vessels of the artistic work. It is their conviction, in fact, that they create the very works of art that lay claim to them. In a manner that might give us insight into the character of Mary's relationship to God, they give themselves over to carrying and birthing something other than themselves that has entered in and laid claim to their persons. It is only in creating that they are who they really are; it is only in being artists that they are free.

With the analogy of God's artistry in play, I turn now to consideration of the impossibility of the divine/human cooperation, the scandalous truth that what is impossible has been made possible.

## TWO-SIDED SCANDAL: THE DIVINE/HUMAN HANDIWORK

### God As Artist, Becoming Flesh

Few people today seem scandalized by John's pronouncement that the Word became flesh (John 1:14). Some of us have written it off as an archaic idea that is incommensurate with our twenty-first-century context and not worthy of lingering attention. Those of us who do claim to believe it have often become overly comfortable with its inexplicability, refusing to be surprised because we wrongly understand the questions associated with surprise to compromise our faith.[21] Others, trying to find ways of grasping the incarnation that circumvent surprise, inadvertently subscribe to one of the age-old christological heresies. We may think of the humanity of Christ as more of a "disguise" than something God actually became,[22] for example, or we may think of Jesus' "divinity" as referencing his exceptionally virtuous character.[23] Either of these approaches enables us to escape the conundrum of full humanity and full divinity existing in one person. Another factor contributing to the absence of surprise might be that it does not impress us as absurd (as it did the believers of the early church) that the God who created the universe would enter the womb of a woman. Since the Enlightenment, we have ostensibly valued who we are as human beings enough to accept that God would desire to share existence with us.

Something crucial is lost when making sense of something extraordinary is privileged at the expense of being surprised by it. Encouraging us not to confine what we know to what we can explain, L'Engle tells the story of a young woman who, as a girl, read *A Wrinkle in Time*. "I didn't understand it," she said, "but I knew what it was about."[24] The great theologians have never claimed to understand the incarnation, but they have sought to know what it is about. One way they have done this is to explore what they identify as "the scandal of particularity" evidenced in the incarnation. This theological concept highlights our conviction that God did not enter into creatureliness in general but into humanity; God did not enter into humanity in general but as the particular human being, Jesus of Nazareth. Jesus of Nazareth was one height and not another, one race and not another, and one gender and not another. He was born, lived, and died at a particular time and in a particular place. Theologians through the centuries have been scandalized when they contemplate that the God who is omnipotent, omniscient, and omnipresent is incarnate in one person, with that one person's particularities and limitations.

The scandal associated with God's entry into creaturely existence is nowhere more evident than in God's selection of Mary. God did not elect to be born of *some* woman but of a particular woman. Again, to think of Mary as having a *choice* at this point might evidence a resistance to the scandalous fact that Jesus is Son of God only as the son of Mary.[25] As Janice Capel Anderson puts it, working with the Matthean text, "[t]hrough Mary Jesus is Son of God."[26] A particular woman gave of her humanity to the being of the God-human. This peasant woman nurtured, raised, trained, and even shaped the personality of the One who is God. In the words of Luther, "Mary suckled God, rocked God to sleep, prepared broth and soup for God...."[27] How scandalous it is to think that God was affected by a particular, historical figure!

Harriet Beecher Stowe,[28] reveling in this mystery, points out that Jesus grew up to be quite like Mary. "Mary seems," she writes,

from the little we see of her, to have been one of those silent, brood-
ing women who seek solitude and meditation,[29] whose thoughts are
expressed only confidentially to congenial natures. There is every evidence that our Lord's individual and human nature was in this respect
sympathetic with that of his mother.[30]

In a fascinating passage that overviews Stowe's understanding of the relationship between Jesus Christ and Mary, Eileen Razzari Elrod notes that
Stowe thought Mary taught Jesus frugality: "[H]e gathered up the left-over
pieces after miraculously feeding the crowd . . . [h]is parable of the leaven con-
vinces her he had watched his mother make bread . . . the parable of the woman
and the lost coin demonstrate that for Jesus 'every penny [had] its value.'"[31]
So seriously does Stowe consider that Jesus is "bone of [Mary's] bone and flesh
of her flesh" that she argues Mary must have known him "perfectly . . . inti-
mately." Because Mary, as virgin, is the only contributor to the humanity of
Christ, Stowe concludes that Jesus must have "more of the pure feminine element than in any other man."[32]

This is the point at which many Protestants might become suspicious. Just
how far *are* we willing to go in identifying Jesus with his mother, Mary?
Regardless of whether or not we might agree with the particulars of Stowe's
comments, it is reflections like these that indeed push us to remember what
the incarnation is about by reminding us how absurd it is to think that the God
of the universe would be taught by a peasant woman how to bake bread and
save money.

Reflection on the creation of art might again be of some help in contemplating the inextricable relationship between the sacred and the profane in the
event of God's coming through Mary. When students of art go to the museum,
they strive to reproduce the work of the great masters. They know that the
genius of a work is not encompassed by the sum of the artist's techniques. Yet
apart from the certain blending of color, the use of a special brush, the unusual
use of light, the hours of presketching and relayering of paint, there is no art.
Students sit with their easels and ponder the scandalous reality that *something
else* has entered into the details of the picture, and that this *something else* is
known only in and through the details themselves. The more they draw, the
more they recognize the unfathomability of it, and the more they know what
it is about.

The Word became flesh, entering the womb of Mary. To be surprised at
what we have witnessed and to contemplate the scandalous details of this mystery is to begin to realize our participation. With Mary, we are called to stand
ready to recognize that the impossible has been made possible, that the order
of things has been reversed,[33] and that we are genuinely included.

## Mary As Artist, Bearing God

"How can this be, since I am a virgin?," Mary asks Gabriel (Luke 1:34). While Zechariah asks for proof of the promise that he will have a son (2:18), Mary wonders at the impossibility of it. While Zechariah disbelieves the prophecy because he cannot understand it (2:20), Mary accepts it even though she knows it is impossible (2:18). While Mary is confused by what is happening to her (2:34), she knows what it is about. "God has brought the powerful from their thrones," she says, "and lifted up the lowly" (2:52). Unlike so many of us, Mary does not get so caught up in trying to make sense of the virgin birth that she loses sight of its significance. She knows that she, as a virgin, is incapable of giving birth. Similarly, we too are "virgins" who are incapable of bearing God, in and of ourselves. As artists cannot create merely with raw materials and technique, but must serve the story, song, or picture that claims them, so we cannot participate in the life of God by means of sheer will and effort. Mary understands this. Her participation in the work of God is founded not in the possibility inherent to herself but in God making the impossible possible (2:37).

Drawing from Barth's understanding, Trevor Hart explains that the surprised Mary's words, "How can this be, since I am a virgin?," mark "the question of all humanity in the face of that work of redemption and regeneration wrought in them by Christ."[34] It is in light of her acceptance of the message that she has been chosen by God that Mary recognizes her own inadequacy. But (in the words of Stowe), "she does not sink under the honor." She is "neither confused nor overcome." Instead, scandalously enough, she "exults in her glory."[35] Mary does not struggle for power, challenging, choosing against, or submitting to the message of the angel. Nor does she abdicate power. As a child of God, she instead engages Gabriel, showing neither pride nor self-deprecation, willing to serve as the very Bearer of God.

Nelson Mandela could have had the God-bearing Mary in mind when he offered the following challenge to survivors of apartheid:

> Our greatest fear is not that we are inadequate.
> Our greatest fear is that we are powerful beyond measure.
> It is our light, not our darkness that most frightens us.
> We ask ourselves, "Who am I to be brilliant, talented, fabulous?"
> Actually, who are you not to be? You are a child of God.
> Your playing small doesn't serve the world.[36]

For Mandela, to choose against being a child of God is no choice. To live as who we are, manifesting the glory of the God who made us, is to be creaturely creators.

What is not explicit in Mandela's exhortation is the recognition that the power, talent, and glory of the "artist" is not realized independently of the Other. Mary's participation in the artistry of God begins not with the recognition that the glory of God is "within" but that it is first transcendent, entering into life with humanity and lifting us up. It is known in relationship, in the dynamic of the divine humiliation/human exaltation revealed to us in Jesus Christ.[37]

It is in recognizing that she, as a virgin, has done nothing to facilitate the coming of God that Mary knows her power as the servant of God. Mary's work as *theotokos* thus begins. As an artist participating in the divine artistry, as the God-bearer into whom Christ has entered in the flesh, she enters creatively into her role. Traveling to meet with Elizabeth, she crafts the words of the Magnificat. Learning to be the mother of God, she revels in the scandal. "Pondering . . . in her heart,"[38] she marvels that this child she has carried and nurtured is, somehow, the promised Messiah. *How can this be?* To ask this question, ever again, is to recommit to participation.

## LIVING AS ARTISTS:
## BEING BEARERS OF THE BECOMING-FLESH

Did Mary choose to accept her role in God's plan? Could she have rejected it? I hope that, by this point in the essay, these questions seem unacceptably inattentive to the character of the divine artistry and our participation in it. The coming of God to the womb of Mary, who receives and attends, is not merely the story of a punctiliar event in which God acted, then Mary acted, and we are left to figure out how to list the credits. It is not, first and foremost, a testimony to what God and human beings *do* but to who we are (when we are being who we are) in relationship to one another.

A writer writes. The Word becomes flesh. Mary bears God. The writer writes because she is a writer. To write (for the writer) is to exist in consistency with essence. It is to be free, to be an artist. The Word becomes flesh because God, in the divine freedom, wills not to be without us but with us and for us. The event of the incarnation reveals who God is: the Word born of Mary, eternally united with the person of Jesus of Nazareth. Mary bears God in freely acting out of who she is as *theotokos*. To choose against God's coming would be a choice against freedom, a denial of self. Like the writer who keeps her daily appointment with the word processor, Mary reminds us that it is in particular concrete actions undertaken in particular moments that finite creatures realize their participation in the artistry of God.

Protestant Christian theology has historically identified Mary as the model Christian believer, the embodiment of the church.[39] Consistent with this, I have suggested that Mary reminds us of who we are as bearers of God, humbly submitting to and courageously claiming our place in relationship to the Art that overshadows us, lays claim to us, and continues both to grow in and remain distinct from us. Will we live, with Mary, as artists who participate in the artistry of God? Will we engage, as she did, the pushing, acting, creating life of the Spirit that birthed, nurtured, and stood by the One who is the salvation of the world? When we embrace our election as God-bearers, the reality proclaimed in the Magnificat is once again made manifest. God enters into existence with us in the person of Jesus Christ, and we participate, in and through him, in the very life of God (Col. 3:3). We realize the forgiveness that is ours, readily forgiving those who sin against us. We know that God is the one Subject in the event of revelation and that we are, also, genuine partners with God.

If we insist on making sense of this, we miss what it is about. If we believe we can generate, in and of ourselves, something to contribute, our relationship to God is nothing but a relationship of uneven exchange. God has done great things for us, we might think, so we should try to reciprocate as best we can, given our limitations. This contractual way of relating to God can be logically extended to human relationships: God forgives us, we should respond by forgiving others; if we don't forgive, God has every right to withdraw forgiveness. When we live by what sense we can make of God's actions toward us, rather than being surprised by the scandal of the incarnation, we have forgotten grace.

If we recognize that virgin birth is impossible, on the other hand, we stand ready to benefit from the covenental character of our relationship to God. To name the impossibility of it is to recognize that we do not have what it takes, in and of ourselves, to bear the God who has entered into our midst. We cannot generate children in and of ourselves; we cannot participate in creation apart from relationship to the one who empowers all of our creative acts.

If we, with Mary, "do not sink"[40] in the face of this impossibility, we have come farther still. Facing the double scandal head-on, we recognize that God has entered into our existence to draw us into existence with God. In becoming a particular, finite being, God conveys that God is not only for humanity in general (*pro nobis*: "for us") but for each of us in particular (*pro me*: "for me"). As Mary is called, by name, to participate in the work of God, so we are also called by name. What is impossible is made possible: we are capable, creative, willing, irreplaceable companions of the God who claims us in Jesus Christ. We are included, as creaturely creators, in the artistry—the providence—of God.

With Mary, then, we shape our words into poetry; we nurture the life that is in us; we ponder what is going on around us. We refuse to stop wondering, to give up on mystery, to abdicate who we are as God's creative servants. We live as artists participating in the artistry of God, wondering how our fragile efforts can be essential, marveling that they yield such beauty. And indeed they are and they do, for God has lifted us up in our lowliness and called us blessed.

## Notes

1. Words inscribed on a tag attached to a piece by artist Vivian Harris-Bonham.
2. Mary is credited with having "found favor" with God—this is more a statement about *who she is* than an evaluation of a choice she has made.
3. Madeleine L'Engle makes this point on page 26 of *Walking on Water: Reflections on Faith and Art* (New York: North Point Press, 1995). Mary, she says, "is free to say *No*," but such a "choice" would jeopardize the incarnational event (22). In my view, such a "choice" is against freedom and humanization: it is, in short, not a real choice but a resistance to the only free choice.
4. See, for example, Jane Schaberg's controversial work, *The Illegitimacy of Jesus: A Feminist Theological Interpretation of the Infancy Narratives* (San Francisco: Harper and Row, 1987).
5. For example, the October–December 2001 issue of *The Living Pulpit* (10:4) makes constant reference to Mary's freedom to choose among options. Mary Hunt praises "a poster supporting reproductive choice in Latin America" that reads, "Mary was consulted about being the mother of God" (26). Elizabeth Rankin Geitz assures us that "it is possible that Mary could have said 'no'" (47). Marvin A. McMickle refers to the angel's words as an "invitation" from God (39). Avery Dulles insists that "God deals with [Mary] as a free agent" (30). Peter Daino points out that Mary did know how to say "no"—"to the mighty on their thrones . . . to the well-fed . . . to the oppressor who exploits the poor and hungry" (34, citing Daino's *Mary: Mother of Sorrows, Mother of Defiance* [Maryknoll: Orbis Books, 1993]). All of these writers challenge the characteristic depiction of Mary as passive, nonagential, and nonwilling.
6. This is the position taken by theologians such as Karl Barth, for example, who argues that Mary is (as should be all human beings in relationship to God's revelation) "non-willing, non-achieving, non-creative . . . merely ready . . .merely receptive" (*Church Dogmatics*, I/2 [Edinburgh: T & T Clark, 1956], 191).
7. That is, God had a job that needed to be done and was commissioning Mary to do it, versus the idea that Mary was chosen to be an integral participant in the divine work of the incarnation.
8. For more on contemporary misconceptions about the character of freedom, see my essay "Limits, Possibilities, and the Sovereignty of God" (*Theology Today* [April, 1996]: 47–62).
9. Methodologically, I am bringing to bear in my reading of the text the theological assessments that (1) the One whom Mary bore is of the "same substance" (*homoousious*) as God (this was decided by the church in 325, at the Council of Nicea) and (2) Mary is "God-bearer" (*theotokos;* declared at the Council of Chalcedon in 451).
10. For more on this, see Augustine's *City of God*, Book XXII, ch. 30, ed. Vernon J. Bourke (New York: Doubleday, 1958), 540–545. Here, Augustine explains that "in eternity, freedom is that more potent freedom which makes sin impossible" (544). When sin is no longer a possibility, Christian believers "will be more free than ever—so free, in fact, from all delight in sinning as to find, in not sinning, an unfailing source of joy" (543).

11. Schüssler Fiorenza, with these words, laments this common portrayal of Mary in "Feminist Theology as a Critical Theology of Liberation," (in *Churches in Struggle: Liberation Theology and Social Change in North America*, ed. W. Tabb [New York: Monthly Review Press, 1986], 58).
12. Here, I have in mind the Kierkegaardian model of conversion. A person faced with the choice of submitting to God or not submitting is also choosing between letting go of self and clinging to self. To take the leap of faith into the arms of God is to die to self; once landed in God's arms, however, the true self (true freedom) is discovered. The "catch" to all this is, of course, that you cannot know you will discover your "true self" until after you have renounced the only self you do know in order to take the leap (see, for example, Kierkegaard's *The Concept of Anxiety*, ed. Reidar Thomte [Princeton: Princeton University Press, 1980] and *The Sickness Unto Death*, eds. Howard V. Hong and Edna H. Hong [Princeton: Princeton University Press, 1980]).

 Mary, in Luke 1, is not struggling with choosing for or against God; for and against self. She has clearly already taken the leap of faith: she knows her true self in relationship with God. She is free to be who she is, as creature in relationship with her Creator.
13. Adams's numerous works include *The Sexual Politics of Meat* (1998) and *Living Among Meat-Eaters* (2001).
14. The information in the above paragraph comes from an informal conversation I had with Carol Adams in November of 2001.
15. "Among Our Key People," *The Key Reporter* 61, no. 1 (Fall 2001): 8.
16. Stephen King, *On Writing: A Memoir of the Craft* (New York: Scribner, 2000), 163–164.
17. See Timothy Gorringe, *God's Theatre: A Theology of Providence* (London: SCM Press, 1991), 77–81, paraphrasing Brook, *The Empty Space* (New York: Penguin Books, 1972).
18. L'Engle, *Walking on Water* 178, citing Williams without referencing the source.
19. Ibid.
20. Ibid., 179.
21. Mary's question, "How can this be, since I am a virgin?" (Luke 1:34) seems to me to be a manifestation of surprise, an indication of her faith.
22. This is the heresy of docetism (it denies the full humanity of Jesus Christ).
23. This is the heresy of Ebionitism (it denies the full divinity of Jesus Christ).
24. L'Engle, *Walking on Water*, 23.
25. In other words (to risk thinking hypothetically!), if another woman had been *theotokos*, "Jesus" would have been a different person.
26. Janice Capel Anderson, "Mary's Difference: Gender and Patriarchy in the Birth Narratives," *Journal of Religion* 67 (April 1987), 190 (183–202).
27. Martin Luther, "On the Councils and the Church," *Luther's Works*, vol. 41, ed. Eric W. Gritsch, trans. E. Gordon Rupp (Philadelphia: Fortress Press, 1966), 100.
28. Harriet Beecher Stowe, daughter of the Presbyterian revivalist preacher Lyman Beecher, was a theologian in her own right. While she is best known for *Uncle Tom's Cabin*, she also authored numerous devotional essays.
29. For further reflection on the character and implications of Mary's pondering see, in this volume, Bonnie Miller-McLemore's essay.
30. Harriet Beecher Stowe, *Footsteps of the Master* (New York: J. B. Ford & Co., 1877), 69.
31. Eileen Razzari Elrod, "'Exactly Like My Father': Feminist Hermeneutics in Harriet Beecher Stowe's Non-fiction," *Journal of the American Academy of*

*Religion* 63 (Winter 1995): 714 (695–719). Citing Stowe, *Footsteps*, 34–35 (From vol. 15 of *The Writings of Harriet Beecher Stowe*, Riverside ed.) For discussion of Stowe's Mariology, see 709–717.

32. Stowe, *Footsteps* (1877), 70.

33. For more on this reversal, proclaimed in the Magnificat, see the essays by Nora Lozano-Díaz and Daniel Migliore in this volume.

34. Trevor Hart, *Regarding Karl Barth* (Carlisle, Pa.: Paternoster Press, 1999), 163; citing Barth, *Natural Theology* (London: Geoffrey Bles: Centenary Press, 1946), 93–94, 123–124.

35. Stowe, *Footsteps of the Master* (1877), 72–73.

36. These words, frequently attributed to Nelson Mandela on the worldwide web, are also claimed by Marianne Williamson. They appear on page 191 of Williamson's *A Return To Love: Reflections on the Principles of a Course in Miracles* (New York: HarperCollins, 1996; first published 1992). It seems probable that Williamson wrote the words and Mandela cited her in speeches given in the mid-90s. It is crucial to note that Mandela chose to share these words in a very particular context, to a particular group of people who were suffering apartheid. The "sin" of these people is not that they think of themselves more highly than they ought, but that they do not recognize themselves as beloved children of God and live accordingly.

37. This is the dialectic used by Karl Barth to frame his Doctrine of Reconciliation (vol. 4 of the *Church Dogmatics*). Jesus Christ is the "Lord who is Servant" ("emptying" himself in the incarnation); he is also the "Servant Who is Lord" (and in this, all humanity is exalted. Mary represents this!).

38. See Luke 2:19, 51.

39. See, for example, Joseph A. Fitzmyer, *The Gospel According to Luke I–IX*, The Anchor Bible Series (New York: Doubleday & Co., 1979), 341.

40. Stowe's words, cited earlier.